For Anthony, Janina and Linda

HARDLY WORKING

Nancy,
You are the Queen of Reviews!
Thanks again for
taking the time to
read the book.
Cheers,
Roger

How did I reach this point and what came after?

HARDLY WORKING

HOW I FOUND A CAREER AND KEPT MY SOUL

By Roger Day Bain

The characters in this book are real
although a few names have been altered.

Printed by IngramSpark.com., in the United States of America.

First printing, 2022.

www.rogerdaybain.com

CONTENTS

INTRODUCTION

IN 1960 I AM TWELVE YEARS OLD and certain that when I grow up, I will become a professional baseball player. We live in Clarendon Hills, a small western suburb of Chicago on the Burlington Rail line. Every day that summer I wait for my dad to come home from work so we can grab our mitts and toss the pill, catching the scent of city exhaust and perspiration on his business clothes as I run up the block to greet him after work. After he changes out of his suit and we have dinner, it's time.

The screen door bangs as we head down our short driveway toward the street. We take our places on the sidewalk at either end of our lot line, about sixty feet apart, and I begin to pitch. We use the sidewalk because my dad doesn't want to wear out the lawn.

I begin throwing my usual assortment of fastballs and jug handle curves. Over my shoulder, I notice our neighbor from a few houses down walking toward us. He's with a vaguely familiar guy.

"Hey, Roger," our neighbor calls. My dad and I both are named Roger. "I want you to meet Cal Nieman."

Cal Nieman is the second-string catcher for the Chicago Cubs. I have his baseball card in a shoebox in my bedroom. Cal and the neighbor were college buddies. Do I want Cal to catch a few of my curveballs? *Do I?* Even the backup catcher for a seventh-place team like the Cubs is a god to my twelve-year-old eyes. Just like that, Cal Nieman, Chicago Cub, assumes his position on our chalked home plate. In front of my house!

A crowd of neighborhood kids gathers. Slowly, they inch closer to the action. I don't dare make eye contact with any of them. "Stay cool," I tell myself. A couple of adults step onto their own lawns to witness twelve-year-old Roger—now more convinced than ever that he will become a professional baseball player—throw the first pitch a bit outside, making Cal lunge for it.

"Put it right here, kid," says Cal, holding up his mitt. I feel as if I'm in a dream. Like I'm in the majors. After 15 or 20 throws, it's over—the closest I would come to the big leagues. "You've got a good curveball," Cal says.

♫ ♫ ♫

My arm gave out at age fifteen. All those Little-League no-hitters and American Legion all-star appearances amounted to faded glory. It was too many curveballs for a young arm. I would not become a baseball player. What would I be? Other than my father—moms were still staying at home—I had little idea what the dads on leafy Blodgett Street did to earn a living. Two friends had fathers who were airline pilots. You could picture those dads at work, in the cockpit, flipping switches, checking altitude, flying a plane. Another dad moonlighted as a clown. I had seen him in clown drag and it was easy to picture him flopping around in oversized shoes. But most wore business suits and commuted into downtown Chicago. What type of work required a suit and what exactly was "business?"

My dad sold classified advertising space for the *Chicago Daily News*. Want ads. Why should I care that a huge percentage of a newspaper's revenue came from classified advertising? One Saturday, my dad drove me into the Loop for a visit. His office was deserted except for us. He flipped on the lights and I sat at his desk. We went into the supply room and gathered up some pencils, paper clips, and notepads. Pretty cool, I thought, to be able to get this stuff without going to the store. Was this his job? Sitting at a desk with a pencil?

On the drive home, we cruised along West Madison Street, or skid row, as my father referred to it. I stared at the bums milling amidst the grit.

"Why are they bums?" I asked. My father explained that many had lost their jobs, or they drank too much booze, or they were crazy.

"If you have no job, you're a bum?" I asked.

"Well, you never know," replied dad.

There was something about these bums; like they were a different species living by different rules. Outcasts or rebels. Like they didn't care to participate. There were no bums in Clarendon Hills. There weren't any poor folks at all, much less people living on the street. At the time, little boys aspired to be cowboys or firemen. No one aspired to be a bum. I was fascinated and next Halloween I dressed as a hobo.

♫   ♫   ♫

Work defines us. As life progresses from youth to adulthood, we spend more time on the job, preparing for work and commuting to work, than we do eating and sleeping. It took me years to figure out how I wanted to fill this giant slice of life—but I knew early on I didn't want to do the same thing, day in and day out, and have the monotony define me. I have done many things for a paycheck, worn numerous hats and collected many experiences along my way. Some of my jobs can be measured in years, some in days, some in hours. I've avoided work, freelanced, vagabonded, observed, learned to play the country blues guitar, experimented with writing, and experienced frustrations and close calls with success, until finally, I forged a path to something I could call my own.

Throughout my journey, I've always sought out that sweet spot: to have just enough without being possessed by my possessions, or by "the man," and to always have time for my own creative pursuits. We shape our own path, our own definition of success. Each of us must decide to partake in a pre-programmed destiny based upon the circumstances of our birth, or forge something that is more personal. We can't all have our name on the building, but we can all build a rewarding life through work—and what we do when we get home from work. To live is to work. To work is to learn. To learn is to live.

Let's get to work

I. IN THE BEGINNING
1960–1970
(Ages 12-21)

MOOSE, DOC, AND THE MEMBERS

Caddy in Clarendon Hills, IL, 1960

A FEW MONTHS BEFORE MY THIRTEENTH BIRTHDAY, I began to caddy at the Hinsdale Golf Club—my very first paying job. The club was a ten-minute walk from my house, but no club member lived where I did, in Clarendon Hills. That was against the rules. Members had to reside in Hinsdale, home of the rich uncle, the corporate titan, the live-in housekeeper, the afternoon martini, the sprawling, manicured lawn. Coach houses. Brick streets. Columns. A few old money families still employed butlers. Although it had a large section of ordinary middle-class neighborhoods, the town's reputation was predicated on wealth.

Soon after I began caddying, I started at Hinsdale junior high. On Saturday afternoons my father drove me in the Rambler wagon over to the proverbial "other side of the tracks," to a newfound friend's house.

I recall one occasion when, during our pickup football game on the lush front lawn, a live-in housekeeper called to my new friend: "Hubbard. It's time for your lunch." Hubbard went into the house with his shoulder pads still on, to dine on pork chops prepared by the cook and dab the corners of

3

his mouth with linen napkins. Although this rather elaborate lunch struck me as far different than the baloney sandwich I might have had at my house, it mattered little to me at the time—wealth made a scant impression on me as a kid. Most of my new friends from Hinsdale took their lives for granted, as did I.

My town was modestly middle class. Most homes had one bathroom and three or four kids who shared bedrooms. It would be several decades before Clarendon Hills transformed into Hinsdale Lite, though the new muscular, trophy homes—too big for their lots—would never be the rambling mansions of an earlier era's wealth.

For residents of Hinsdale, club membership was a must. "The Club," as it was referred to, was a gathering place for those who had *arrived*. It was where like-minded, well-bred folks with similar aspirations gathered; folks eager to showcase their faith in the status quo while being catered to and smiled at. Club members shared a belief that they were blessed, that there was a divine element involved in their good fortune. Sure, hard work had got them to this exalted position—maybe not *their* hard work, but someone's. "We are so blessed to have all this," was a frequent mantra. These were God's creatures, steeped in an aura of entitlement and a knack for conversations about golf swing mechanics, the renovation of the fourteenth tee, membership rules, recent purchases, investments, the Aspen real estate market, and how swell things are if we can just keep them this way.

To caddy at the Hinsdale Golf Club, you had to be at least 13. Because I was tall for my age, I passed. Caddies were divided into three descending classes—A, B, and C—subject to the judgement of the caddy master. Most of the C caddies were pipsqueaks. Numbers were then assigned to us, ranging from one to ninety-nine and the lower the number, the more qualified the caddy. At least, that was the theory. Somehow, I was assigned number A-13. Class A!

What I remember most was the caddy master, Doc, and his cohorts Moose and Harry. Doc was in his forties, and clearly not from Hinsdale. He dressed like a golfer, wore thick glasses, and his beard was a permanent five o'clock shadow. He reminded me of Sergeant Bilko from the 1950s TV show; a bit of a hustler and a schemer, and a gambler. Club members had a winking appreciation for this rogue in their midst. It was Doc who decided which little creep was going to carry which golf bag for 18 holes at the going rate of $3.00, a sum large enough to keep me thick in baseball cards and milkshakes from Parker's drugstore, where I had begun to ogle Darlene, the 15-year-old, tight-sweatered soda jerk.

Moose was Doc's enforcer. He had a world-class menacing stare and didn't hesitate to frighten a suburban caddy. Looking back, I'm not sure he *had* any function other than terrorizing us. His black hair was well-greased, and his gut pushed out over the waistline of sans-a-belt slacks. He wore shiny shirts of a pattern and color unknown to the dads on my block. He was from an entirely different world. He was Moose.

Harry was downright scary—gaunt, way tall, and a pock-marked complexion. It was doubtful that he'd ever seen a dentist, and he had the demeanor of Frankenstein. He was a professional caddy and a golf hustler who spoke in double negatives through broken teeth. In downtown Clarendon Hills I had glimpsed him getting off the train in his cracked, wingtip golf shoes then followed him at a safe distance as he strode up Blodgett—right past my house—to his job at the Club. I wondered where he lived. Skid row? And how had he learned a rich man's sport? I never found out.

When things were slow, Doc, Moose, and Harry played cards and swore and accused each other of cheating or bluffing.

"You folded when I knocked. That's 20 for me, asshole."

This was my first exposure to real cursing. It wasn't practiced in my neighborhood—or, at least not in front of the kids. When word came that a member was ready to golf, Doc leaned out of his office and peered through his thick glasses at the pathetic collection of caddy boys, all of us cooling our heels on the bench that lined the walls of the shack. He seemed to delight in this moment. He knew which members were ball-busters, and which ones had low handicaps and needed a competent caddy. Which scrawny kid would he pair with a captain of industry or the well-coiffed wife of the bank president?

"Here, Bain," he'd say, handing me a card with a member's name and my number 13 on it. "Go pick up the clubs for Mrs. Templeton. They're on the first tee."

I was always gripped with a moment of anxiety on the way to the pro shop to pick up the clubs, knowing that I was about to undergo a three-hour golf etiquette examination.

The club had a no-tipping policy, with signs posted in the pro shop to reinforce the idea. Seemed a bit cheap even to my young mind. On occasion, though, a member handed me twenty-five cents at the turn, which I'd spend on a Baby Ruth and a Coke in the caddy shack. A quarter was a small amount to truly consider a tip, but it still fostered a minor conspiracy between the member and me. In my eyes, we were bending the rules together.

I recall a general air of indifference when it came to the members' relationships with caddies. Some tolerated my existence. Some ignored me altogether, like I was but an arm handing them a club. Occasionally one would ask where I lived or where I went to school or if I played golf, pleased to be displaying a concern for the welfare of the help. Some wore plaid pants. Some had wives who drank too much. Many owned the firm. All believed that golf was what civilized people did.

I had played golf a few times with my uncle—a real ace—and on public courses with kids in my neighborhood, picking up a sense of the rules. Further training came from the occasional tidbit from Doc or Moose about how to hold the flag or to be sure that my shadow didn't cross paths with the line of the putt. Doc grew serious when he was instructing us, like perhaps he had been a teacher or a priest in a previous life.

"Always keep your eye on the ball. That's your job. You always gotta know where the ball is. Speak when spoken to. Never laugh at a duffed shot. Laugh when you get home. Don't make your player wait for you. And keep the clubs from clanking. I hear that you were clanking, I'll send you home."

Walking down the fairway was a good opportunity to sing under your breath, whenever your golfer was at least twenty yards away. If the member was good enough and he hit the ball far enough, I'd get to sing a whole song between the drive and his next shot. Most radio songs were two minutes or less. How long did it take to explain that *Betty Lou Got a New Pair of Shoes* or that it was *Finger Poppin' Time*? I didn't yet know about Blind Blake or Muddy Waters or Robert Johnson. The Rolling Stones weren't on the radio yet.

One nice caddy perk was free golf at the Club on Mondays when the course was closed for maintenance. We had to dodge the sprinklers and skip any greens that were being repaired, but who cared? We played 18 or 27 holes, practiced our cheating, and tried out some of the cuss words. Although I wasn't aware of it at the time, my growing mind was being exposed to two sides of America: hanging around Doc, Moose, and Harry one minute, then handing a club to Mr. Comiskey or Mrs. Johnson the next. Right off the bat, I'd stumbled into a job that revealed a swath of our social strata. As I matriculated through Hinsdale junior high and then high school, I became friends with many club members' kids, but I never thought to myself, "One day, *I'll* become a member." Not because I felt that I couldn't, but because I found Doc more intriguing than any of the members. He was a character. Through the eyes of a 12-year-old caddy, members were caricatures. Doc and Moose were on the hustle. The members were trying to hold on to what they had. Chalk one up for the salt of the earth.

ME AND MY UNCLE

Glasner Bros. LaGrange, IL, 1962-63
At the beginning of the 1960s, one sixth of American workers
were employed by the auto industry.

THE MINGLED SCENT OF MOTOR OIL. MECHANIC'S grease, cigarette smoke, and exhaust fumes permeated the garage behind the showroom of Glasner Brothers, where I detailed used cars for my uncle, Lee Glasner, who owned the American Motors dealership with his brother. The scent was intoxicating; the smell of modern civilization on the march.

It was an era of mom-and-pop car dealerships, unlike the multi-acre superstores of today. The showroom had just enough space for three new cars and a slightly uncomfortable Naugahyde couch, flanked by two chrome ashtray stands. Sales were handled by Uncle Lee and his son, my cousin, Bob. I was fourteen or fifteen, and it was my first experience witnessing the true art of selling: the eye contact, the good-natured joshing and guffawing, the practiced sincerity that implies the salesman is in the customer's corner. My Aunt Helen came in a few hours a day do the books in the tiny glass-walled office and was the only woman on the scene. She gushed every time she saw me, like I was a prince.

The centerpiece of the American Motors lineup was the Rambler Classic Custom Six. It wasn't a car that cool guys and high school gearheads craved. They wanted the Ford with three deuces, or the newly introduced Chevy

409—the car rhapsodized by the Beach Boys. The Rambler was a better fit for everybody's Uncle Louie, the guy who could smoke his cigar while driving the old lady to the beauty parlor, a damn poodle in the back seat. Frugal Uncle Louie didn't care about trends, design, beauty or truth. He was an American Motors customer.

Working for relatives is tricky. Do they expect more, or do they tolerate less? I'm not sure what Uncle Lee expected of me, but I could never deliver a car detailed to his specifications. The detailer had to buff, polish, vacuum, and wipe down every inch of chrome, metal, rubber, and upholstery until the car shouted, "Buy Me!" My uncle had a certain method to be adhered to at each step of the process, from the soaking to the wax application to the buffing technique.

"Work the buffer like this. Counter-clockwise!"

I would take over and after about six seconds he'd grab the buffer to again demonstrate his technique, then he was off to the back lot or the showroom or the small front office. I was paranoid about leaving buff swirls that could ruin a finish, so I overcorrected and buffed too lightly. Between customers, Uncle Lee might duck back into the garage to put the final touches on whatever car I was detailing. This version of Uncle Lee was different from the guy at family gatherings, where he was always loose and jovial. At work, he was driven and slightly impatient.

One of the mechanics was black. The only black people I'd known were basketball opponents from mixed-race schools. We might exchange a two-second handshake at the opening jump, a glance, or a grunt during the game, but that was it. The Chicago suburbs were segregated. My father once drove our monthly housekeeper, Maggie, home to the Southside, and though it was only a twenty-mile drive, it was worlds away. My whole damn town was white, and my experience with people of color was through media: athletes, musicians, or stereotypical portrayals like Buckwheat from *The Little Rascals*. I knew that my favorite baseball player, Ernie Banks, had first played in the Negro Leagues, but I hadn't processed what that meant. I knew that Jackie Robinson had broken the "color barrier" in baseball but had no grasp of the courage involved in making that happen. I had overheard my parents mention the Civil Rights Act, but like many fourteen-year-old kids, I was more into Motown and RBIs than racial politics. I can't imagine what the black mechanic must have thought of my white bread self, but I for one felt my horizons expanding.

Another step on my journey to adulthood: for the very first time in my life, I ate at a lunch counter all by myself. What freedom I felt, moseying down the street to the local lunch counter and plopping down onto one of five or six stools. Funny how that made you feel grown up. Giving your order to a middle-aged woman who called you sweetie and then watching the cook, some hard scrabble hash slinger, prepare your order—that was grown up stuff.

"You sure made short work of that, sweetie," said the counter gal as I wolfed down my hamburger, fries, and a coke.

"I was hungry," was about all I could muster at first. Eventually, though, I mastered the art of shooting the breeze with whoever seemed to want to talk at the counter, the common topics being the weather, baseball, the price of anything and everything, and maybe the upcoming Pet Parade.

The LaGrange Pet Parade was a slightly kooky bit of Americana that every year travelled down Burlington Avenue right past Glasner Bros, a zany gaggle of pets and pet owners: Chihuahuas in baby carriages, Angora rabbits on leashes, Siamese cats in wheeled cages, a monkey on a stick, a turtle or two, plus the high school bands, Little League teams, Campfire Girls, a formidable contingent of clowns, (not my neighbor) and always the sputtering magic of the Glasner Brothers 1902 Rambler replica.

As a parade sponsor, Glasner Brothers provided the car for the obligatory parade celebrity to ride in. WGN-TV had been covering the parade since the early 1950s, and each year a celebrity served as the official parade marshal, often television stars from hit shows like *Bonanza, Dennis the Menace*, and *The Beverly Hillbillies*. In 1958 my mother had the pleasure of driving a sporty Nash convertible with Dick Simmons perched in back with his dog, King. Mr. Simmons was the star of *Sergeant Preston of the Yukon,* which had been a radio show, then a hit TV series in the mid '50s. Mom was lucky that the Nash Rambler made it through the parade without overheating or breaking down. That much at least could be said about American Motors products: they were tough enough to handle a parade.

While working this job, I took the train by myself, experienced what it was like to work for a relative, learned to detail cars, witnessed firsthand the art of selling, and worked alongside a black mechanic, who, I imagine, thought of me as the privileged nephew of the owner. Which I was. But nothing could beat the thrill of eating lunch on my own. What more could I ask from a job? Work was providing an opportunity to educate myself in ways that school could not.

Courtesy LaGrange Historical Society

CAR HIKER

"Z" Frank Rent-a-Car, Chicago, IL, 1965

THE SUMMER OF MY SIXTEENTH YEAR, I hiked cars for "Z" Frank Chevrolet in Chicago, my first job with full time hours. It was a glimpse of the world beyond my pastoral suburb of Clarendon Hills, and a chance to become a part of the daily fabric of big-shouldered, bad-assed Chicago and all its poetic grit. I had not yet read Nelson Algren or Studs Terkel, but for a summer I would be a bit player—an extra—in their legendary city.

A friend of my folks got me the job and provided my ride into the city. Every workday, Mr. Burr picked me up and drove me to a six-story garage on Federal Street on the south edge of the Loop, a monumentally congested slice of urbanity where Z Frank Chevrolet had leased space. My only duty was to drive rental cars from Federal Street to the Peterson Avenue service center on the far north side and then make a return trip.

Although I didn't know it then, "Z" Frank Chevrolet was about to become the largest volume Chevy dealer in the world. For all I knew, every job I would have from here unto forever would be for the biggest something-or-other. The thought of compiling a resume hadn't entered my thinking but had it, I could put "hiked cars for the biggest Chevy dealer on the planet." Everything I knew about "Z" was from their commercials that barraged the airwaves. It was a musical stinger that played at the end of each commercial:

female singers:

Z Frank (beat)
Z Frank (Honk sound effect. Two honks.)
Z Frank before you buy

I had always paid attention to these little ad songs. They became part of my mental soundtrack. The John's Bargain Store jingle, *where your dollars had the sense to buy you more*, was on equal footing with *Chapel of Love* by the Dixie Cups.

My assignments on Federal Street were given to me by Hardy, a short black man in a gray shirt and pants—the hiker uniform, which I wasn't required to wear. He had a limp caused by one leg being shorter, and a boat-load of swagger, telling it like it was and would forever be. He looked at you three degrees to the left of your eyes. He jangled keys and barked orders and the entire staff obeyed. His position reminded me of Doc at the Club. They were each masters of their domain, emperors of their fiefdom.

"There's a customer up on Peterson who needs this Malibu Sport Coupe." He'd point to a blue Malibu that had just squealed down from somewhere up the ramp as the driver got out and took a powder.

"Here the keys. Go on, now," Hardy would say to the white kid. "Yes sir," I thought. More fun than driving the Rambler station wagon we had at home.

This job had me in constant motion, threading my way through downtown congestion, cruising Lake Shore Drive, riding the el train and the bus, and walking all around the loop. I learned that the intersection of State and Madison was the epicenter of the city's grid. Street names became familiar. Wacker Drive runs in near every direction. Even underground! I began to recognize traffic cops and street refugees from West Madison Street looking for a donation, to see the city as a place of real people rather than faceless masses, the way it looked in schoolbooks. I gained a feeling of being part of something much bigger than anything I had previously felt. The soundtrack of

13

screeching el tracks overhead, honking horns, accelerating taxis, cop whistles, and shouts, pigeon flutter and street preacher rantings; the gaudy display of signs and lights, sun glinting off metal and glass, whizzing traffic and towering buildings, and a million people going a million places, like they all knew where they were headed—I now felt part of this. It was intoxicating. I began to feel like a "grown up."

I often lunched at one of the joints under the el tracks that served tough, greasy steak with baked potato for $1.29, then partook in my near-daily ritual: gazing at the electric guitars that hung behind the counter or in the window of the pawn shops on Van Buren Street. These Fenders, Gibsons, and Silvertones were as exotic as any Ford or Chevy. They were mesmerizing. Just to be standing in front of a shabby, gaudy store filled with random stuff and a Get Cash Now neon sign above the door was a thrill—and somehow felt like a privilege.

Since Elvis shook up my life at about age eight, I had been a big fan of rock and roll, though it never occurred to me to buy a guitar. The main reason: I played sports. There is only so much youthful energy to be parsed out and mine was on the hardwood court or the baseball diamond. But I had always loved rock 'n roll music. The Rolling Stones were my current favorite and I often filled my head with little snatches of melody and rhymes. On occasion, I sang improvised lyrics with a band—the Cavaliers—in the cramped basement where they practiced or on a Friday night gig at the Hinsdale Youth Center. I just sang anything that came to mind, at times wearing a bathrobe because it seemed like a good idea. I didn't yet grasp that those who are drawn to this sort of thing—improvising lyrics with a band; public absurdity—have an inkling for the arts. I hadn't yet acknowledged my own inkling.

One day after leaving Peterson Avenue, I heard *Satisfaction* for the first time while on Bryn Mawr Avenue where it feeds into Lake Shore Drive heading into the Loop. Nothing like turning up the radio to a killer song while cruising The Drive in a shiny new Impala when you were 16 years old! Roll down the window. Sing along. Pound the wheel. Slap the seat. This hazy recollection of where I was when Keith Richards' holy grail of a riff first bit me is akin to remembering where I was when JFK was assassinated (in study hall during my sophomore year in high school). And to think I was getting paid for this!

♪ ♫ ♪

At the Federal Street garage, a half-dozen levels were connected by an impossibly tight spiral ramp. I was not required or permitted to drive up these dark tunnels scarred by countless bumper scrapes. That was for the professionals. I just dropped the car off or picked it up, the same as a regular parking customer. I was the only white kid working at Federal Street. I was also the only one still in school. Every other hiker was an adult or at least past high school age. None were getting ready for college. None lived in the suburbs. None listened to the Beatles. All were black.

On occasion, I chatted about music on the radio with the guys closer to my age. In addition to WLS, the go-to station for white kids, I listened to WVON (The Voice of the Negro) late at night, so I was familiar with Chicago soul artists like Syl Johnson, The Dells, Tyrone Davis, the Chi-Lites and Jimmy Reed. A shared taste in music can be a momentary equalizer for those from vastly different points on the opportunity spectrum. Take Mary Wells' *The One Who Really Loves You*, a song on the playlists of both WLS and WVON that summer. In the record biz, this was referred to as a crossover hit: black stations and white stations playing the same tune. When that song came on the little radio in the Federal Street office and I began popping my fingers to the beat ... if I liked what he liked, we had something in common.

There was one other thing I had noticed on WVON: the commercials. Mister King's auto dealership on South Stony Island—about twenty miles south from Peterson Avenue—didn't tout their selection or price. They touted the fact that they would give credit to anyone, "even if you've been turned down all over town." Few people where I lived had been turned down "all over town." On Chicago's southside, I guessed that nearly everyone had been turned down.

This was the summer of the Watts riots in LA. Chicago was also a tinderbox of racial tension. One day, Hardy needed me to drive a van to a garage on the south side, a vast swath of Chicago I had only visited a couple of times prior, to see the Yankees play the White Sox at Comiskey Park. But this was a different experience. I was by myself, not surrounded by throngs of baseball fans. And I wasn't sure where I was going. To make things shakier, this was the first time I'd driven a van—with a manual transmission no less—and there I was, going into a neighborhood where everybody was black. It felt like a different country. It *was* a different country. I glanced at the directions I'd scribbled on a piece of paper. Was I going the right way? At an intersection, I had to slam on the brakes to avoid hitting a mother and her kids who were crossing against the light. Time stopped. For a moment, I got an inkling of what it must feel like to be in the minority. With the neighborhood watching, the woman glared then shouted something at me. As I shrunk behind the wheel, I had that feeling you get when you think your bowels might evacuate. Tomorrow's headline could have been: "Shitting White Kid Runs Over Black Family, Ignites Race Riot." The light could not turn in my favor fast enough. Back on Federal Street, I explained the incident to Hardy.

"You were lucky," he said, jangling his keys, all nonchalant. "Next time, I'll have someone else go there."

On August 14 that summer a real riot ensued when a hook and ladder fire truck lost control on the city's west side, hitting a street sign that fell onto and killed a young black woman. The truck was from an all-white fire station in an all-black neighborhood. The Governor alerted 2,000 National Guard troops. Yes, Hardy, I had been mighty lucky.

♪ ♪ ♪

There are flashpoints on the American timeline when everything seems to be unraveling. When something new might replace, for better or worse, what had been. Race was often the cause of such eruptions. I had never wished revenge on an entire race. I had never felt hatred toward an entire race. It had never occurred to me. Mainly because my parents weren't racists. But summer in the city of 1965 was a world where such disdain bubbled to the surface. At the time, it didn't dominate my thinking. I was still in my chrysalis phase, still in my high school bubble of carefree hanging out, but I began to realize that I could be hated for the color of my skin. My workmates and their ancestors had suffered centuries of cruelty and suppression from those of my skin color. Did they hate me—even though I dug James Brown? We aren't born to hate.

How was I to know that a person currently making headlines at the epi-center of this racial animus and fear would soon come to Federal Street?

♪   ♪   ♪

Muhammad Ali's white convertible Cadillac with red leather upholstery pulled into the Federal Street garage. Like an urban mirage, the heavyweight champ of the world was in the building. A couple months prior he had knocked out badass Sonny Liston in the first round. Amid great controversy, he had recently changed his name from Cassius Clay to Muhammad Ali—a Black Muslim name—which upset much of the adult population, both black and white, including his own father *and* Martin Luther King.

We had been tipped that he was coming. Hardy instructed all of us *not* to call him Cassius Clay.

"His name is now Muhammad Ali."

When the big white Caddy convertible whooshed into the garage, five or six car hikers gathered around. Ali sat in the middle of the back seat, both arms spread out along the top of the red leather seat: the King of the world. A driver and a bodyguard, both in black suits, sat in the front seat, keep-ing tabs on the scene. Ali emerged in one effortless movement. Graceful. In command. In the moment. Alert. We gathered briefly in the tiny office, and each shook the hand of the champ, the hand that had delivered the phantom punch to Sonny Liston. I felt no hatred or disdain emanating from him. He was gracious and quiet, different from his bombastic public persona. I have no idea where he was going or why he parked his car at our garage, but I had just met the Champ, the most famous person in the world, an emerging voice for his race. It never occurred to me to get his autograph.

A few weeks later I was back in high school for my senior year. I knew I would never hike cars again.

♪   ♪   ♪

1966. The year you graduate high school is a watershed year. It is the fulcrum; the point where you look ahead or begin to long for the past; when you join the fulltime workforce or the army or you go to college; a year when you might begin to entertain career options—what you want to be when you grow up. In this moment, all the possibilities afforded by the American Dream stretched before me—a thru line from stable home to good education to high school athlete to college grad to career and marriage, kids, nice home, two-week vacations, and everlasting happiness. This pre-programed path was my cultural DNA, and at that moment I didn't question it. Everything would fall into place if I didn't make waves. My career thoughts fell somewhere between vague and non-existent: possibly work in a building in the city dressed in a business suit? Practice the art of appearing professional. Put on a little show. But that was still a few years off. My next stop on this timeline would be the University of Kansas in Lawrence, recommended by my high school counselor because of the quality vs. the cost of the education. Good value! And a good draft deferment. And they had a great basketball team starring Jo Jo White.

My summertime fling with the city had given me a greater frame of reference through which to view myself and the world; an education that school could never duplicate. For a summer I had become a player in world beyond Clarendon Hills. I had noticed that my skin color and my street address gave me opportunities that many didn't have. While my high school classmates and I benefited from college and the resulting cascade of opportunities, my Federal Street workmates would be stuck in low wage jobs. I had begun to comprehend the circumstances of others. It's the least we can do as social beings.

THE FLANGE LADIES

Magnetrol machine shop, Downers Grove, IL
Summer 1966

WHENEVER MY FATHER MENTIONED HIS JOB AT the Schick Shaver factory, before his career in advertising sales, his voice took on a tonal wistfulness bordering on pride. Now it would be my turn to discover the *romance* of factory work, although I doubted that Dad's romance was about the joy of factory work but instead more about the rapture of youth.

Magnetrol Industries billed itself as a manufacturer of instruments for level and flow control. I got the job because the plant manager (or owner?) was a Ruth Lake Country Club friend of my Uncle Lee. My main duty was drilling holes into flanges. I didn't know what a flange was prior to this job. There had never been an opportunity for me to use a flange or buy a flange or even ponder a flange. I had never considered the importance of the flange or uttered the word *flange*.

"These circular discs of steel connect the guts of our nation." That's what the foreman told me on my first day. Welcome to flange world.

Each workday, I arrived on the train, walked a few blocks to the factory, grabbed a clean, denim shop apron from a stack folded against the wall, proceeded to my drill press station—one of about twenty—said hello to the ladies with eastern European accents who worked alongside me, picked up my first oily flange of the day from a large tub that sat on a battered metal table, and began drilling, an exercise in precision mindlessness. My only previous experience with a drill press had been in junior high school shop class. I think I got a "B" in the course.

Now, I found myself surrounded by factory ladies. It could have been Blanche who advised that I "Put de flange right here and clamp it down so it never move." She was a flange professional with a cigarette dangling from her lip and a babushka hiding her hair. She pointed to the X marks that were on each flange. Someone had scored the Xs and now all I had to do—like a good automaton—was bring the spinning drill bit to the X and pull the drill lever downward as the bit bored through about an inch of cast iron flange.

I can't remember doing anything on this job other than picking up flanges—most were ten inches in diameter—clamping them, drilling them, then putting them into what was referred to as a tub. Where the flanges went next was of no concern to me. Madge or Flo or Doreen likely knew, but I can't recall asking them. The narrow skill of drilling flanges would not be my main takeaway from this job. What made a greater impression on me was my co-workers.

The flange drilling ladies of Magnetrol seemed to have come from a different planet than mine. Their families had not arrived on the Mayflower. They were a breed apart from the moms I knew. Their financial circumstances didn't allow them to stay home while hubby worked. They were coarse and real. Not dainty. They ate sandwiches of pimento loaf and cheese and pickles and canned fish. And man, they were intense smokers. Two cigarettes in a ten-minute break. They also smoked while working, cigarette clinging to the lower lip, while efficiently pressing a half-inch drill bit through an oily flange. Steel shavings clung to smudged spots on their shop aprons. They wore babushkas to protect their hair from factory grit. After work, when I spied one with her hair flowing freely, it dawned upon me that she had a life apart from Magnetrol.

It would be nice to say I felt privileged to be part of the proletariat but in fact I just needed a job to supply me with gas, beer, cigarettes, the occasional date, and spending money for the looming college semester. These ladies worked for a very different reason. They were adults who needed to make rent, buy groceries, and pay for transportation. They were of the working class. I was not.

Working with people from a different class, a different culture, seeing up close how others eat and live and converse: these were the lessons of much of my early work experience. I was learning that not everybody talked like me or sounded like me or had the same opportunities that I did. We may be created equal in terms of the number of teeth, bones, and organs, but where we are born and to whom dominates our destiny soon after conception. The salt-of-the-earth female drill team had earned my respect and I hope that they enjoyed me, their flange pupil. I wish that I had been more inquisitive and learned more about them. This was their life. I was but a tourist.

I had no idea what became of the flanges that I drilled, what role in our great, industrial nation they fulfilled, what mechanical systems or contraptions they held together. Hats off to the flange. And to the ladies who drilled them. And the ladies who are still drilling them. Or have they been replaced by robots? A-h-h-h-h-h, the flange.

ROGER BAIN, who hails from Clarendon Hills, will study liberal arts at the University of Kansas. A 1966 graduate of Hinsdale high, he is a member of the Magnetrol machine shop.

STONE ALONE

For someone as moved by rock & roll as I was, it is difficult to ponder what would have happened to my life had I begun to seriously play guitar the moment I was grabbed by Elvis, Buddy Holly and Jerry Lee Lewis. But I didn't. I've already mentioned that athletics consumed most of my energy. And it had yet to dawn on me that I should, as sung by The Who, "pick up a guitar and play." In my high school, you were either a Stones, Beatles, or Beach Boys adherent. Of course, we all loved Motown. The Stones were my overwhelming fave. I owned their albums, knew the lyrics, and had fine-tuned a pretty good imitation of Mick. In modern parlance, the Stones were part of my brand. In terms of making a living, how could you beat being a Rolling Stone in 1966? Imagine if your work routine involved sneering for album cover photo shoots, playing music all night with your band, and hanging out with Marianne Faithful? In July, the Stones played the Arie Crown Theater in McCormick Place. What would it feel like to hear *Paint It Black* in person rather than just over the car radio? I got tickets—maybe $10 for a pair—and invited a girl from Lake Forest I had been dating. (She never showed up and we never spoke again.) In that moment, though, as Mick rose from a bridge lift beneath the stage floor to the Bo Diddly beat of the Buddy Holly song, *Not Fade Away*, I didn't care that I was by myself; the audience shrieks seemed part of the band. We all became part of the show. Anyone who attended was in the cult of the Stones. They were the bad boys of rock—a totally contrived image as I would eventually learn—and here they were, right before my eyes in all their glory: Mick gesticulating and sashaying; Keith breaking into a Chuck Berry duck walk; Bill Wyman off to the side, standing straight and never moving; Brian Jones in a flopping page boy haircut and Edwardian puff sleeves, bobbing up and down to the beat; Charlie Watts driving like a time machine. They were still a club band, not yet a stadium act.

Later, at home in my basement bedroom, still buzzing from the show, the phone rang. My room's phone was a recent addition and allowed me to have conversations out of earshot of my family. It also afforded privacy whenever I summoned up the courage to call a girl for a date. I often chose the Stones *Tell Me (You're Coming Back)* as a soundtrack to ramp up my swagger for these date calls. But a ringing phone late on a Sunday night was alarming. I picked up in the middle of the first ring.

"Roger," said a breathy, familiar voice. "It's me, Judy. Do you know where I am?" From my bed, I could hear a stirring through the heat ducts above, indicating my mother was now also awake.

I pressed the mouthpiece to my chest and whisper-shouted: "It's okay, Mom. Go back to sleep!" Judy was a couple grades behind me and a well-known Stones fan, now an official groupie. She preferred tight skirts and mascara and was considered loose for no other reason than her appearance. I thought she was cute and sassy, although I never told her that. I probably liked at least twenty girls at the time but kept those feelings to myself, as a typical young male hesitant to show feelings.

"Where are you?" I asked, though I had already sensed the answer.

"I'm sitting on Bill Wyman's lap." I bolted upright. She gushed that she was at the Stones' hotel somewhere near O'Hare and from her perch on Bill's lap began to provide a first-hand report: Brian Jones was running from room to room, drunk on rum—I remember that she specified it was rum—and acting obnoxious; Charlie Watts was at a jazz club somewhere in the city; Mick and Keith were in the next room listening to Dylan records, looking for songwriting inspiration; and here she was with Bill. Judy should have been a reporter for Teen World. She giggled as she passed the phone to Bill, who now had a question for me.

Bill got on the line and right away wanted to know about Judy the 15-year-old sophomore.

"Tell me, Roger, what kind of girl is she?" The bass player of the Rolling Stones—with that Brit accent I often imitated—had just uttered my name and now he was asking for my opinion!

"She's a good girl but not a nice girl," I blurted. Whatever that meant. I suppose that I was implying that she might "put out." This answer puzzled the thirty-year-old rock star with the fifteen-year-old gal on his lap. Had I spontaneously created some meaningless American aphorism?

"A good girl but not a nice girl?" repeated Bill. I heard Judy scream-laugh in the background. She knew what I meant. I began to congratulate Bill on the concert, but discussing the Stones seemed to bore him. He was more interested in Judy, who got back on the phone and told me I could meet the band at the hotel. But it was late Sunday night, and I knew there was no way I was getting permission to drive the family Rambler station wagon to an airport hotel, and I wasn't enough of a rebel to hijack the car. I hung up, dazed, coursing with questions for the next time I saw Judy, but I can't recall ever seeing her again. In that moment I thought it was okay that she was with the Old Stone twice her age, but years later would have freaked out if my own teenage daughter was with a celebrity lecher.

THE BOSSMAN
EATS GARBAGE

Naismith Hall, Lawrence, KS, Fall, 1966

WITHIN A COUPLE OF WEEKS OF MY ARRIVAL AT KU, I snagged a kitchen job at the recently opened private dormitory, Naismith Hall, named after basketball's founder and eventual KU Athletic Director, James Naismith. If I wasn't good enough to play big time college hoops, might as well work at a place named after its inventor.

Had the term upscale been used in 1966, this ten-story tower would be in the upscale category. It was billed as "luxurious living." Naismith students came from families with dough—many from Chicago's North Shore—who believed that their precious offspring deserved living conditions a cut above the typical dorm rat.

"We will never run out of food," stated a brochure for Naismith Hall. That sounded good to me. The prospect of delicious, plentiful meals was a motivating factor for choosing to work at Naismith. I was given a choice of compensation: either $1.00 per hour or ... free meals. A buck an hour was below the federal minimum wage standard, but Naismith Hall didn't bother with this compliance. I chose the money option. What 18-year-old didn't want an extra $15-$20 bucks in their pocket in 1966?

When you are on KP duty, you quickly learn what constitutes garbage. I witnessed trays of perfectly good chicken fried steak, meatloaf and mashed potatoes, and triple decker club sandwiches being tossed into garbage bins: a close up look at blatant American waste. At what point in our timeline did it become necessary to throw so much stuff away? Was this the byproduct or the goal of an affluent society? I hadn't yet grasped that money leaves a trail of garbage. More money, more waste. "That guy has a lot of garbage. He must be doing well." The food I was expected to throw away could have fed a legion of the hungry. A costly lunch item one minute became garbage the next. Delicious garbage. To do my small part in combatting this wasteful behavior, I decided to save some of the "garbage" for my own sustenance while on trash detail.

My system was simple: I placed paper napkins inside an empty five-gallon industrial vegetable can then nonchalantly filled it with uneaten cheeseburgers. When no supervisor was looking, I placed the can in the trash barrel then wheeled it to the back dock, reached into the huge can of cheeseburgers and took one bite of 25 different burgers. Seemed less wasteful than eating two entire burgers and throwing away 23 whole ones. I tore into each burger as if in a cheeseburger speed eating contest. There was little time to savor each bite as I was expected back inside in a minute or two. I also ravaged the day-old cakes and pies, doing my part to at least get some of the food into a human digestive system rather than a one-way ticket to the dump. The trick was to refrain from stuffing so much into my ever-hungry maw that I would be unable to swallow it if anyone surprised me.

Another distinct memory from this job was instigated by a magazine article (Time?) about how "today's youth" were experimenting with various methods of catching a buzz. When the staff bakers made banana bread for the dorm, I requested that they save the peels for me. The inside of the banana peel was purported to have a psychedelic component. Sounded like bullshit, but I was game. The baker ladies rightfully thought I was crazy when I scraped the insides of a dozen peels, placed the scrapings on a tray, baked them for a few minutes, emptied the tobacco from a filter cigarette, filled it with the baked inner peel stuff, went out on the back dock, lit up and proceeded to give myself a sore throat. The sensual pleasure of eating a banana beats smoking one. Obviously, I had no weed connection yet. In 1966, nobody smoked grass in the Phi Psi house where I lived. It was more of a study-and-get-drunk atmosphere.

My boss at Naismith Hall, the food service manager, was a short guy with a crew cut named Dalton. This guy was the archetype of a square. He had a white face, a flat top haircut, rosy cheeks and always wore a gray suit. Or maybe any suit turned gray when he put it on. He also had inordinately large shoes, of almost clown-like proportions, and what I considered to be a misplaced enthusiasm for his stupid job. I had just turned 18; he was about 28. He thought I was some cool guy because instead of saying "cool," I said "boss," a term I had picked up listening to WVON in Chicago. It may have been DJ Herb Kent the Cool Gent who said boss. Or Pervis Spann the Blues Man during his late-night shift. Or E. Rodney Jones. In any case, it was a boss station. (Was boss a play on, "Yes, boss?" Or did it mean, "that rules!" Or was it from the Jimmy Reed song? *Big Boss Man, can't you hear me when I call.*)

"Hey, Dalton. You're looking mighty boss today," I said to my boss. "I think a string tie might go well with your new suit." I always encouraged him to wear string ties because he was befuddled by the suggestion, and I enjoyed befuddling others. When he found out my nickname was Bossman, recently given to me at my fraternity, he relished calling me Bossman.

"Hey, Bossman," said Dalton. "How was the lunch rush today?" I suspected that during the rush he had been reading food service magazines in his office.

"It was fairly boss," was my reply.

During one back dock feast, after I had shoved a substantial amount of yesterday's strawberry cream cake into my pie hole, Dalton burst through the back-dock door like he was Superman ready to take off. But it was me who soared off the dock with my back to Dalton.

"Hey, Bossman," he said. "Do we need to do something about all the sweat bees out here?" He was seeking my counsel, but my mouth was too full of cake for a reply, so I began to furiously swat at imaginary sweat bees while slinking out of sight behind the dumpster, where I bent down low and spit out the contraband.

"Yes, the bees are bad today," I answered wiping a smear of cake from my face. "That's why I jumped."

Seeing how quickly he picked up on *boss,* I decided to coin a new adjective just for Dalton—*book*. Man, that's *book*. A short while later, Dalton eagerly informed me that he was feeling *book*. He was not putting me on. He was feeling *book*. I could see it in his strut.

My boss was calling me Bossman and now I wanted him to proclaim something to be *book*. What possessed me to propagate this put on? There was a lesson here, but what? How easy it can be to manipulate? How persuasion and manipulation are cousins? How ridicule is the root of ridiculous? Or, how everything's *book* when you're young and well-fed and managing Cs in most of your classes? Or, how people who don't *get it* are fodder for wise asses?

Of course, as far as manipulations go, this was relatively benign. Far greater ruses awaited in my future.

The Bossman

MOVING STRANGERS

Beltman North American Van Lines,
Chicagoland, 1967

BACK IN CLARENDON HILLS AFTER MY FRESHMAN YEAR AT KU, I worked as a mover for North American Van Lines, giving me a brief glimpse into the reality of folks on the verge of change, in the midst of disruption. The mover is a stranger who invades the most private parts of a family's home and gets paid to turn their lives inside out. When moving a family *into* a home, you lug the furniture and boxes from the trailer and place each item in the appropriate room, but you don't see what's inside the boxes. *Removing* a family from their home is more revealing. You pack up their drawers full of crap and mementos, their exquisite furniture, priceless heirlooms, and collections of implements and strategically wedge them into a truck. You see the booze they drink and the cereal they eat. You see the stains on the carpet and the messes they have failed to clean up. You spot the mouse turds. You go through their entire assortment of plates, wrapping each one in newspaper, then putting them into a box marked "kitchen." You empty drawers of corkscrews, hole punches and batteries into a box marked "miscellaneous." You get grease all over your shirt from the filthy back of the refrigerator, the grimy tangle of steel coils unseen after being shoved against the wall 20 years ago.

Some of the folks appeared wistful or anxious about the impending move, while others seemed as if they couldn't wait to leave.

"The people in this neighborhood all have a stick up their ass," one lady sniffed to no one in particular as she watched her purple couch get carried up the ramp and into the truck headed for San Diego. And most of the customers were nervous about having a stranger—like me—touching all their stuff. Some made excuses about the condition of their stuff.

"I just couldn't leave this," said a man pointing to a battered tool chest that was missing a leg. "It was my father's."

It was too heavy to move until I emptied the drawers into a few boxes. And I soon learned about books and records and how much they can weigh when you put them all into one big box.

This job introduced me to the fiercely independent long-haul drivers I worked alongside. They were at times irascible and often possessed a crafty intelligence. Sometimes I'd meet them at the moving site, other times I'd climb into the semi-trailer cab and drive with them to the site. It could be anywhere in Chicagoland. One time in a far south suburb, we got stuck beneath a viaduct. It had obviously happened to the driver before. He jumped out of the cab, and I could tell he had a plan. He got his pressure gauge and let the air out of every damn tire until we were low enough to scrape through. And then he lit up a Camel and told me he was suffering from a bit of a hangover.

Most drivers leased their own rigs, made their own decisions, and had freedom from the daily grind. Every day presented a new adventure, a behind-the-scenes look at America on the move. In the mid-1960s some twenty percent of the country made a move in any particular year, twice the rate of modern times.

The long-haul mover had mastered the art and science of making the necessary calculations to achieve a balanced load that wouldn't slide around during the long haul and would be easy to unload. During the house walk-through, the driver sized up what to load first.

"Okay. Let's put a couple of mattresses against the back wall of the trailer and then we're gonna nudge the piano right next to 'em," he'd bark. "Wrap the piano nice and tight. And take off that belt! That piano gets scratched and it's my ass not yours!"

Pianos were a problem—especially high-end grand pianos that had to be carefully blanketed and bungeed. And that was to say nothing of how damn heavy they were.

Moving a hide-a-bed down three flights of rickety wooden back porch stairs is the definition of backbreaking work. One summer was enough for me. This was another job that was not exactly greasing the skids to a future that still never stretched more than the next semester. But I had been introduced to an American archetype: the independent contractor. The road warrior.

For years afterward, when I was in someone's home, I might look around at their stuff and inwardly determine what should load first and what they should get rid of right now because it wasn't worth moving.

HOT GREASE AND THE ACE FLIPPER

Lum's fast food restaurant, Lawrence, KS, 1967

THE FAST-FOOD ERA WAS UPON US. SPEED RULED. Meals no longer needed to be respites of relaxation. Why wait for your order when you could get it in less than two minutes at McDonald's, whose goal was to deliver a near identical experience at every location across the country? Cookie cutter sameness was touted as a *good* thing. This new breed of restaurant didn't need tablecloths or waitresses. That was old school. For those in a big hurry—like most productive members of the rat race should be—you could even eat while standing at the counter. Salt, sugar, and grease joined forces to create a mid-century American umami thing, delivered to you in a bag, a minute or two after having placed your order.

As this culinary revolution unfolded, I was working in the kitchen of my fraternity, a job that reduced my room and board, but paid me no hard cash. I needed money I could spend. That's how I found myself at a joint called Lum's, which may be the worst name ever for a fast-food franchise. Compare the name Lum's to, say, Dairy Queen. DQ is a good name. It sounds inviting and wholesome. The cow and the queen. Americana. Lum's, however, rhymes with the popular antacid, Tums. And it sounds too much like bums. In my imagination, the Lum's were a family of losers: a smelly daughter, an out-of-control son, a chowderhead father and an alcoholic ma who lived in a ramshackle house in some 1930s black and white Mickey Rooney movie. You'll be surprised to know Lum's doesn't exist anymore.

But you can't blame the Lum's brain trust for wanting in on the action. The company began as a small hot dog stand in Miami and by the late '60s had locations in many states, including one in Lawrence. I spotted a help wanted sign in the Lum's window and was quickly offered a job. There was no angst-filled waiting period to see if you'd got the job. Lumsters were hired on the spot. The main qualification was your availability to work right away. Could you start *now*? Here's a mop.

I willingly took these food service jobs to earn spending money for things like 3.2 beer at The Wagon Wheel or donuts from the iconic Lawrence establishment, Joe's Donuts, that served hot and greasy donuts to sloshed students. It never dawned on me that I could be more ambitious. I still had no idea what I wanted to be when I grew up.

You needed mirthless determination to make it through a shift. Lumsters punched in, without joy, then punched out four hours later and slid through the door to whatever banal pleasures awaited. I made no friends on the job and cannot now recall a single co-worker. But it was here that I witnessed the Ace Flipper, brought in to handle the grill during the busiest two hours of the year: from 9:30 – 11:30 prior to the noon kickoff of the KU/K-State football game. College kids like me had not acquired the skills to keep up with the riotous demand for hot, greasy burgers craved by the rah-rah crowd. This day required the ace.

The legend drove in from some faraway place—a version of a Kansas gunslinger. When he slipped in the back door, the manager proclaimed, "There he is!" All eyes turned to a gaunt, slightly agitated dude who looked like Harry Dean Stanton's half-brother. I couldn't get the notion out of my head that he also looked a bit Speck-ish—as in Richard Speck, the nurse killer. I nodded in his direction, but the Flipping Ace was already headed to the break room to put on his apron. He carried what appeared to be a mini violin case that turned out to house his customized spatula. It had his name and a date engraved on the handle, commemorating a flipping milestone. It was said that he had flipped a million burgers—a true American hero.

Things were about to get crazy. As throngs poured into Lum's, all hankering a dose of morning grease, I was at my station: a tank of boiling oil. After two weeks on the job, this vat of hot oil had become my domain. My task was to dip a French Cheesie into the tank. The French Cheesie was a Lum's original, one of the unhealthiest sandwiches yet perpetrated upon our species. Before their baptism in boiling oil, they were frozen little sandwich quarters filled with either cheese product or what was purported to be tuna—the Tuna Cheesie. The thing was coated with frozen batter and a dusting of meal; industrial food for those eager to shove anything down their gullets. Deep frying makes most things palatable.

As the orders piled up, I dropped a wire basket of Cheesies into the bubbling vat. The tiles beneath me had a veneer of grease, as did my face. It permeated my clothes and ruined a perfectly good pair of Chukka Boots. It was like peering through a Vaseline smeared lens.

While waiting the 45 seconds or so that it took for a basket of Cheesies to brown, I glanced toward the Ace Flipper, who had about 83 burgers going at the same time. Every square inch on the steaming, smoking grill slab was filled with burger patties. Ace lit the occasional Pall Mall and usually, but not always, kept the ash from landing on his work. Hunching over the rows of hot meat, he found a flipping rhythm, like the conductor of a sizzling patty orchestra. Sweat dripped through the bandana tied above his brow and hissed when it hit the grill, creating a salty mist that mixed with the greasy burger smoke and the robust odor of Cheesie oil, an olfactory onslaught that I can still conjure, though not with relish.

By game time Lum's had emptied, save for us shift workers. The thin, weaselly Flipping Ace threw his apron into the laundry bin, wiped off his spatula, placed it in the case, and rode off into the early afternoon sun. There was no time for small talk. He didn't even eat. I waited until after his departure to consume my self-made Cheesie.

Lum's was pure rah-rah, white bread, Kansas, but a parallel culture in Lawrence had also begun to take shape, one that I would soon join. This was the hip Lawrence where William Burroughs eventually came to live and give readings in his gravelly voice to a handful of aficionados at the student union, stopping every few paragraphs to take a sip from a glass of water, his only stage prop. This was the Lawrence of Pig Newton and the Wizards playing acid rock at Potters Lake on a warm spring day to a lawn full of tripping hippies who had recently discovered that the state of bliss and the state of Kansas could be one and the same. The Lawrence where the Barking Geckos—my future band—yipped at Off the Wall Hall during the National Surrealist Party's 1976 Convention, playing songs with titles like *Far Eastern Supermarket Opening'* and *There's a Dead Mouse Resting on My Conscience.* The Lawrence where Abbie Hoffman told a field house full of students that they should kill their parents (metaphorically, of course) and then, after his performance, crashed overnight at the house with the rotting couch on the ramshackle front porch at the corner of 13th and Tennessee. The Lawrence where the Kaw Valley Hemp Pickers staged their annual Big Eat just outside the city limit, a counter-culture celebration of the illegal weed harvest. The Lawrence of Mike Barlow—The Barl—and his Husky puppies and his cartoon illustrations, his perpetual Marlboro and cowboy hat and greasy duster, and his attempt to kayak down the Kaw to the Missouri to the Mississippi to New Orleans in the dead of winter. The Lawrence where I would idle away jobless afternoons dashing off poems for the dustbin in a dimly lit booth at the Bierstube tavern.

It was only a matter of time before I lost my taste for Cheesies. When I left Lum's at the end of the school year, I never again set foot in the place—though I'll never forget the Flipping Ace. He was a master. Being really good at something, no matter how trivial, sets you apart.

My next work experience with the fast-food industry would be under profoundly different circumstances some twenty-five years in the future, doing something I was really good at.

THE THREE JOB SUMMER OF 1968

Western suburbs of Chicago

EVERYONE WAS WORKING IN 1968. SINCE WORLD WAR II, America had experienced two decades of prosperity. Unemployment was hovering around three percent. Manufacturing was still strong. You could buy a VW Beetle for about $1,700. The minimum wage was $1.60. A pack of Old Gold Filters was a quarter. Coca-Cola was a dime. And, oh yes, Martin Luther King was assassinated in April and Bobby Kennedy in June. A lot of people were bummed out, angry or feeling hopeless. The riots at the Democratic Convention exploded in late August. Haight Ashbury was turning away from LSD in favor of speed—or so said the underground newspapers that I would soon begin reading.

As the country heaved with uncertainty, I plugged away in three short-lived summer jobs, doing things I would hopefully never have to do again. My friends and I all worked without being particularly thankful for the opportunity. For us, summer jobs grew on trees. Our only impediment was the Vietnam War. Work, drink and be merry for tomorrow you might die in a rice paddy 5,000 miles away.

My first gig that summer was as a carpenter's apprentice at a Del Webb development in booming Oak Brook, Illinois, a few miles north of Clarendon Hills. This was the domain of Paul Butler, Oak Brook's founder and godfather, a wealthy guy of the polo set who had convinced the state to run two tollways through his land, increasing its value by a gazillion. My high school friend, Bill, got me the job and he provided my ride to work.

This turned out to be a laborer position, but to management, calling us laborers meant dealing with the labor union and having to pay higher wages. By creating an apprentice classification, the money men saw a way to get cheap labor. An apprentice carpenter had to do what he was told for minimum wage. I used my hammer mostly for pulling nails, not pounding them. That was a task for real carpenters.

One hot, humid day about six weeks into the job, with the temperature climbing well into the 90s, I was tasked with lining a foundation pit with pea gravel. First, shovel the gravel into the wheelbarrow, then trudge it over to the pit and dump. Repeat. Heat waves shimmered above the pit. It was grueling work and after a full day I was officially gassed. My justice-seeking mind told me that something didn't feel right. Shoveling pea was laborer union work, I told the foreman. Which paid twice what I was making. I quit, on principle. My parents were not overly pleased with my stand against injustice because the result was a son without a job.

♫ ♫ ♫

I couldn't be idle, so I teamed up with a gal I knew from KU who had been stenciling addresses onto the curbs of unsuspecting suburban homeowners then asking for a donation. We had no permits and never investigated the legality of unauthorized curb stenciling. Our one rule: never stencil anywhere near where we lived. Clarendon Hills had no curbs, so I was safe. After painting one side of a street—whether the residents liked it or not—we put envelopes into their mailboxes (technically a federal offense but who knew?) with a message suggesting a two-dollar donation for hard-working college kids earning money for tuition and books. (And beer.) At the end of a good day we might split 30 bucks. This endeavor was part con/part begging and I suppose it opened my eyes to the myriad ways one can make money.

37

Another takeaway from this so-called job: oil-based paint cannot be removed from cloth upholstery. One day I spilled a half-gallon of white paint onto the backseat of my family's first ever second car, a 1962 Pontiac Catalina. I had convinced my mother to loan it to me for a trial period. My dad's reaction encompassed exasperation and scorn, feelings that I eventually experienced with my own kids' follies in the hazy future. "I can't *wait* until you have kids," my dad taunted.

Years later I inherited the Pontiac and the paint stain.

♫   ♫   ♫

Next. Door-to-door selling is an ancient commercial art that I had witnessed on Blodgett Street when an encyclopedia salesman knocked on our door. Although I had gone curb-to-curb during my last gig, I had never aspired to go door-to-door until an unlikely opportunity appeared. A guy I knew was selling Fuller Brush and he recruited me to join in the fun: my brief brush with an iconic American tradition.

Growing up I remember the Fuller Brush man coming to our house. That was when Fuller Brush men were just that—men. Grown men. Adult men. Men with hopes and dreams. Not summer break college kids. For me to even consider knocking on doors uninvited with a suitcase full of brushes took an attitude adjustment. Are you kidding me? asked the sensible part of my brain. Give it a try, said one of the other parts.

To the 1950s housewife, the Fuller Brush man provided a diversion. She could turn off the vacuum cleaner and blithely welcome a strange man wearing a suit into her home, one who carried a valise similar to a medical doctor's. It may have even titillated her. It provided a momentary escape from removing dry cleaner plastic from a kid's windpipe or carrying out the endless tasks required to run a household. Purchasing a good brush—after hearing all about its construction, bristle count and durability—was an investment for the family, not just a frivolous expenditure. That's how she explained the new purchase to her husband when he arrived home after a hard day at the office, loosening his necktie and ready for martinis and meatloaf before falling asleep on the couch.

At the tail end of the 1960s an increasing number of housewives were joining the workforce. This caused Fuller Brush to change strategies and target storefront businesses rather than residences. On my one training day, I walked a route with the guy who had hired me and listened to his spiel. He was very smooth. Unflappable. He knew when to scram because there was no hope of a sale, but he also knew the signs of hope, when a "not right now" could be turned into an "oh ... okay. I'll have that one."

My boss told me that he was making a "killing." "It's a piece of cake if you know how to sell." Eat cake and kill: the capitalist manifesto. After one day of witnessing how to sell brushes to strangers, I was on my own. My insoluble problem was that carrying a large briefcase stuffed with brushes made me feel like a dork. One who feels dork-ish will not succeed. Attitude is everything, the saying goes. If anyone I knew saw me, I might drop the case and run. But we were in a suburb where I knew no one.

I have always remembered—that I managed to sell toilet bowl cleaner to a Chinese laundry. I thought it the salesperson's duty to push for more but when I suggested that they double their order the woman behind the counter told me to leave. "You go now!" With my black case of products now a few ounces lighter, I shuffled to the next block, where, after a long deliberation, I managed to sell a hairbrush to a couple of women who ran a poodle parlor. They got to brushing little Frenchie as I made a quick getaway in case they changed their minds.

After a half day this felt like drudgery. With a finite amount of time on the planet, I reasoned, why spend it doing things that I was not cut out for? Not that I could define just what it was that I might be cut out for. With each step, my case of brushes grew heavier and my self-image more cartoon-ish. My heart wasn't in it. Nor my head or my soul. By high noon, using the power of negative thinking, I decided that it wasn't worth my time or talent to remain a Fuller Brush Man. I fired myself and headed to Wrigley Field for the afternoon Cubs game. I had earned about $6.00, enough for a Wrigley Field bleacher ticket, two hot dogs, a couple bucks of gas, a pack of Old Gold Filters and a dollar or two to save for my future.

♪ ♪ ♪

I was beginning to realize that everything before our eyes has required selling. It is a fundamental concept: a combination of psychology, persuasion, and confidence. The salesman stereotype is that of the much-maligned con man in league with the devil: the slippery used car salesman; the bible selling huckster; the glib politician; the Moroccan rug merchant. The reality is that we all enjoy being sold to if the seller is masterful. Selling is a form of performance art on display in every corner of the world. Go into a restaurant and find the toothpicks. Somewhere, a toothpick salesperson has convinced a manager of the durability, comfort, and exceptional price of his toothpicks. Had I joined this pantheon of sales sharpies? Although I can be cheerfully persuasive, I am not a born salesman. I am not a "he could sell ice to the Eskimos" salesman. I am more of a thoughtful salesman. The problem with being a thoughtful salesperson, however, is that it requires a thoughtful buyer, not a buyer who wishes you would just shut up and leave their poodle parlor.

♫ ♫ ♫

During this job-hopping summer of 1968, while protestors were getting their heads bloodied by the police at the Democratic Convention in Chicago, while US troop levels in Vietnam were escalating past a half-million, as the Apollo 8 crew trained to become the first humans to leave earth's orbit, I had remained in my safe bubble of suburbia and a draft deferment while shoveling, stenciling, selling, and quitting.

SIGN READER

3-M National Advertising, Bedford Park, IL
Summer 1969

"PEACE. BROTHER."

The nation was, going through some changes in 1969. In August, an event for the ages featured youth culture gone pleasantly wild in upstate New York at the Woodstock Peace and Music Festival. Never had so many been so high in one place at the same time. Marijuana, music, mud and naked tripping. Peace may have been *the* word for 1969. There were college kids for peace, mothers for peace, clergy for peace, soldiers for peace, even Senators for peace. John and Yoko recommended that we give peace a chance, while Nixon bombed the bejesus out of Vietnam in the name of "peace with honor," meaning peace that he and Kissinger could sell as victory to the American public. But change was coming—or had come. You could feel it in the air. The left was no longer the province of workers. Now it was populated by kids in their twenties. Moratorium Day on October 15, a mass protest against the Vietnam War, would see millions marching in cities and college campuses.

That summer was the final fling for my life on Blodgett, but I hadn't consciously realized that I would soon join this disaffected youth brigade.

I continued living on the fumes of my past. I had not yet shed my skin. For now, I was still an ex-jock, ex-frat boy enrolled in a pre-ordained life of orthodoxy, but I felt a growing tug of disillusionment with this path. The Vietnam War was a catalyst to question authority and the white picket fence version of the American Dream, but I hadn't yet begun to voice—or live—my inchoate opinions. How could you listen to *Street Fighting Man* or *Sympathy for The Devil* and wish to remain an upstanding young citizen.

I caught wind of a paid marketing internship at the 3-M Corporation in Bedford Park, a near southwest suburb of Chicago. Other than the fact that they manufactured Scotch Tape, I knew little about the company, whose full name was Minnesota Mining & Manufacturing. A paid internship there would keep my options open. It would look good on my resume I imagined.

From a pool of about 15 hopefuls, 3M selected me. It seemed so easy. Some candidates undoubtedly had more career ambition, but I had a confidence generated by nonchalance. If I didn't get the job, so what? I could find something else to do. At my nonchalant interview I realized what a stellar contender I was. I had been the vice president of my fraternity, I was enrolled in the KU Journalism School majoring in advertising with a minor in speech, I had been a basketball starter in high school. I was tall. I had a winning smile that fell somewhere between a smirk and a chuckle. Also, I lived in Clarendon Hills,where a 3M division head resided. That couldn't hurt my chances. I would have hired me.

One of the guys I beat out went on to become Worldwide President of marketing at Disney. He was a high school friend of mine, and years later—possibly at our 30th high school reunion—when he was mega successful, he recalled that he'd lost out to me. I had no idea that he had even applied for the internship.. Getting beat out of this internship obviously had no effect on his career.

My random guess of the other thirteen applicants: three or four were drafted into the army, one may have been wounded in Vietnam, two might have experimented with LSD, and maybe one joined a commune and learned how to make tofu. Six certainly turned into good suburban dads, and three found happiness in a sales career. There may have been one or two females amongst the candidates but there may also have been none.

The building where I was to work was situated amongst huge warehouses, freight yards, a railroad, and a landscape of smoke, fumes and industry, a tableu only a pigeon could love but an ideal setting for the office salt mine. Instead of a pick and shovel, it was a phone and a report every Wednesday by 9:00 a.m. Everyone in the office wore business attire purchased at Wieboldt's or Carson's or Sears: many shades of off-brown and almost-gray. No pinstripes, no sharkskin, nothing flamboyant or sartorial. The entire floor exuded monochromatic blandness, a fluorescent wasteland of identical cubicles from which rose the low hum of conversation or phone talk, unpunctuated by guffaws, shouts, exclamations, or transistor radios. A snapshot of the office slog of existence.

Into this stepped the chuckling prince of nonchalance. I was assigned a desk that was barren except for a telephone and a scotch tape dispenser. The only items in the drawers were little scotch tape dispensers. If at the time I didn't find this hilarious, I do now. Scotch tape was everywhere. This was a great place to repair torn book pages or ripped five-dollar bills.

Scotch Tape was all about the quick fix. But my first task required no tape. In the name of market research, I was to phone 100 motels in California to ask if they belonged to a certain travel association. The reasoning behind this assignment wasn't explained and I didn't ask. "Hello, motel clerk. I am a marketing research whiz kid who has no idea what he's doing and I would like to know if you belong to the California Motel Association." Every call prompted the same response: the association had ceased operation. About 20 calls in, I thought it sensible to report my findings.

"Keep making the calls, " instructed my boss, whose shirt collars were too tight, making his head look like it was being squeezed upward, like someone should step in and loosen his tie or he might asphyxiate. " Always look like you're working," he concluded, as he returned to his office and picked up the phone.

This was my first brush with menial office labor. "Look like you're working" is a mantra for many, if not most jobs. Either I continue to make fruitless calls, or my boss would have to figure something else for me to do—and just like that I would become a pain in the ass to him. I continued to make the calls until they found something else for me to do.

Busy work can be a form of torture, but I was in luck. The marketing division I worked for had a map product named *Travelaid* that listed the exact text on each exit sign of each Interstate highway throughout much of the nation. The maps were distributed free at gas stations within a quarter mile of each interstate interchange. One key to the operation's success was to have accurate, updated exit sign copy. I would be the updater.

The balance of the summer I gathered exit sign copy, cruising the interstates, driving through each interchange and writing down copy while speeding behind the wheel—true distracted driving. I often wrote without looking at the paper or drove without looking at the road—in a time before seat belt laws. As a fast-approaching sign appeared, I glanced down at the clipboard on the passenger seat and furiously scribbled. This was no job for lefties. I often drove the same interchange a bunch of times to make sure I got the wording right. *Foxboro North .5 miles.* I rented cars and drove interstate highways from Illinois to Minnesota, Kentucky, Pennsylvania, Boston—most of the time by myself. This sealed the deal: I wasn't an office guy. I preferred the freedom of the road.

A *Travelaid* sales force beat the bushes for local businesses in order to sell little ads on the maps, often nothing more than the name, address, and phone number of the business plus a phrase like, "in business since 1956" or "best burger within a mile of the Interstate" or "24-hour tow service." After a couple weeks I accompanied one of the salesmen to see how he worked his magic. It wasn't magic. More like persistence and persuasion. Writing down sign copy with my life unfurling before me was profoundly different from what the salesman was doing. His life already seemed to be unfurled. I stood next to him—we both wore business suits because this was business—as he went through the numbers with an assistant manager at a gas station Kwik mart.

"It's all about targeting your advertising," he explained to the disinterested clerk, who replied that any ad spending decisions required the approval of the manager, who wouldn't be in until late tomorrow afternoon or the day after or the twelfth of never. If this was different selling than Fuller Brush, it seemed to require a similar acceptance of rejection.

Had my short-term partner settled on this job because he wasn't qualified for anything better than hectoring bored clerks? Was this his dream job and if not, what was? Was he trapped by a family and mortgage? Was my dad, also an ad salesman, trapped? Would I, one day, be trapped? Are we trapped the moment we're born? Or are we let loose? These questions ran through my mind as the salesman and I made small talk, gazing out the windshield at the Interstate. When I asked if he liked the job, I didn't get a straightforward answer. He instead outlined his service in the Korean War. Then he brought up the Vietnam War and protests. He couldn't figure how anyone wouldn't want to serve his country. I told him that if I joined, I wouldn't be serving my country but instead would be serving a deadly, wrong-headed policy.

"I don't believe the war should even be taking place," I said—one of the first times I had voiced aloud that sentiment to anyone other than family or friends. He didn't agree with my assessment. Life was about duty. Do what you're told. Don't question authority. Neither of our minds changed.

This was my last office work until I reached my thirties. I had tasted the corporate world. For a summer, it was a good experience. For a lifetime career, it gave me a "Is this all there is?" feeling. I had a growing realization that my path was my own decision and to hell with expectations—a liberating feeling.

♫ ♫ ♫

One Saturday morning that summer my friend Steve sauntered down our driveway on Blodgett while I was helping my dad with some household project in our one-car garage. For the past ten summers Steve and I had played catch, ridden bikes, talked about girls, and listened to Del Shannon records together. We played furious games of one-on-one hoops in his driveway. We had both been Little League all-stars, getting our names in the *Clarendon Hills Doings*.

"Guess what?" said Steve. Before I could answer the world's most ridiculous question, he said, "I enlisted."

I gulped. My dad coughed. Steve looked sheepish. He tried to downplay the seriousness of the situation by explaining how he hadn't really been ready for college, how young he would be when he got out of the army, how he could then go to college on the GI Bill and how his dad thought it was the right decision. Steve's reasons for enlisting were not because of politics or patriotism or a belief in the war, but instead because his dad was a World War II vet and an American Legion officer. Steve felt that he'd already raised so much hell in his young life that he now owed this penance to his gung-ho father. He never mentioned the possibility of cradling a dying comrade in the jungle or contracting malaria, although he would soon experience both things. I didn't know what else to say other than, "good luck." I felt blindsided.

As Steve walked back down the driveway, my dad turned to me and said, "Don't you get any ideas." No problem, Dad. I had no ideas.

My dad had been denied enlistment in WWII due to asthma. I would never be pressured by a gung ho father. In fact, both he and my mother were on the side of the anti-war protestors. We weren't a military family, unless you count Colonel Jehiel Day, a distant ancestor on my father's side who had been a hero in the War of 1812.

Like much else, I hadn't yet given my impending date with the draft board much thought. I still had a student deferment, allowing me to float along on my sea of privilege. But Steve's announcement had given me a dose of unease: my Little League buddy going off to war to please his dad. Would I put my life on the line to please my own father?

I MUST BE CRAZY

Lawrence, KS, 1969-70

IN MY FINAL YEAR AT THE UNIVERSITY OF KANSAS, I was ready to have my mind blown or blow it myself. I never thought, "I'll become a hippie." I simply quit getting haircuts and got high with astonishing frequency. This transformation had been inevitable. I was attracted to the free form, counterculture life beginning freshman year when I had staged a couple of "be-ins" in my fraternity house basement. I recited self-penned absurdist poems like *Pink Labels of Garb* while accompanied by guitar feedback supplied by a brother as another rapidly turned the light switch on and off to mimic a strobe light. Yet another brother popped his fingers. In a certain sense these were Mad Magazine-esque parodies of Bob Dylan, Alan Ginsburg and the beat/hipster scene.

Now, in my final year, flush with a $1,500 student loan (nearly $14,000 in 2022 dollars), after paying my tuition, I bought an ounce of hashish from a scraggily long hair who I had recently met then spent a chunk on the four-way ownership of a 1956 yellow International Harvester school bus. Tom Wolfe's The Electric Kool-Aid Acid Test about Ken Kesey, the merry pranksters and their bus Furthur, served as inspiration. In our bus, referred to as "the bus," we crunched along the gravel roads outside of Lawrence, going

47

nowhere in particular but feeling like we were headed in the right direction. My fraternity days were in the rear-view mirror, and I would never again reside on Blodgett Street.

Stepping off the bus after a cruise in my band jacket

I lived with three roommates—two were fellow bus owners—in a dusty old house that was considered upscale in 1920 but for a long while had been rented to students; meaning it was in a state of neglect. We called it the crash pad because someone was always visiting from somewhere and curling up in a corner at bedtime. Anyone was welcome to our party—hippies, athletes, misfits, grad students, future football coaches, shabby old men who roamed the neighborhood alley: the more the merrier. At one gathering, while demonstrating a Mick Jagger stage move, I fell backward onto the lumpy couch where an empty glass awaited, slicing into my right kidney region. The resulting laceration required internal stitches. I could have bled out to *Let It Bleed*.

My part-time occupation was bussing tables at a sorority house, where I filled up on thoughtless calories from the chocolate milk machine—a dream of my five-year-old self. Even sorority sisters were becoming radicalized. It was chic. Jaunty. A few went braless and dated guys with long hair who lived off campus and smoked weed. Two years prior, these guys might have worn short hair and belonged to a fraternity; or they were hedonists, cosmic intellectuals, or smart kid misfits. Outward appearances, including my own, were morphing into a look that was *anything goes.* I remember wearing my first pair of bell bottoms to class, like I was "coming out." Then I bought a well-used high school band jacket at a thrift store and a frayed waistcoat that was most likely part of a three-piece ensemble. Goodbye button-down shirts. It was 1969.

My rapid awakening was stoked by literature, music, underground newspapers, Zap Comics and psychedelics. I read Kerouac, Abbie Hoffman, Joseph Heller, Kurt Vonnegut, the occasional issue of *Ramparts, The Village Voice,* the *Berkeley Barb,* the local underground rag, *Vortex,* and I tore through every issue of *Rolling Stone Magazine.* The journey of self-discovery that Herman Hesse chronicled in *Siddhartha* now made sense. My expanding musical tastes included the anti-pop records of Captain Beefheart, especially *Trout Mask Replica,* so deliciously bizarre and such a big thumb in the eye of convention. My favorite university course was Cases in Persuasion, where we sat in a circle and said whatever was in our minds. My existential contributions were something like: "we're on a small rock spinning around in the middle of infinity, so why worry?" Like some cosmic Alfred E. Neuman.

But the shadow of Vietnam loomed over all young males.

Throughout the past six years, U.S. troop levels in Vietnam had swelled to half a million. I remained in the sunshine of my student draft deferment, but how much longer before it got cloudy and started to rain on my parade of good times and chocolate milk and bus joy rides?

I didn't know any commies, so I wasn't frightened of them, but fear of communism—any communism, even in a tiny country like North Vietnam—had ruled U.S. foreign policy for decades. Shouldn't I learn more about this fear? In a nod to the fear of getting my head blown off for reasons I couldn't fathom, I considered it my civic duty, my moral duty, my patriotic duty, to understand why we were fighting the Vietnamese in their own country. Was it worth dying for? Killing for? After a diet of pamphlets, articles, teach-ins, be-ins, speeches, and rallies, I concluded that the war was futile and wrong. (Defense Secretary Robert McNamara, an architect of the war, published the same conclusion several decades later.)

Ho Chi Minh, the North Vietnamese leader, our ally during WWII, didn't want colonialists—the USA and before us the French—from a distant land to shape the soul of his country. Nor did he want China, their historic enemy, to dictate terms. Ho wanted North and South Vietnam to be unified. Meanwhile, our leaders told us that if South Vietnam *fell* to communism, the next country and the one after that would fall, like so many dominoes, a game played with human lives. Uncle Sam was sending hundreds of thousands of its youth to fight in the name of this domino theory, employing hideous chemicals and defoliants, bombing the countryside into oblivion, and racking up staggering civilian casualties, all while misleading the American public from behind the flag.

As America propped up a series of corrupt South Vietnamese governments with little regard to what the Vietnamese people wanted, our stated strategy was to win the hearts and minds of these people of whom we knew so little. The Pentagon brain trust had overlooked one ageless principle: you can't occupy and expect to win the hearts and minds of the occupied.

With the war grinding on in Southeast Asia, a different one was taking place at home. Pot smoking, long haired students had become the enemy of President Richard Nixon and the so-called *moral majority,* who professed: "If you're against the war you're *for* the enemy." This postulate presupposes that the war is a just and necessary one. Many disagreed. Radicals, hippies, yippies, Black Panthers, students, clergy, folk singers, and a few senators fueled a resistance movement that squared off against Nixon, the Generals, most of Congress and the "America, right or wrong" crowd. By fall of 1969, college students were almost twice as likely as the general population to oppose Nixon's war policies and a bazillion times more likely to smoke weed. That's why Tricky Dick changed marijuana classification to a Schedule I drug—the same as heroin—to make it easier to bust his youthful opposition. Questions of patriotism and morality were debated on campuses, at workplaces and in the media. The nightly news featured carnage and meaningless enemy body counts, like a scorecard in a game of Grim Reaper. (We killed a thousand of them last week and they only killed five hundred of ours. We must be winning!) Esteemed CBS anchor, Walter Cronkite, had publicly concluded the war to be unwinnable. Meanwhile, the defense industry was making a killing.

My transition from high school athlete to college fraternity brother to poster boy for everything Nixon detested was now complete. I marched along Memorial Drive on National Vietnam Moratorium Day, October 15. I didn't wear a button-down shirt, and instead I wore discarded clothing from the Salvation Army store. I didn't drive a respectable sedan, I careened around in an old school bus. I didn't drink scotch and soda, I smoked hash. My American dream did not include volunteering to be a pawn in a tragedy.

The army had an insatiable need for conscript pawns. A government official had the idea of creating a draft lottery to be randomly *fair* about which clueless youngsters would be sent to the jungle halfway around the globe. On December 1, 1969, with much fanfare, this lottery was conducted on national television and radio. On that date I found myself alone at the crash pad—as alone as I had ever felt—tuned in to a Kansas City radio station broadcasting the lottery. If your number was 200 or below, induction was guaranteed. Maybe I would be #365 and avoid this whole mess?

The reality show began. The announcer intoned, "Number one," and then grabbed one of 366 blue plastic capsules, each containing a birth date. "September 14th," the announcer continued. Guys born on September 14th immediately knew they were toast. They had lottery number one. As each number and corresponding birthdate was announced I felt an uneasy sorrow for the unknown names attached. This was fate playing out on national TV and radio. Beethoven's unfinished ninth symphony, which he described as grabbing fate by the throat, would have provided the perfect soundtrack for the broadcast.

With each number called that wasn't mine, I relaxed by a factor of 1/366th. After a weird, sizable unit of time went by, the lottery show reached number 82. Then, the voice coming over the radio clearly stated the exact date that *I* was born. My birthday. The date that my mother always circled on the calendar. The date I brought cupcakes for the kindergarten class in

1953. My birthday was lottery number 82. My fate had been grabbed by the throat. Unless I was deemed unfit for military service, I would be inducted. Back home, my mother was crying, my father was pacing, and my siblings were stunned. I was defiant.

A few months later, at my draft physical in Chicago, I was unruly, purposely dropping my urine specimen on the table of war clerks. I shouted gibberish. I laughed maniacally. I showed the war doctor a note stating that I had a grand mal seizure when I was five years old. (My mother reminded me of this and secured the note.) I made quite a show of the lack of mobility in my shoulder that had been dislocated several years before while playing summer league basketball and pulled out another doctor's note. The notes were flying but it didn't matter. I passed. They were passing everybody.

The next move was mine.

We choose our own paths but have less of a say in the path that the leaders of our country choose. Would the world be a better place with a population that followed their informed conscience or their elected leaders? The conundrum: conscience or country?

My only certainty at this point—with the full backing of my parents—was that under no circumstance would I volunteer to kill strangers in their own country, strangers who had never threatened me or my fellow citizens. I also wasn't wild about getting shot and I was allergic to authority, never a good trait for a service member. I read pamphlets about going to Canada, where my father said he would move the entire family if necessary. I read about becoming a conscientious objector or going to prison.

Forget it, I thought. I'll go crazy.

With the guidance of two older friends, one a clinical psychologist, the other a Doctor of Pharmacology, we hatched a crazy scheme. Under the tutelage of my "crazy coaches," I studied how to become a paranoid, messed up, depressed, dysfunctional, maladjusted, mixed-up college kid. I would be the kid that the army deemed unfit for service. A 4-F or 1-Y classification would do.

I remember the scent of incense on a sleepy afternoon at the collaborating psychologist's ramshackle house, where my coaches laid out the plan—a real-life escapade. I would create a history of psychological problems of such a degree that the army wouldn't dare accept me. One determinate would be the MMPI personality test, a thing I had never heard of. My collaborators coached me on how to take this true/false test with 551 questions. It apparently had a built-in detection key designed to catch those trying to fake a psychiatric disorder. As I recall, there were seven or eight questions embedded within the test that needed to be answered a certain way. My clinical psychologist friend provided me with the numbers of these embedded questions and how I was to answer each one. He told me that I could answer the rest of the test however I normally would. If those seven or eight questions were answered correctly, no one would suspect what I was up to. But I couldn't just ask to take the test. I needed a licensed practitioner to prescribe it.

Phase one of our plan: with the help of lysergic acid 25, I stayed up all night reading *Case Studies in Deviant Behavior*. If you've ever dropped acid, you know that reading while zonked out is a waste of time. You are too engrossed in the universal, or the molecular, or the infinite, or the hilarity of existence, or the sound of your breathing and how it is the perfect match for the thrum of the cosmos. This trip was a tactic in a caper from which I learned many life lessons. The next day, when the psychedelic effects wore off, I was haggard and ineloquent: the perfect state for my performance as a maladjusted misfit. A truly epic role for a fake actor.

In the morning, exhausted, and after downing a bowl of shredded wheat—which I somehow still recall—I traipsed up the hill to the student health center. I shuffled to the sign-in window in the small lobby and, avoiding eye contact with the receptionist, explained that I could no longer sleep. After that I shut up and stared at the shiny floor tiles. I managed a quick peek at the receptionist because she sounded cute.

"Please have a seat," she said, as I looked away. I remained standing. "It's okay to sit down," she assured me. "Someone will be right with you." I took one more peek while she wasn't looking. She *was* cute. Maybe she was attracted to disturbed misfits?

Within a few minutes, I was directed to the office of a counselor. I lit a cigarette, then another. My instructions were to look no one in the eye. Sigh at the right time. Search for my words after long pauses. Project a feeling that it was all too much. Slowly, stumblingly reveal that I had been unable to sleep with my girlfriend; that I had little interest in school; that I was being supported by my aunt, which had in turn caused a rift with her brother, my father; that last week I had wet my bed. I would lie my way out of my predicament. It was more like acting than lying. A performance.

Eventually, the counselor brought up the subject of the war. I volunteered that I didn't want to be inducted but I didn't know what I should do. After my litany of tribulations, the specter of military induction was just one of many problems I owned.

"I'm not going to commit you," said the counselor, (Commit me? Whoa! My plan was working!) "but would you voluntarily like to spend the night in the student health facility?"

I glanced downward and let out a small gasp, as if the idea of self-commitment freaked me out. I didn't wish to appear to be too willing. "Not today. Maybe if things don't get better," was my weak rejoinder.

A couple of weeks later, after another meeting with the same counselor at the student health center, and after my disappointment that the cute receptionist wasn't on duty, I "submitted" to an overnight stay. As I climbed into my hospital bed, a nurse brought me a dose of Thorazine, a drug used to treat mood disorders and acid freak-outs. It had little effect on my non-freaked out state, but it was good for my record.

A one-night stay seemed enough to me. The next day, I flew over the cuckoo's nest, slipping out when no one was looking. Breaking out would also be a good black mark on my growing record. And Quicksilver Messenger Service was playing that night at the Freedom Palace in Kansas City. I didn't want to miss John Cipollina's trippy guitar solos that made you forget where you were, even though this was where you wanted to be.

My next step was to find a second opinion from a psychologist licensed to administer the MMPI, one who might be, *wink-wink*, sympathetic to my situation. The entire mental health industry was aware of the avoiding-the-draft-by-pretending–you're-crazy phenomenon. But such notions could never be uttered by either patient or doctor. The counselor at the health center gave me the name of a psychologist in Kansas City, who my collaborators confirmed would be a good choice. I set up an appointment and took my true/false test. It was the weirdest test I have ever taken. Here are some examples:

- I am very seldom troubled by constipation. (True or false)
- At times, I feel like swearing. (True or false)
- Evil spirits possess me at times. (True or false)
- Everything is turning out to be just like the prophets in the bible said it would. (True or false)
- When I am with people, I am bothered by hearing very queer things. (True or false)
- I loved my father. (True or false)
- It would be better if almost all laws were thrown away. (True or false)
- I think I would like the work of a librarian. (True or false)

The test results came in and I "passed." I was on my way to certification! The following week I received a note that I could show to the army. The note stated that I might be "harmful to myself and others." That covered a lot of ground. Everybody steer clear of this guy. He's a harm to everybody. (The note may be in a memory box in my attic right now.)

I soon landed an appointment with the army shrink so he could make a final assessment of how much harm I might cause to the military. His bedside manor was brusque and dismissive. With a touch of sadistic glee, he ordered me into a tiny room to re-take the MMPI. It was the kind of room where the walls seem to be closing in on you. The thought of re-taking this soul-crushing test almost made me think that I should have just joined the army. Answer yes/no to 551 questions like these and you, too, will go crazy. Especially in a tiny stinking room, surrounded by those who could swoop in and throw me onto a cargo plane bound for Da Nang.

- I have often had to take orders from someone who didn't know as much as I did. (True or false)
- I have often wished I were a girl. (True or false)
- I used to like drop-the-handkerchief. (True or false)
- My judgement is better than it ever was. (True or false)
- I wish I could be as happy as others seem to be. (True or false)

I finished the damn test. The army shrink made me wait for his decision:

the waiting was torture. Time stands still while you fidget. He knew I was on trial. He was the judge and the jury. Guilty, your honor. I'm guilty of an elaborate scam to avoid becoming fodder.

After a jittery hour in the waiting room, a uniformed dude about my age walked in, stood in front of me and, with a straight delivery, said, "Congratulations."

"Congratulations, what?" I asked.

"The army rejected you," he answered, turned on his heels and strode away.

It took a few seconds to sink in, sort of like an honest sip of good bourbon that goes down hot and finishes warm and fuzzy. Never have I so loved being called a reject. I had achieved my goal. This similar-aged, uniformed Army dude knew that I was the lucky one. Had he been secretly rooting for me? I was rooting for him. I was rooting for every dude in uniform. Not rooting for them to kill the Viet Cong but rooting for the killing to cease. Rooting for peace.

This entire caper taught me the power of selling, performance, persuasion, research, gaming the system, making it happen, and creating your own rules when necessary. Maybe I had a future as an actor or a con man or in the advertising industry? I couldn't stop the war, but I could stop myself from participating in it. Following my conscience was more important to me than following the political whims of later-to-be-proven-wrong mongers in Washington. Many consider this reasoning to be blasphemous and unpatriotic. I am not saying what I did was absolutely right. It was a path I chose. I have never regretted my decision. I did what was within the scope of my own power. The unfortunate notion that there is glory for those who die in a senseless war has led to slaughter through the ages.

Wars often rely upon nationalism, blind obedience to leaders, and the naivete of the youth required to fill the battle zone. Never did I think less of the souls who went to Vietnam. Their decisions were formulated within their own minds, though many never considered it a decision. They just went along with it. I doubt that most draftees had studied the history of Vietnam or why we were there. We were but a couple of decades removed from the nightmare of WWII, the *Great War*. The prevailing feeling was that you did what your country asked of you. If Uncle Sam wanted you to kill some Cong, you did. Young men were on a conveyor belt. Few considered the alternatives because the alternatives—Canada, prison, going crazy—were as scary as the war was frightening.

One classmate in a human relations course at KU, an ROTC kid from a small Kansas town, had become intrigued by the views I had expressed in class. He visited my house and we discussed the history and politics of Vietnam and the USA, and what the country's options were as well as his own. He challenged me on my thinking, but I could tell that at the same time he was challenging his own views. When he finally shipped out, it was to a war that he now had many questions about. I hope he made it.

Some who went to Vietnam were old friends. My long-time friend, Smock, spent his final two-week leave with me prior to shipping out. When he left my house in Kansas, very conflicted, neither of us were sure if he would rejoin his battalion or go underground. He joined, gutted it out and survived. My childhood friend, Steve, who had enlisted to please his father, made it home from Vietnam with a pound of Thai sticks and told me how he had cradled a dying friend in the jungle after a fire fight. I can't recall if he told me that last part before or after we got stoned. A few years later, he introduced me to my future wife, and served as best man at our wedding before he began a ten-year descent into freebasing and other unhealthy habits. He died of a heart attack at age 42. Another classmate, who had celebrated kindergarten birthdays with me, died in Vietnam from something other than enemy fire. Either his truck slid off the road or he got a jungle infection? He was dead, and his death had occurred in Vietnam while wearing United States Army issued boots.

I checked the archives and had I been born one day earlier I would have had lottery number 232. I most likely would have escaped induction without having to go crazy. And had I been born a couple of years prior, who knows, my political awakening might never have bloomed, and I would have accepted the draft. Timing is everything. As it played out, I did what I thought was right. My life was in my own hands.

II. HARDLY WORKING
ENJOYING MY EARLY RETIREMENT...
WHILE YOUNG AND HEALTHY 1970-79

Typical middle-class American life plan:

SCHOOL
WORK
RETIRE
DIE

♫

My plan:

SCHOOL
EARLY RETIREMENT
WORK
RETIRE AGAIN
EVAPORATE INTO THE ETHER

FRIED PIE & THE REDNECK BROTHERS

Lawrence, KS, 1970

MY FIRST KANSAS SUMMER FOUND ME AT A CROSSROADS. By now, it was easier for me to list the things I didn't believe in than those that I did. I was skeptical of marriage, careers, the Vietnam War, government—in short, most of society's institutions. That was for squares, man. I wanted no one to tell me what to do or to think. The choices I made had to be mine. All mine. In a notebook I scribbled, *live as if your life depended on it*.

I hatched a plan, a life map where I would "retire" at the *beginning* of adulthood. Of course, I would need to work, but as little as possible. And nothing career oriented. Hell, I had no idea what I might do.

♫ ♫ ♫

I found a meaningless temporary job in the want ads section of *The Lawrence Daily Journal World*: Help Wanted: Bakery Work. My mind conjured cakes ... pies ... sweet rolls. I applied, interviewed with the owners—two large, surly, unkempt brothers—convinced them of my sincere desire to get into the baking trade, and got the job. They took whomever they could get. Not many wanted to work in an un-airconditioned bakery during the Kansas summer. They simply needed a warm body. Even a hippie vermin body with a beard and long hair would do.

It would be generous to refer to the place as a bakery. The operation centered around deep frying those little turnover-style pies of fruit or chocolate that are wrapped in waxy paper and sold at grocery and convenience stores: they're sweet, processed, and cheap, advertised as a snack or lunchbox treat, and have nutritional value akin to licking a bowl of frosting. Growing up, I wolfed down these pies in four or five bites. You could close your eyes and not be sure if you were eating apple or blueberry or peach. It was just sweet goop, offering a momentary rush of sugar.

The brothers bought truckloads of pre-made frozen pies from an industrial baking operation, executed the final deep frying and wrapping, then shipped them to wherever worthless calories were sold. This was hardly baking. There was no mixing of ingredients. No braiding the dough. No brushing with egg white to achieve a post-bake sheen. These pies were manufactured, not baked. I was certainly gaining an insider view of the American appetite for industrial, institutional food, like I had witnessed at Naismith Hall and Lum's. We had transitioned from being a nation of eaters to a nation of consumers. These pies were meant to be consumed, not eaten.

The job required a hairnet to keep my long hair out of the pies. The brothers were not in the business of selling hair pie. It was their running joke. I was also compelled to wear a beard net. The brothers got a kick out of this. A beard net is akin to wearing a feedbag or a drool cup. I might as well have pulled a ladies' stocking down over my head like a bank robber.

My main task was shuttling trays of pies from the deep fryers to the racks and the stainless-steel cooling tables that lined the oppressive warehouse. I was a fried goop shuttler. There was no clock to watch. No countdown to quitting time as the second hand ticked away. You were done for the day when the pie bros had fried enough pie.

This job taught me little about bakeries or pie, but I learned what it felt like to work for bigots who were proud of their bigotry, which they believed to be homespun wisdom. They weren't *trying* to be evil but simply thought that assigning the problems of the world, their problems, to various races and classes—of which they weren't members—was logical.

"Do you really think that black people's smart as us?" one might ask me.

What does a young white guy employee say to his boss in this situation?

"Black people are as smart as they care to be but they're not willfully ignorant."

Properly confused, the pie bro strokes his chin, and the world went 'round.

The redneck brothers believed that their ideology was the only true path for real Americans. They drove pickup trucks sporting American flag bumper stickers. The flag belongs to us, not you. Hippies didn't put flags on their bumpers. Instead, they sewed them on to the ass of their frayed jeans. The American flag bumper sticker was proof that the driver supported Nixon and the Vietnam War, was against hippies and liberals and believed in God, not LSD. This was the period when the American flag was appropriated by belligerent assholes. It continues.

All that patriotism required constant vigilance. An air of fatigue often cloaked the brothers. It was draining to always be on alert for disrupters. They detested hippies, but I got a pass because I worked for them. They knew me. This must have twisted them into knots. It was the hippies they *didn't* know that they hated. They spouted off about killing some damn hippies, both to show their patriotic cred and to rile me. I never truly thought they would kill anyone, and they never tried to physically harm me, but their venting often included descriptions of mayhem.

Quite a few other subcultures sparked the ire of the brothers. The usual suspects: Indians from any hemisphere, dark skinned people, and kinky-haired New Yorkers. But it was their damn business and their damn warehouse, they could say whatever they damn well pleased and if I didn't like it, I could get a damn job somewhere else because this was America, dammit! Just check out old glory on their truck bumpers.

We developed an understanding, an acceptance that we were of different minds. I wasn't going to change their way of thinking. For my own amusement I might ask a brother:

"Who's number one on your hate list today?"

"Those fuckers that hang North Vietnamese flags on their wall."

"And who is that?"

"Some hippies on Tennessee Street. I read about it in the *Journal World*. Believe me, they couldn't get away with that in Russia."

"So, we should be more like Russia?"

"When it comes to hippies, we should."

"Am I a hippie?"

"I hope not."

Though I never referred to myself as a hippie, that was my stereotype. If you had long hair and wore threadbare clothes, you were a hippie. It was a look. Simple as that. You are how you look. In 1971, if you *looked* like a hippie, one could extrapolate that you smoked grass, were anti-war and laughed at the American Dream. Being a hippie made you feel like an outsider in a culture that you didn't wish to fully participate in. And that made you feel kind of good, like it was your best chance to experience the heroic status of the minority. Minority heroes were the hip heroes. Rosa Parks, Caesar Chavez, Huey Newton, the New York rabble rouser, Abbie Hoffman, and Jerry Garcia, the acid guitar shaman with the Latino last name.

If I cut my hair, shaved, put on a golf shirt, slacks, and tassel loafers (footwear I abhorred and still do), I could have landed a job befitting my upbringing and education. I would have no longer been an outsider. I would have become part of the system. But real minorities needed more than a haircut and a job to fit in. I could fool the rednecks on account of my skin. Bigotry and racism are simply a disdain for the *other*, always a surefire way to attract a collection of haters and dimwits. And votes.

The next election, 1972, would pit Nixon against George McGovern. Tricky Dick appealed to the "moral majority." God was on their side. McGovern appealed to the disgruntled minority. Not enough were on his side. Nixon won, which only heightened my disdain for *the establishment*. Blatant bigotry has been a constant in this land of immigrants. From sea to shining sea high profile politicians have tapped into this vein of disdain for the other. They have often been sadly successful.

I didn't believe in society's institutions, but I did have my beliefs. Very strong ones. I believed in the magic of existence; the magic around every corner; the magic of the moment. And now, the magic of guitar playing. During that melting summer of 1970, alongside teaching myself to seem crazy, I began the lifelong endeavor of teaching myself to play the guitar. I wanted to write songs. My inner voice needed an outlet. Because I hadn't begun playing during the typical teenage timeframe, I had a lot of ground to make up. A girlfriend bought me a cheap acoustic, I picked up a few songbooks—one by Donovan, I remember—had guitarist friends show me chord changes, and I was hooked. Nothing has had a more profound effect on my life.

A MEMBER OF
THE CONGREGATION

Minneapolis, MN, 1971

AS LIFE ROLLED BY IN LAWRENCE. MY ONE-TIME CRASH PAD roommate and fellow bus owner, Stew Rose, called me. I had lost track of him. "Hey, Ozzie. I'm in Minneapolis." Stew had nicknamed me Ozzie because of my wizardry, I guessed. "George and I leased a church here on Seven Corners and we're living in it. We have a leather store and we're starting to sell waterbeds. You'd be perfect to manage the waterbed store." A job offer? Sounded wacky enough for my tastes. Say no more. I slipped out of Lawrence.

Leather goods were the rage. Handmade leather sandals, purses and belts were in most young wardrobes. George and Stew selected Minneapolis because one of them had a love interest in the Twin Cities. They had also negotiated a sales territory with a California waterbed distributor. Thus, was born the Funk & Rose Leather Goods and Waterbed Emporium. Belts of leather and beds of water. Cutting edge retail at the time.

My new neighborhood was a downtrodden district with seven corners. The seven converging streets had nowhere else to go. It was a screwed-up jumble of urban planning defined by empty lots overgrown with weeds, parked semi-trailers, tarpaper shacks, chain link fencing, abandoned ware-houses, a biker saloon, a retail appliance store, and the Band Box Café.

Boozing, both indoor and outdoor, was a popular sport. Broken glass lay scattered everywhere, a coat of sad glitter that sparkled when the sun came out, giving the corners the appearance of a twinkling wasteland, an urban Oz. Instead of munchkins, there were the elderly, the diminished, the hus-tlers and a smattering of students, artists, and hippies.

The building that housed Funk & Rose had been a Slavic Baptist Church until its parishioners fled to the promised land. It then morphed into a chair fac-tory. Dusty stacks of partially finished chairs and seat caning machinery lined one wall. A large punch press idled in back by the loading dock, gathering dust. A few church pews were crammed together in what had been the choir loft. A series of makeshift rooms in the one-time choir loft housed a fluid cast of residents: draft dodgers, runaways, hitch hikers, writers, dreamers, and an ex-cop who had been kicked out of the force due to his love of psychedelic recreation. All the remodel-ing handiwork was George's, including the basement platform shower.

My private quarters were quite public. I slept in the front display room window on the first waterbed I had ever seen. My bed also served as the test bed for customers. My roommate was a mannequin outfitted in a leather vest and leather cap. Only a plate glass window separated me from the nighttime scene of ghastly shadows and patches of neon. More than one time I awoke in the early hours to find myself mere inches from a retching wino on the other side of the glass. I had never lived in such a profound environment. This was a long way from Clarendon Hills or Lawrence. It reminded me of the skid row I had witnessed with my father when I was very young but now I was a participant rather than an ogler.

The Church occupancy changed on a weekly basis. When all were pres-ent there was a hum, a vibe: George tinkering with the wiring or the plumb-ing or the carpentry; Stew reading the Wall Street Journal, talking business over the phone; Lars the ex-cop tooling a belt; Natasha sewing a leather coat; Banjo Bob, the draft dodger, just back from Canada, frailing away upstairs; the South Dakota gals accompanied by their sled dogs, dropping by with some afternoon tequila; and Sherlock the Basset hound hugging the floor-boards. I had stepped into a warped fairy tale.

All church residents were expected to craft something of leather, if not daily, at least occasionally. It's hard to say that I had a boss. I received no official training in crafting leather goods nor, as far as I could tell, did any of my fellow crafters. We were a parish of auto-didacts. Customers at times joined in and made their own leather thing.

Most nights at the church featured a party of sorts with a menu of—drum roll—crummy weed, the cheapest beer available, and Boone's Farm Apple wine, resulting in the Seven Corners Buzz. The ex-cop got wasted every night on quarts of Boone's Farm while playing the electric bass guitar at full volume. Sherlock the Basset Hound provided the vocals. You could either leave the building or join in.

Across Seven Corners from the church sat The Clifton House, a flophouse for indigents run by Ralph Mayhood, who lost both times he ran for the state senate. We still referred to him as the Senator. He housed the sad men who staggered, stumbled, bled and puked their way to the short end of the stick, while he collected their social security and disability monthlies. Senator M employed two, nearly seven-foot Native Americans who, for reasons only imagined, were often on crutches or wearing casts. These were the Senator's driver and his body man. Their resemblance to kin of Frankenstein was uncanny. The senator was like a character out of some 1950s Republic serial, driven about by twin behemoths in a grotesque, chopped and elongated 1950s Cadillac, an evil menace to the universe who must be stopped. If one of us spotted the senator or his chopped caddy, we would drop our belts and rush to the front door of the church for a look: a senator spotting. It should be noted that seven or eight years later, the Senator was murdered by drunken residents in his own hotel.

♩ ♩ ♩

A focal point of Church life was the Band Box, a tiny art deco style café squeezed in front of an expressway overpass. The Box had four counter stools and a pair of two tops. The cook was a hairless, 80-year-old deaf dude with hearing aids. The only vegetables served at the Box were potatoes and onions. Nothing grown above ground. Nothing green. It was a salad free zone.

George and Stew were connoisseurs of greasy spoon fare and could be found in the Box at least seven times a week. Stew wore button-down shirts as he frequented the diner, the Wall Street Journal tucked under his arm, keeping up with the world of corporate finance, a world that one day he would join. Reading the Journal dressed in an oxford button down while consuming "three tacos for a dollar," he was just another Box regular. George was like a kid in a candy store, surrounded by a relentless supply of colorful street characters to carry on with.

The Box interior was busy with signs of butcher paper and shirt cardboard, drawn with crayons and magic marker, each done, quite obviously, by the same hand, with the same graphic: a pointing finger. Like you see in clip art. On some signs, the finger pointed to the prices: "Tacos 3 for $1.00." Others had the finger pointing to instructions: "No spitting on premises." Others provided lunchroom philosophy embellished with a pointing finger: "We are not responsible for our food once it is in your mouth." The sign maker was Harold S, self-proclaimed Mayor of Seven Corners.

Harold was frail and well into his 70s. He had the appearance of someone who had been given a shrinking pill yet retained the clothes of his previous weight. His worn gray overcoat was cut for a man twice his size. His hair seemed to be blackened with what? Shoe polish? His pale-yellow facial skin was dotted with liver spots. On the bridge of his schnoz rested a pair of bifocals usually in need of a cleaning. Beneath his overcoat he wore a buttoned business suit. Writing instruments peaked from the breast pocket. Harold claimed that in the old days in Chicago he had been a trouble shooter and ward boss for Big Bill Thompson, the mayor, hushing up political scandals, collecting payoffs and hanging out at The Hanging Gardens, a bar in Cicero run by the kid brother of notorious mobster, Frank Nitti. Harold's business card identified him as a "locator." What did a locator do?

"I locate! People need to find things." Harold was a bit miffed at the question.

Harold the chef cooked for us in the Church basement. Due to decades of sucking on cheap stogies, the only tastebud he had left was the one that detected heat. He used extraordinary amounts of pepper and hot sauce in whatever he concocted. Extraordinary! An entire family-size black pepper container poured into a boiling vat before your watering eyes. Add a bottle of hot sauce and, Voila! Hungarian Stew ala Harold. Watching somebody sample Hal's food for the first time was a treat for fans of sardonic slapstick. One time a hitchhiker from North Dakota gagged so energetically on Hal's chicken soup that we thought he would choke to death. I had learned to fill my bowl with ketchup and crackers to counterbalance the pepper effect.

George and Stew had become Hal's, keepers. (We referred to him as Hal when not in his presence.) They took him shopping or wherever he needed to go, always addressing him in loud voices because he was hard of hearing. The Church gave Hal an unlikely social scene that hadn't existed for him before Funk & Rose. And Hal, in turn, gave us an endearing yet irascible—and unlikely—colleague, foil, talisman. I commend Stew and George for their generous outreach to one who is far outside their upbringing. And Hal appreciated the attention. A cross-pollination of both backgrounds and generations is helpful if our species is to survive and flourish.

Hal serving George and Stew a fiery fish head stew

♪   ♪   ♪

The ravages of alcoholism were everywhere on the Corners. While taking a morning stroll down Cedar Avenue, I came upon a disheveled mess of a man—a bum you might call him—clinging to the chain link fence next to the sidewalk that spanned the expressway overpass behind the Box. His gnarled hands clutched the links, his grimy shoes kicked at the fence, his tattered overcoat whipped in the wind. As I helped him off the fence, he shoved me, thinking I wanted to filch his brown bag of Tokay that rested on the sidewalk. A witness may have had difficulty determining my role in this skid row scene. My scruffy appearance almost put me in the same league as the other guy. Which one was the bum? In 1971, more than half of the country would have considered *me* to be a bum. I gave the guy his wine bag and resumed my walk.

♪   ♪   ♪

SUBSTANCE ABUSE COUNSELOR FOR A DAY

One afternoon, George summoned me to Mixers, a Seven Corners bar that catered to anyone who wanted to drink. I walked past the afternoon pool game and spotted George in a corner booth with an unshaven man in his late forties who looked disheveled, but one step above the clientele from The Clifton House.

"Ozzie, I want you to meet Bill Gaylord." George, who had been drying out the past few months, was sipping a coke. "Bill here wants to get turned on."

In front of Bill Gaylord sat a row of empty shot glasses. George was a magnet for fringe characters. Bill waved George into silence.

"I'll take it from here," said Bill, as his bloodshot eyes met my gaze. "Ya see, Mr. Oz ... I won't make any bones about it. I'm an alcoholic."

"Could have fooled me," I said with good humored sarcasm.

"That obvious, huh? I've been trying to kick the stuff for seventeen years," he said with an air of bemused pain. "But it's only gotten worse. I lost my job, my wife left me, and my kids won't speak to me. My life's a mess. But I can't stop. See this hand." He held up a slightly tremorous hand.

71

"Steady as a rock," I said.

"Took six shots of scotch to steady it. I'll try anything to stop. George here says I should try pot and you might be able to help me."

This put me in the rather exalted position of healer. "Have you ever tried it before?" I asked, sounding to myself like a doctor.

"No. I never tried it and I don't want anybody to know. My wife can't find out."

"I thought you said she left you?"

"She might as well have left me, but we still live in the same house. She calls me her disgrace. Last week, she gave me the ultimatum for about the fiftieth time. 'Quit the booze or I'm kicking you out.' I think this time she means it."

"Well, I guess I could find a little something. Come back tomorrow and—"

"No. I want it right now. Get some and follow me to my house. I don't know how to smoke it or anything."

"It's alright, Ozzie. Bill here is cool," said George, who seemed to be enjoying this intervention, coarse correction, underground therapy, whatever it was.

Trying to turn on a drunk was precisely the kind of off-the-wall adventure that gave me a sense of purpose. Of engagement. I went to the Church to grab my small stash and get the communal rattletrap van, ready to follow a middle-aged alcoholic who I had known for ten minutes to his suburban home, an act of both do-goodery and adventure. My mother would have been proud. Maybe.

Bill pulled his baby blue T-bird into the shoveled driveway of an expensive looking white brick ranch house on Red Bud Lane. A rush of amazement and understanding dawned upon me: those souls I had seen on West Madison Street in Chicago and Seven Corners may not have been born into a life of wretchedness. Many drank their way there, making me wonder about the wino I encountered on the chain link fence. Is this how Bill could end up? He was in a limbo: one foot in the suburbs and one on the Corners. Was I his latest hope? His only hope? Me, with a little bag of reefer?

"Is your wife home?"

"She's at work. Come in. I need a drink."

"Look, Mister Gaylord. If you're trying to quit, you can't keep drinking. You can't just think about quitting."

"I know. I've tried."

His hangdog expression touched me. "Take your shoes off, please," he said. The place was immaculate. And quiet. The living room and dining room appeared to be off limits to humans. You could almost hear the dust settle on the polished dining room table.

The stairwell to the finished basement was lined with pictures of happy, well-scrubbed Americans. Model citizens. The son in graduation robes, daughter at a beach; mom—a very young mom—with a young, smiling dude: Bill Gaylord, the happy husband. What promise life held, said their smiles. Bring on the future.

At the bottom of the stairs, Bill knocked the last picture askew. I straightened it, a large-framed color shot of two young men posing with a Giant Marlin hanging between them. They held drinks and looked very pleased, a scene to make Hemingway proud. The caption read: *Havana 1957.* Marlin fishing in Cuba was a sport for the rich. A different life. Bill had earned a lot of money at one time. He lived in a suburban showplace but hung out at Mixers, where he was just another booze hound.

Bill said, "If I'm going to smoke pot, I need a drink."

"If you keep drinking, you won't know what reefer feels like," I explained. I was the doctor. He was the patient.

"Okay. Let's see what it looks like," he said.

I'd had some experience getting the older generation stoned. I had turned on both of my parents—and even my mom's girlfriends—to somewhat hilarious results. After taking a few hits, the girlfriends all dove behind the couch when a delivery man came to the door. I wasn't sure this time would be as hilarious. I had a joint already rolled.

"Smoke it like you would a cigarette," I instructed, "but when you inhale, keep it down a couple of seconds." I torched it and took a drag.

"Here." I offered it to him.

"Well, give me my own."

"Just try this one."

"I want my own for Christ sakes. You don't go passing cigarettes around. Make me my own. Do you want a beer?" he asked.

"Sure. I'll have one." What was the use? I sat on the barstool rolling another joint as Bill Gaylord tended bar.

"A beer ain't even drinking," offered Bill in his sandpaper voice. He struck a match and took a small, hesitant hit off the joint. For a moment, the long look of eternal despair, his normal countenance, vanished. In its place was one of curiosity. Perhaps his only change in expression in years. It was no small accomplishment, and I silently congratulated myself. C'mon Doctor Ozzie.

"Hey! This ain't bad." Mrs. Gaylord must have flinched when her husband started using the word ain't. The Corners had rubbed off on him. "Yeah ... I think I feel something. What's it supposed to feel like, cuz I think I feel something?"

"Don't even think about it. Just smoke it."

He took another hit and gazed out the sliding glass doors with a look of bleary contemplation as I began to consider the prospect of his wife's return.

"Yeah ... I feel it. I'm sure I feel something. It's like ... I need a drink."

"You didn't finish your beer. Why don't you just relax a while," I said.

"Roll another one," he demanded. "Roll a couple. You think someone who drinks as much as me can get high on one little cigarette? Roll, Mr. Oz."

"Okay. But I don't have that much," I said. There had yet to be any mention of reimbursement for my house call, but what the heck, I was Dr. Oz from Kansas, and wouldn't my mother be proud? Or worried. I rolled a few numbers as Bill Gaylord alternately expressed that he could feel it, no he couldn't feel anything, did I want another beer, where could he hide it so his wife wouldn't find it and on and on. He was stoned. Finally, he wondered how much this stuff cost. I gave a quick rundown of the preferred countries of origin, how many seeds and stems were in a bag and the different weight increments available, all the way up to a pound.

"I want a pound. How much is a pound?"

"Anywhere from $100 to $300," I guessed. I had seen a kilo brick (2.2 lbs.) a couple of times but had never bought more than a lid for myself—an ounce. This was getting into felony territory. I had little idea where to even get a pound, although I thought that Lars might.

"Get me a pound of the finest," he said, absently reaching for the bottle of scotch.

I offered him three big joints, which he thought wasn't near enough for his needs. Then he again wondered where he should hide them. I said the freezer. He said behind the wall clock. I thought I heard a sound from upstairs. What would I tell his wife or kids if they came in on this scene: a hippie smoking weed with dad?

"Look, Mr. Gaylord. I gotta go."

"How will you get me the stuff?" he asked.

I told him to speak with George tomorrow. I had no intention of being a middleman. Social work was tough and maybe I wasn't cut out for it. I fingered the shrunken baggie of weed in my coat pocket as he accompanied me upstairs.

Outside, the sun was a red sliver on the horizon, a few pink clouds in the pale sky. The van started right up. As I drove down Redbud Lane, several sets of headlights passed by, and I wondered if one of them was Mrs. Gaylord and what she would think when she came home to the weed stink in her basement rumpus room. When I got back to the Church, I told George what had gone down, and he seemed proud.

♫ ♫ ♫

What awaited around the bend? Like others of my generation, I had been inspired by Kerouac's, *On the Road*. My trip to California during spring break of my college senior year had only whetted my appetite. With my friend, Spider, we had tasted America, witnessing the deciduous hills of eastern Kansas give way to the plains, then the dark green conifers of the mountains, the vastness, the unfurling possibilities; we roared through the Petrified Forest at dawn with no sleep; had our car searched at the California border while I concealed a lid of weed in my armpit; were denied entry to Tijuana because our hair was too long; saw a Tennessee Williams play, Camino Royal, performed by an offbeat theater company that served marijuana tea in Newport Beach; scored weed from a Malibu dealer who lived on a houseboat, wore a toga, and practiced his aim with a blow gun while being served scrambled eggs by his topless, ample girlfriend; watched a nameless lead singer sniff something from a bag at the Fillmore West; got rousted by the cops on a rooftop overlooking the San Francisco Bay. We were smoking weed under a blanket when they confronted us. Someone had called in a report that suspicious looking characters were on a rooftop: snipers? The cop smelled the weed and reasonably concluded that we were hippies getting stoned, not a cell of SDS. How could I settle for an office job when all of this was waiting? More west coast travel seemed inevitable. Most likely nothing planned. It would just happen.

My eyes continued to open. There was simply too much to see and do. I wanted more, the "more" that a job couldn't give me. At least, not any job that I was able to conjure. Through experience and a commitment to self-discovery, I craved an understanding of how the world worked. Seven Corners, with its collection of misfits and characters was a window into this grand, romantic notion. Or at least it seemed that way to a twenty-two-year-old kid. Church life was magical, illogical, and financially unsustainable for me, but I was grateful to be a member of the congregation. It provided a foundation for my restless American Dream.

Because I had no car, paid no rent, and shopped at thrift stores and the Salvation Army, I required little money. When I needed a new winter coat, I went to the Hall of Rags and purchased a vintage, fur collared winter coat for two dollars—it gave me the look of an extra in *Doctor Zhivago*. I could live frugally on the fumes of my upbringing and a low threshold of material desires. And an occasional $25 check from home. I didn't respond to the bank notices—sent to Blodgett Street and relayed to me by my parents—requesting that repayment begin on my student loans totaling $4500. The bank had enough money, I reasoned.

SLOSHING IN ST. PAUL

The Twin Cities' first Waterbed Store, 1971

WHEN GEORGE AND STEW PURCHASED THE TWIN CITIES waterbed territory from a California company, their grand plan called for a separate waterbed location, not just a tiny space at the Church. The "display" waterbed in the Church window—my bedroom of sorts—was hardly an inspirational setting for prospective buyers, so George and Stew rented a storefront on University Avenue in St. Paul, not exactly a thriving retail corridor. Who better to manage the store than me? My qualifications: I knew George and Stew. I spoke English. I had slept on a waterbed. I hoped that being the first waterbed store manager in the Twin Cities might sound promising to my family, but I can't recall that they were overjoyed. There would be no waterbeds on Blodgett Street.

Waterbeds had splashed into popularity in the early 1970s and rapidly spread east from California. Buy a waterbed and catch a little of the west coast vibe. Buy a waterbed and you could be an early adapter, a member of the ongoing movement to upend cultural norms by sleeping on water. The beds quickly became an accessory for a society always on the lookout for the new and different. In place of firmness and stability, the waterbed moved when you moved. It heaved when you turned over, it swelled when you sat upright, it rippled while you dreamed. It was marginally kinky. It sloshed.

My managerial duties included unlocking the front door, reversing the sign from Closed to Open, sweeping the floor and making sure the posters hung straight on the wall. We sold the posters, too, featuring psychedelic imagery, swirling neon peace signs, or trippy sayings, like Make Love Not War. If someone bought a waterbed, which was not a daily occurrence, I collected the cash or held the personal check up to the light, as per Stew's instructions, although I was never sure what I was looking for. I often brought my guitar to work to pass the time between customers. When I felt the urge for a different perspective, I put the "Back In 15 Minutes" sign on the front door and ducked into the basement for a quick puff and a few licks.

I can't recall the exact price but I'm pretty sure the beds were less than $40 for a queen size. My sales pitch stressed that water sleeping was good for back pain. No dust mites could penetrate the mattress. If you were bed-ridden, it provided a way to avoid bedsores. And please, don't worry about falling through the floor. Though the California King weighed about a ton when filled, I glibly explained that a two-hundred-pound man or a refrigerator exerts more load per square foot on a floor than a waterbed. This was my first job selling to the public, unless you count my one-day brush with Fuller Brush. I tried to be polite, avoided hyperbole and was patient with nitwits. I also didn't sell many beds.

Those early waterbeds were basically prototypes: a couple of sheets of plastic bonded together and a closeable hole where you could insert the hose. But you also needed a frame, built by George at the Church. The frame kept the waterbed from spreading out too much, alleviating pressure on the questionable seams. George's frames would have received at least a "B+" in high school shop class: sanded 2x8s, a plywood bottom, and a strip of carpet glued to the top edge of the boards, so you wouldn't bruise your knees and shins too badly upon arrival or departure. We recommended a liner in case of leaks. I also recall an additive that was necessary to keep the water from growing algae. Then there was the optional electric heater for the long Twin Cities winter, although I never trusted electricity around water.

Most beds eventually developed leaks. When a slightly disgruntled customer arrived with tales of water soaking their shag carpeting, I handed over a free patch kit. It was the same patch kit used for bicycle tire inner tubes. The patch kits didn't work any better than the waterbeds. George, the handyman savant, was the only one who could occasionally get the patch to hold. The California company assured us that the next generation of beds would be a lot stronger—although a little pricier—and soon there would be special, fitted sheets and even a water pillow.

"Won't I drown on this thing?" That was the most popular comment in 1971. To overcome this common objection, I demonstrated the strength of our beds by executing a running back flop onto the water sack and encouraging customers under three hundred pounds to do the same. The neighborhood cops dropped by to wonder aloud what would happen if someone unloaded their firearm at the waterbed, as they guffawed at the wildly hilarious scenario of water spurting out of the bed and ruining everything. The firemen from the station down University Avenue discussed the safety of smoking on a bed of water. If the smoker fell asleep with a lit cigarette, would the result be a conflagration or a flood?

The Faust Adult Movie Theater was directly across University Avenue. The day manager of the Faust often wandered over to slosh for a few minutes on his break. He had a porn mustache and wouldn't have looked out of place in *Ding Dong Schlong*. From his wavy perch on the display bed, he would look out the window commenting on each incoming and outgoing Faust customer.

"He comes at three o'clock every afternoon and buys a large box of malted milk balls."

"That guy always sits in the front row."

"This guy complains that the AC is too cold."

The Faust manager told me that anytime I wanted free popcorn, to just come over. The one time I ventured across the street to the Faust lobby, I pushed through the padded doors, peeked inside the theater, and glimpsed the backs of the heads of a smattering of patrons, bathed in porn-glow from the screen. That was my only visit to an adult theater until years later, while visiting Middlesbrough, England, I made a roots pilgrimage to the ancient theater where my grandfather had provided organ accompaniment to silent movies the night my mother was born in 1922. It had since been repurposed into a porn showcase.

♫ ♫ ♫

After a couple of months on the job, I assumed I had experienced every customer type, until the day a small group of plain, country-looking folks came into our store, looking like they might have pulled up in a buggy: bonnets and beards and overalls and long skirts. I greeted them with one of my waterbed salutations for all occasions, like, "You folks sure look like you could use a waterbed. Feel free to jump on it." My sales patter didn't seem to register. The lead man tipped his wide brimmed black hat and nodded his head. The group clustered around the bed, sizing it up, pushing on it. The oldest woman in the group, probably in her late fifties, had an extra strange vibe, a slightly dazed countenance, as if focused on something I was unable to see. She sat on the edge of a bed, sprawled onto her back, and began the inevitable sloshing and jiggling. Then she spotted the Jimi Hendrix psychedelic poster on the wall. One look caused her to bolt upright to a standing position. As the bed sloshed, she began to emit some impossible to identify ululations, nonsensical syllables of fevered gibberish. I had never seen a person in a trance, which is what she seemed to be in.

"She's speaking in tongues," offered the man who had tipped his hat. I couldn't be sure if he was their leader or her keeper. He matter-of-factly explained something about how she was channeling the mysteries of Jesus. The tongue-talker clutched at my wrist, spouted a few more phrases, then fell backwards onto the waterbed, spent from her other-worldly orgasm. As the bed rippled, she flopped along until finally she regained consciousness. I asked if she was okay and made awkward small talk with her party. When the tongue-talker had fully regained her balance, the entire group herded out of the store. I bade them farewell and put the "Back in 15 Minutes" sign on the front door.

Like so much of what I had been experiencing, this was an incident of note for me, widening my worldview, revealing the disparate elements and factions of the human stew, convincing me that I was learning something, that I was carrying out an experiment and not just bumming around, hardly working.

♪ ♪ ♪

Whenever Stew—my boss, my friend, my Church mate—made a surprise visit and found the "Back in 15 minutes" sign hanging in the door window, he reprimanded me.

"We've got to stay open all day, Ozzie," Stew implored, picturing the slew of imaginary customers who had been turned away. Since college and magic bus days, Stew had called me Ozzie, as in the Wizard of Ozzie, due to my shaggy appearance, and my appetite for the high life. He knew that I was a back-in-15-minutes kind of guy. He was surrounded by hippies, underachievers, dreamers, and drop-outs, none of which he considered himself to be. But he handled it.

When he drove me to work in the rattling company van, always accompanied by Sherlock, we often stopped for a tuna sub at a little joint that was on the way. When he picked me up at closing time, he was eager to hear if I had sold a bed. Many days I hadn't, but when I had, we celebrated with another tuna sub. Sherlock felt the vibe in the back of the van and gave off his victory smell.

Sherlock

A BLAZER IN THE NORTH WOODS

A guitarist who had gone to Canada to avoid the draft had slipped back into the country and was now living at the Church. I was practicing some licks he taught me when George called me downstairs from my Church stall. (I had moved from the front window.) It was his birthday and there was cake. As I descended the stairs, I heard a note from a pitch pipe followed quickly by the opening lines of the most over-the-top, enthusiasm-on-steroids, opera-style rendition of "Happy Birthday" I had ever heard. Belting it out was a short gentleman dressed in a blue blazer and red bow tie, his eyes ready to jump out of their sockets, his dark hair slicked back. The performance was post-eccentric. The volume he achieved was astonishing. He could have filled an auditorium. "Ozzie," said George. "I want you to meet John-John."

John was an opera singing tenor who could hit a high "C." He was a friend from George's Baker University days in Kansas—just the sort of person who would fall into George's orbit. George had served as John's protector from the louts who populated the pinball parlor near Baker University. John was the kind of person who had been mocked all his life for being too boisterous, too different, too unique, too much.

How could I have possibly known that in a decade I would utilize John's talents to promote a television channel that no one had yet conceived, in an industry that few had heard of, that was barely in its infancy? At that moment, I was not thinking about anything beyond the birthday cake that John was devouring. This guy could eat.

The next day George drove us about 50 miles northwest to the Twin Cities Waterbed Association's first annual picnic. I rode shotgun while John shared the backseat with Sherlock. In the northern woods of Wisconsin, we swatted mosquitoes, drank beer and played volleyball while John ate multiple steaks, burgers, and cake slices. The waterbed association folks—a collection of laid back, scruffy entrepreneurs—weren't sure what to think of this bow-tied guy in a blazer with a giant appetite, sweaty brow and eyes that appeared to be straining from their sockets, and this was to say nothing of his loud, vociferous behavior. His rendition of *The Drinking Song*, a popular German Lieder, rattled the pinecones, provoking Sherlock to yowl.

With John in front of the Church

GO WEST, YOUNG MAN

Goodbye Waterbeds ... California Beckons, 1971

IN 1971, THE MICROPROCESSOR WAS INVENTED, KICKSTARTING the digital age—although none of us realized it at the time. The war in Vietnam slogged on without me. The 26th amendment was ratified, lowering the voting age from 21 to 18. I was already 22. Disneyworld was set to open. Yawn. I had now been a Church member for about five months and my universe didn't reach much beyond where various Twin City girlfriends lived. My lack of career was sailing along splendidly, yet I knew that the Twin Cities would not be my permanent home.

In June, a friend from Lawrence, Brian McKinney, drove up in his 1964 VW bus, quickly fitting into the Church milieu, crafting belts and guitar straps, singing songs in a high Neil Young voice, and generally lounging around. Like me, Brian was restless and wanted to do a whole lot more than build a vertical career. Maybe he'd become a singer-songwriter with those mutton chop sideburns?

Brian's visit to the Twin Cities was a friendly detour preceding a 2,000-mile drive to San Francisco to pick up his girlfriend and take her back to Kansas. He aimed to arrive in San Francisco by the beginning of July. Would

I like to join him on this cross-country odyssey, he wondered? Of course I would!

My few months as waterbed store manager had provided enough cash for a drive out west, and then some. Meanwhile, Brian was down to his last few bucks. I had an idea: Brian could assume my duties for a couple of weeks to bankroll his trip. When I informed Stew of this plan, he tried to talk me out of it but admitted that I probably didn't have a future in the waterbed industry. Or the leather industry. Or any industry. It was true. My future stretched no further than the planned road trip to San Francisco.

For two weeks, I became Brian's unpaid supervisor at the waterbed store. The responsibility was daunting. We played our guitars in the showroom during the frequent spells when there were no customers. This interim arrangement allowed Stew time to find a replacement. On departure day in late June, Brian and I took about three minutes to pack our belongings and head into the great wide open.

♪   ♪   ♪

Life on the road! Brian's VW bus had no starter. For two thousand miles, wherever we turned off the engine had to be on a downward incline so we could push the bus and pop the clutch to jump start the thing. Night driving was impossible because the alternator was too weak to run the lights for more than a few minutes. No starter. No headlights. These were minor inconveniences for pilgrims. At least the brakes seemed to work. We were nervous about getting rousted for loitering the night we parked behind a gas station in some desolate, middle-of-nowhere outpost, but no one called the sheriff. At least gas was cheap. Thirty or forty cents a gallon, as little as nineteen cents in some spots.

Barreling down Interstate 80, we took turns playing my cheapo acoustic in the back seat. I attempted to write a song but never got past the first line: *Long ago I saw the buffalo rumble thunder across the plains.* In my mind we were part of the great tradition of western trailblazers. When an interstate hitchhiker flashed the peace sign, we pulled over, he jumped in, and we became fast friends for a few hundred miles before he hopped off to continue his own trip. (The peace sign lost all relevance a few years later when Nixon flashed it upon his resignation in 1974.) We detoured to Boulder to visit a high school friend who lived in a silo, but not for long. We were on a mission. I wondered if I would ever again live in the Midwest. My inchoate life plan was unfurling on the road, putting me in a fine state of exultation, thrilled to be part of the vastness, to ogle the magical tumbleweed, the otherworldly gas rigs dotting Wyoming like industrial art, the mirage-like salt flats in Utah where the Green Monster had broken the land speed record, and the endless sky jammed with stars. The sense of freedom was exhilarating. When I had driven to the west coast during spring break of my senior year at KU, it wasn't an open-ended trip. We only had eight days. Now, I had a one-way ticket to the rest of my life. I could do anything. I could do nothing. I could be anybody. I could write my own life.

♫ ♫ ♫

We arrived in San Francisco at the beginning of July. The city still possessed a roguish charm—a place of poets, longshoremen and radical thinkers, of eccentric shopkeepers and descendants of the gold rush, of those looking for something and those who thought they had found it. Rent was no more nor less reasonable than in Kansas or Minneapolis. The Haight Ashbury neighborhood, at one time the epicenter of flower power, hippies, and free love, now had more speed freaks than pot-smokers. More bad vibes and less bliss. But the city was still a hotbed of bohemianism and radical thought; a city of hills, little shops, psychics, collectives, gay culture, free concerts, the scent of eucalyptus and dreamy, rolling fog. The city felt different to me than when I had spent those few days here during spring break. I now felt more like I belonged.

A bonus awaited: Brian's girlfriend, Sally, had tickets to the Grateful Dead Show at the Fillmore West taking place on the long 4th of July weekend. We would experience the ultimate San Francisco acid band at the shrine of counter-culture acid rock. The Fillmore West would then close forever, unable to keep up with the burgeoning rock arena industry. But we would always be able to say that we were there and always know that we were there, and it would make a permanent deposit on our DNA.

♪ ♪ ♪

The line waiting to get into the Fillmore reeked of patchouli oil, righteous b.o., reefer and incense—the absolute freakiest freak-show the culture could assemble. There were be-robed gurus, barefoot flower girls, speed freaks, acid heads, dropouts, used-to-be-clean-cut-but-now-zonked-out-ex-varsity-athletes and assorted expats from the small towns and suburbs of America, wearing fringed vests and patched jeans, high school band jackets, puffy sleeved Zorro shirts, tank tops, granny dresses and threadbare thrift store garb adorned with feathers and buttons and beads. And many headbands. It was a scene to make most older Americans shake their collective head in befuddlement and beeline for the liquor cabinet. My reason for coming to San Francisco was to simply experience what was out there. This was definitely out there: a laid-back utopia to some, a dystopian anarchy to others. There may never have been a time so dominated by youth.

Security that night was provided by the Hell's Angels, the respected, feared, and often reviled biker gang that began in Oakland and had now achieved an ironic, almost heroic status with the peace and love crowd. They too were non-conforming California originals who thumbed their filthy noses at anything remotely bourgeois. During the Dead show, I bumped into an Angel as he took a long pull of something in a paper bag. He grunted. My Angel moment.

"Dark Star!" yelled someone from the audience. "Morning Dew!... New Minglewood!!...play something heavy!" Would the performance go on forever, until the building levitated, nirvana achieved? Would the secrets of the universe be revealed to the faithful? Every single person in the joint was high and dancing—or doing what passed for dancing—blissfully shrieking, jumping up and down, gyrating, undulating, inhabiting their own time and space, communing with the spirits, achieving ecstasy, until the entire place melted into a screaming Edvard Munch scene. Visitors from another planet would have been confused. Middle American suburbanites would have been terrified. George Washington might have wondered if crossing the Potomac had been worth it. This wasn't the revolution he had in mind.

Many hours into the show, Brian and Sally told me they were going back to the apartment. I assured them that I could find my way home—although

I had little sense of where the Fillmore was in relation to the apartment on Cole Street just north of the Panhandle—but I didn't care. I would find *the way*. I would improvise, like the Dead. With about a thousand other zapped souls, I stayed until the bittersweet end, adding my whoops and exultations as the swirling pageant of sensory madness throbbed, as each song started and swelled and petered out or hit a dead end only to be resurrected by Jerry or Phil or Bob. Jerry the hipster shaman displayed the constitution of a long-distance runner or one who knew the right chemist, never leaving the stage, playing with The Rowan Brothers, then the New Riders of the Purple Sage and finally a few hours with the Dead. *Johnny B Goode* was the last number and I'm not sure how much more I could have taken.

Somewhere between midnight and daybreak, I loped out of the Fillmore into the other world of an early morning city, quiet and surreal; where tomorrow had already begun and yesterday seemed a thousand years ago. I managed to snag a ride with some revelers in a pick-up who were headed to a donut shop near Sally's apartment. *The way*. I passed on the donuts and scrambled home. When I woke up the next afternoon, Jim Morrison's Parisian death was in the news but all we talked about was the Dead.

Over the next week, Brian busied himself reading *Zen and the Art of Motorcycle Maintenance* to gain an insight into fixing his VW bus's mechanical problems, a wonderfully ridiculous idea that seemed to make sense but didn't pan out. Brian possessed a mad spirit that couldn't be categorized. Later, he and I (Sally, too) would be founders of the Barking Geckos, an absurdist band of musical misfits. We were wavelength brothers. The Kansans jump-started their way back to Kansas, while I took over Sally's room.

♪ ♪ ♪

Although sad to see Brian depart, for the first time in my life I was away from any midwestern connections. No high school or college friends. No one who had ever been to Clarendon Hills, Lawrence, or Minneapolis. I was another immigrant from the Midwest seeking an escape, a good time, new friends, the meaning of life.

As the summer danced, I explored the city at a time before gentrification, before there was a tech sector, before area companies gave themselves edgy, ironic names and handed out extravagant salaries to young people who wanted quartz countertops AND justice, who sought virtual reality more than cosmic consciousness, who focused on a glowing screen that contained their lives.

As the summer danced, I bopped around, maybe stopping for a free vegetarian meal—what is this stuff?— at the Hari Krishna temple, sitting cross-legged in a circle with other freeloaders; maybe heading to Golden Gate Park to watch the old Italian men playing Bocce, the clicking of balls catching the breeze and landing in my ear; maybe rambling through the panhandle, weaving around eucalyptus, coastal redwoods and Monterey pines; maybe the cheap thrill of long-stepping down Haight Street past the panhandlers and burn outs; maybe stopping at Cindy's Market a half block from my place for an ice cream bar and trading pleasantries with the man we called Mister Cindy; maybe trekking (at night) to the fog-bathed Sutro Baths ruins at Lands End on the Bay, a ghostly reminder of a past civilization—our own. Another cheap thrill that cost 25¢—taking the 38 Geary Bus with no particular place to go. Hop off when you feel like it. Or, that time when word on the street had Hot Tuna playing a free show around four o'clock at the corner of wherever and Masonic, immediately springing into action using the only social media that existed at the time—asking strangers on the street if they had any pertinent Tuna info—eventually finding our way to exact spot. Or the many trips across the Bay Bridge for daytime "free concerts for the people" at Provo Park in Berkeley to hear The Youngbloods, Country Joe, Commander Cody and His Lost Planet Airmen, and Asleep at the Wheel.

The Summer of Love had come and gone, but that summer I learned to love pinto beans. Where had they been all my life? One Cole Street roomie, an even-tempered, Chicano dude from east LA, John Lopez, provided simple instructions.

"Put in just enough water to cover the beans about an inch or so, throw in salt, pepper and cumin, bring 'em to a simmer and then just keep 'em covered with water till they're done. To check, just blow on 'em and when the skin puffs, they're ready." Pinto beans have been a cornerstone of my diet ever since and I've passed down this love to my kids. (I'd eventually write two songs celebrating my adoration of the pintos.)

♫   ♫   ♫

Plans had been brewing for a camping trip to Canada. Two years previous I had considered moving to Canada to escape the draft. I was now escaping San Francisco to explore Canada with my new roommates, who had avoided the draft by being too tall or still in school or via the luck of a high lottery number. One, I soon found out, had dodged it because he had a police record.

Four of us crammed into John's compact car for what would be my first taste of the great northwest. Along the way, we cooked pinto beans in a redwood forest in Humboldt, camped at Humbug Mountain, Oregon, and plunged into every snowmelt river we crossed. When we reached the Canadian border, we were denied entry. While filling out the border questionnaire, one of our crew had confessed to getting busted for growing a pot plant in a kitchen window two years prior.

"Why the hell did you admit to that?" we asked. He said that he wanted to be an honest outlaw. We had gone to the trouble of triple wrapping our weed in tin foil then submerging it in a large jar of peanut butter—for nothing. We could have left our honest friend behind but of course we didn't. The border Mounties denied our entry for reasons of "low moral turpitude." Turpitude became the buzz word for the next couple of weeks. This Canadian border trip was a Grateful Dead lyric come to life.

♫   ♫   ♫

I returned to an empty room on Cole Street. Empty because all my worldly possessions had been with me on the trip. The room echoed slightly—a nice reverb. Though the floor was hard wood and the sleeping bag thin, it was a great atmosphere for reading Bram Stoker's *Dracula*, left by Sally, and now making the rounds in the apartment. What a chilling book to read in dim light in a bare room in an old apartment building in a foggy, eerie, ghostly city. If you've ever read *Dracula*, you won't forget it.

Simple pleasures like reading about vampires combined with my growing expertise at not spending money gave me little inclination to look for a job. The future looked bright. If I kept my mind open, everything would work out fine. I had my whole life to work. Just not right now. I still, somehow, had a few bucks from my waterbed gig. Stretching money had become a necessary life skill. I was disillusioned with society, with corporate America, with the white picket fence ... but I was happily disillusioned. Not pissed off. If Jack Kerouac and Ken Kesey could do it, why not me? I, too, was a practicing procrastinator, a seeker, a sleeping bag philosopher, a middle-class dropout with fanciful notions of time and space.

My folks mailed me a random $25 check, out of worry, I supposed. Twenty-five bucks wasn't a huge sum, about a day-and-a-half's wages at the waterbed store. But I welcomed it. And it might have eased their minds to know that at least for a week I could afford food. Kids who worry their parents never feel that the worry is warranted. I sure didn't. Don't worry about me, I'm not worried—I'm the least worried guy ever. I took my cue from Mad Magazine's poster boy, Alfred E. Neumann, whose motto was: What me worry, expressed as a statement, not a question.

My mother had concerns that my footloose ways were motivated by anger at "the system." But I didn't *feel* angry. I felt incurably happy and hopeful, as if I'd unlocked a secret to the universe. Gimme a book to read, a guitar to play, a few friends, some decent weed, an occasional road trip and all would be boss. A-h-h-h, freedom from responsibility. Avoiding the mainstream was an honored American pastime practiced by outcasts, fools, escapees, and poets.

My sister later told me that my dad was so confounded by my wayward lifestyle that he actually broke down crying one night at the small family dinner table in our kitchen, the table where I had consumed countless gallons of whole milk while growing up; the same table where I had concluded each dinnertime by saying, "Please may I be excused," then took my empty plate to the sink, then carried out the garbage. I'm glad I didn't realize the depth of my dad's despair at the time, or I might have suffered guilt. Even if you're not Catholic, guilt can creep into your life.

My parents had come of age during the depression, followed by god awful World War II. Traipsing across the country without a care was not in their playbook. And my dad had lost his father at age seventeen. Security was not a given for them as it had been for me. Getting a college education—something neither of my parents had—then not working or working at jobs with no future was confusing to them. Generations often don't see eye to eye. I was aware of this at the time but felt that I had to do what was right for me. The same goes for my own kids today. However, there can be painful moments, or years.

When my dad forwarded me a letter from the bank that held my student loans, I called the telephone number and explained with barely concealed snark that I was broke but would be happy to pay it off with free guitar lessons. The loan was guaranteed by the state of Illinois and for the remainder of the decade I got dunning notices from them. Had my parents been forced to make repayment, who knows how that might have curtailed my free spirit. I did pay off the loan about ten years later, when I had a family, a job, and a desire for good credit.

♫　♫　♫

I was an Amateur Hitchhiker. If not a job, it provided free transportation. During one aimless week, I hitched from San Francisco to visit a high school friend in Palo Alto. After a couple of nights there—we saw Santana at an outdoor venue—I thumbed my way toward Highway 1, making sure that my route took me through the hills of La Honda, right past Ken Kesey's notorious cabin. When we passed his place, I had a clear view from the back of a pickup that lasted maybe six-seconds. Check that off my list—not that I kept a list.

A day later, I was standing on the side of a breathtaking stretch of Highway 1 with the Pacific at my back, close to where I had spent the previous night in my Boy Scout sleeping bag. Nothing but a few white cloud puffs, cerulean sky, a most magical strip of ocean highway, and the feeling of riding a cosmic wave with a curl that stretches way beyond right now.

A battered old pickup truck—my preferred ride—stopped and I ran to get in, joining three guys from New Jersey in the truck bed. They had all met on the road the day before and to seal the cosmic deal had swallowed mesca-line tabs a few miles up Highway 1. One delightfully frazzled chap had a bat-tered guitar and was playing *Cowgirl in The Sand*. The driver asked me where I was headed. Big Sur, I guessed. He spied my sleeping bag and thought it was rather thin, so he handed me an Army issue blanket with a couple of holes in it and casually told me that a couple of hours ago he had deserted from the Army and was now picking up as many hitchhikers as could fit into the back of his faded green truck.

"I want to help people, not kill people," he explained in a sort of drawl. Next to him was a mutt dog and next to the mutt was a woman he intro-duced as his old lady. A band of tripping, deserting, guitar playing wanderers who did not know each other yesterday, sailed along the stunning scenery of continental America's westernmost highway in a pickup truck from a time before Elvis: everyday alchemy there for the taking.

When the desperado driver realized he would rather be heading toward Canada than Mexico, he let us out and wheeled around. Who knows where the noble fugitive ended up? Our band of irregulars plotted the next move while sunlight danced off the Pacific. The plotting was interrupted when a cop pulled up behind us and put his flasher on. Me and the New Jersey guys made an instinctual dash for the ocean but there was a fence in our way, and we knew that running made us look guilty, so we faced the music and got ticketed for hitchhiking. My driver's license still listed my Clarendon Hills address—23 Blodgett Street. The officer told us that it was illegal for pedes-trians to be on the highway and suggested we were breaking the laws of soci-ety as well. He told us to get out of here. Did he mean California? His beat? The planet? The more we walked the more we got out of here.

In a few minutes, we sprouted thumbs again and caught a ride to the park. Paying to get in Big Sur State Park went against our principals, so we climbed a tall fence near the entrance and dropped down inside. At the first campsite we spotted six girls. Were we in heaven? We waved. They waved back. Like all good campers, they were getting stoned and drinking beer. The campfire girls agreed that the fire was big enough for four more and we all had a good time that night. Nobody seemed to be worried about anything.

♫ ♫ ♫

I was living moment to moment. No one could get in touch with me. I had escaped. Except for my guitar, which was back in my room on Cole St., all my possessions were on my back. If I just kept going, if I climbed far enough out on the limb, it would be impossible to make it back to society's prefab expectations for a college educated, white, suburban, ex-athlete with "lots of potential." A slap in the face of predictability, without rancor and full of hope.

I knew I was lucky. I'd had a comfortable, trouble-free upbringing. But I wanted more from this life. I was on a quest, and the only way to discover what I was looking for was through experience. To become a man of the world. To stand beside Highway 1 near Castroville next to a field of artichokes and forge a fast road friendship with a hitchhiker going the opposite way. "You gotta walk to the end of the curve to get a ride," he shouted from across the pavement. To be with fellow tripsters in the back of a pickup truck sliding down Highway 1. To drop acid at Big Basin State Park, lose our car keys in the redwood needles and then later find the keys, believing that one of us had cashed in a karma chip. To attend a Billy Graham show at the Oakland Coliseum on a lark and be "saved" with thousands of true believers and afterward go to a funeral home in Berkeley where a friend worked and play the pump organ and jump in an empty casket and sign the guest book as Bram Stoker, like we were in a Marx Brothers movie: *A Night at the Funeral Parlor*. To drink it all in like there was no tomorrow.

♫ ♫ ♫

It was now time for a pilgrimage to Desolation Valley in the high Sierras: adventure and spiritual mind expansion right out of *Dharma Bums*. For two weeks, eight of us rambled the trails, ate trout from the glacier ponds, carried on all-day conversations about eastern philosophy (of which I knew very little), the Dead, the Vietnam War, and the importance of bananas. One crew member, Pat, a blonde-bearded spiritual savant, and a very tall ex-basketball player, was noted for his banana-heavy diet, a running joke of sorts.

Lying flat on our backs at night we glimpsed the universe, looked for the Milky Way, and let loose with a "whoa" or a "wow" each time a shooting star zapped by. When I was very young, my father had told me that there are more stars in the sky than grains of sand on all the beaches and deserts of the world. I took his word for it then, but now knew that he was right. The closeness of exploding thunderbolts during nighttime thunderstorms reminded us of how fragile we had been and still were and would always be. And finally, a knowing silence in solemn recognition of our microscopic contribution to infinity. My religion.

We were a very tall group. Slim, was 6'11. Banana Pat was 6'8. So was Redwood City Craig. I was a shade under 6'2. We all had long hair and beards. One day we twice passed a pack of Boy Scouts on the trail. The first time we were clothed. After swimming and fishing at an alpine pond, we thought it would be a good idea to hike naked while drying. The two girls in our group kept their panties on. As our naked procession headed back to camp, we again encountered the scouts, who were heading back to the ranger station. One unfortunate scout had managed to snag a fishing hook in his nostril. He didn't want anyone touching it. We offered help, but the scoutmaster nervously declined our naked offer.

♪ ♪ ♪

Heading down the steep trail from Desolation, after months of living without working, spending $10 a week on communal avocados, hard rolls, cream cheese, tortillas, eggs, cheese, and pinto beans, I was overcome by a sense of my own rootlessness, freaking me out just a little. I had to keep moving, but where to next? With each step I felt the pull of home. I began singing *I'm Going Home*, a Stones song from an album that still rested in my basement bedroom on Blodgett Street.

With little remaining dough and no love interest, I guess I needed a dose of the home fire—a reverse pilgrimage. The thought of home was of comfort to me. The day after we returned to Cole Street, I hitched to Berkeley and found an offer on the ride board at the student union, and in a few days I was headed back east. Just like that. I had no clue what I would do next.

95

♫ ♫ ♫

Back on Blodgett Street, we were all happy to see each other. I'm sure there were questions of how I was managing; maybe a mention of a job opportunity; which neighborhood kids or family friends had started law school or got an assignment from the Peace Corp or grown a beard. I'm sure my dad "loaned" me a few bucks, which I quietly accepted. Although these infrequent handouts were helpful, we all knew it wasn't near enough for me to live on. Parenthood is treacherous. Each child presents a new opportunity to disappoint. At that moment, I don't know if I was disappointing them or angering them. We never had uncivil words. I was always welcome. They had three other kids to raise; to worry about. I knew everything would work out alright for me but how could they know in the same way?

In a letter to Mom and Dad while I was in San Francisco, I had informed them that, "I am learning how to make money stretch. Now all I have to do is find where to get it in the first place so I can practice stretching." I was joking. They were fretting. Such are the joys of parenting a young man of the world. It would be many years before I could imagine the angst-filled conversations they must have had about their footloose, irresponsible, determined, dreamer of a son. What the hell was he doing? He was going back to the Church. I had recently turned 23.

THE DEAL GOES DOWN

Procurement Services,
Minneapolis to Sonoma, 1971

I HAD BEEN BACK AT SEVEN CORNERS a few days when a guitarist acquaintance named Jeff came by the Church asking for my assistance. He told me that his friends wanted to acquire some hashish—two or three pounds. He surmised that the San Francisco Bay Area was a hash hotbed and that I must have connections. Loose thinking on his part. I wasn't in the dope dealing racket. I knew no one who sold hash by the pound, but sensing a possible adventure, I told Jeff my friends might know "people" who could point us in the right direction. Jeff's "people" would cover my expenses, giving me both a job and a caper. All I had to do was guide Jeff to the hash.

Two of my summertime roommates on Cole Street in San Francisco— Pinto Bean John and Banana Pat—had since moved to a non-working chicken farm on the outskirts of Sebastopol (I think) while one attended Sonoma State. We were welcome to sleep on their floor as a base of operations.

Neither Jeff nor I owned a vehicle, but we found an offer on the ride board at the University of Minnesota student union: *Free transportation to the Berkeley area in exchange for driving a medium size Ryder truck.* The note elaborated that on the journey, the truck would be accompanied by a

97

station wagon containing the family moving to the Berkeley area—Walnut Creek to be exact. An East Indian voice answered when I called the number. We arranged a meeting.

The Indian gentleman was pleasant and self-assured. Accompanying him were his wife and two kids. Having just left his job as chemist at Ralston Purina (or Betty Crocker?), he was moving to California to seek his American dream. He had patented a Silly Putty-like substance that may have been called Crazy Stuff or something similar and had concluded that California was the place to roll out a goofy new product. Who could argue with that? California, the incubator of whimsy: Hollywood, waterbeds, hula hoops, frisbees and now, presenting ... Crazy Stuff. The Stuff was gelatinous and malleable and possibly purple. I have no recollection of what you were supposed to do with it.

The chemist's wife sported a traditional, smudged bindi between her eyebrows. Sunjay, their son, was about eleven years old, and their daughter—who I recall was named after some type of jewel—was about eight or nine. Rather than be concerned by the appearance of Jeff and I, the Indian chemist said, "I wish to expose my young children to American hippies," as his children smiled at us. I was rather touched. Many white bread families would have done everything possible to keep their kids from mingling with hippies. But this Indian family patriarch was onto something: be curious, kids. From curiosity grows both wisdom and empathy.

Jeff and I certainly looked like hippies. He had long straight hair, wore wire rimmed glasses and dressed in all denim. Every day. Like a uniform. I too had long, straight hair that hung past my shoulders and wore glasses—not wire rimmed. My wardrobe was a mix of Goodwill treasures, especially vests and western shirts with pearl snaps—the uniform of a middle-class dropout.

On a bright morning, our improbable party of American Dreamers departed Minneapolis for the West coast. The Interstate speed limit was 65 or 70 but our Ryder truck had a governor on the accelerator that kept us from doing more than 50. This would be a long trip. Jeff was not especially talkative. He may have been quietly holding his breath because of the few thousand dollars in his backpack, money that was not his.

Like typical tourists, we detoured to Mount Rushmore because the inventor of Silly Stuff or Goofy Putty or whatever it was called was an American history buff. To pass the citizenship test, immigrants end up knowing more about America than most who are born here. He had switched continents and was now both eager and hopeful for this new country that had allowed him the opportunity to do what he was doing: uprooting his family, changing his life, dreaming of a big financial payoff. I supposed that same country had also allowed me to "do my own thing."

The dad intoned brief verbal sketches of the various presidents whose giant busts graced our vision from Mount Rushmore. I recall that he mentioned Washington's wooden teeth. The odd nature of our caravan was sinking in: a family from the Indian subcontinent accompanied by a couple of hippies, traveling through a state named for an American Indian tribe, the Dakota Sioux, gazing at gigantic busts of four revered American Presidents, two who had owned slaves, one who had freed them, and one who had a well-known animosity toward Native Americans. And the sculptor of the monumental work was rumored to have had sympathies with the Ku Klux Klan back in the 1920s. A uniquely American tableau, baby. After a few minutes of the dead presidents, Jeff and I sneaked a few puffs of an all-American joint—courtesy of Mexico—before heading back to the Interstate.

Sunjay joined us in the Ryder truck for stretches of the drive, pleased to be riding with the big kids. His questions were unrelenting: about our beliefs and experiences and upbringing and education and what foods we liked and what television programs we watched and what music we listened to and what did we know about India. I had worn an Indian madras shirt in high school was all I could muster. By the end of his inquisition, I was mentally exhausted. Jeff thought that the kid was a pain in the ass and didn't respond much. Kids make you think.

One evening after dark, we pulled off the Interstate at Wamsutter, Wyoming, a tiny settlement with a rundown motel and adjoining bar. The lobby walls were adorned with trophy heads of the local ungulates. Dusty antlers infused the small room with a creepy, dead vibe. A clerk slumped behind the front desk looking like he just woke up or was about to go to sleep. On the saggy lobby couch sat a very large, ornery looking bearded dude with a ratty cowboy hat, holstered pistol, and a pyramid of empty beer cans on the cluttered table before him. I could feel his malevolent stare, but I didn't want to look; one of those situations when I wished to be almost anywhere else. We were in enemy territory, where the galoot ruled. The clerk read the room and sensed trouble.

"Settle down, Junior," said the sleepy clerk, who was half Junior's size and twice his age. He wouldn't be much help should Junior do more than just stare at us. I thought of *Easy Rider*, where the hippies are gunned down by rednecks. I didn't want my head on the wall next to the mule deer's.

The family rented a room while Jeff and I slid out to the station wagon for a night in the frigid car. We wedged ourselves between luggage and boxes then pulled blankets over the whole mess to camouflage our circumstance, hoping that Junior wouldn't stumble out for a look. I silently repeated my transcendental meditation mantra, hoping to tamp down my anxiety: the mantra versus the menace.

We considered what to do should Junior start pounding on the station wagon windows. Offer him a joint? Run? To where? Reason with him? Offer him Crazy Stuff? We had no weapons other than karma. I silently promised to be a good lad for the rest of my life should there be a rest of my life. You know you're in some shit when you make that sort of promise.

Denim Jeff and I took turns dozing during the bone chilling night. We were still alive when the sun finally peeped up. The inventor of Crazy Stuff came out to the car and confirmed our suspicion. "There was a very loud pounding on our door in the night. It was that big guy. I told him you hitchhiked to California." Thanks to our chemist client, we had been spared an ugly confrontation.

A few days later we arrived in Walnut Creek and said goodbye to the family. The father gave us a ride to San Francisco, where my friends picked us up and drove us to their place outside Sebastopol. We still had no real plan. After a few days hanging around the chicken ranch making inquiries, friends of friends set up a meeting for us at a hidden homestead nearby that I recall was named the Rolling J Ranch. These guys supposedly knew where to get hash. It was right next to a property where the Grateful Dead were purported to have once lived.

The Rolling J residents were musicians. They had memorized the entire Dead catalog and their leader, Zak, was a Jerry Garcia look-alike. We jammed and shot the shit and concluded that everyone was cool. Jeff handed over the dough from his pack and we left for a fretful night of pondering where the money and the hash would be when morning comes.

When we returned to the Rolling J, two pounds of dark brown, almost black Pakistani hash—pungent slabs wrapped in cellophane—greeted us. I'd never seen anything like it, reminiscent of a Holloway Candy Slo Poke caramel sucker large enough for the entire neighborhood. We pinched off a little piece of the slab. Tasted it. Smelled it. Smoked it. Sweet! Our senses were enhanced. It was good. Paki hash was better than Lebanese, in my opinion, but not as good as Afghani, the hash of the Gods. What would the Indian chemist have thought of this drug deal, made possible in part by Silly Stuff? Or was it Nutty Stuff?

So, the money men back in Minneapolis used Jeff as a connection, Jeff used me, I used my friends, they used their friends, who directed us to the musicians, who knew the guys with the hash. Or maybe they knew guys who knew the guy with the hash. How the hash got from Pakistan to the Bay Area may have required a half-dozen more connections. Black market capitalism at work. My job was over.

Jeff and I said *adios*, and I've neither seen nor heard from him since. No recollection of how he travelled back to the Twin Cities. My cut of the deal was an ounce of hash. On occasion I would sell a gram to friends for $10 when I needed dough. I doubt I had more than thirty dollars in my jeans, the balance of the spending money I'd been fronted for my assignment. I hadn't worked since the waterbed store gig a half year prior.

♫ ♫ ♫

It was late fall, and the weather was crisp and sparkling and full of promise. For a couple of weeks, I lingered at the one-time chicken ranch, dining on apples from a tree on the property and zucchini from their small garden, supplemented with a ten-pound sack of brown rice and a five-pound wheel of cheddar cheese. We had a daily meal of baked zucchinis stuffed with apples, cheese, and brown rice. For culture we had *Bo Diddly's Greatest Hits* and one comic book: *The Fabulous Furry Freak Brothers*. As Fabulous Freewheelin' Franklin says, "Dope will get you through times of no money better than money will get you through times of no dope."

Pinto Bean John and Banana Pat were attending Sonoma State part time. They had almost as much free time as me. One day we joined friends for a float down the Russian River on logs. All of us ingested psilocybin to enhance the float, because why not? This was recreational tripping at its finest. A manageable current, smooth logs, good friends and perfect water temperature, a kaleidoscopic vision of harmony and understanding. We were from the same source as the river proclaimed my psilly mind.

Hours later hunger set in. One floater was of Russian ancestry and knew how to make borscht. Seemed like a serendipitous meal. We headed to town to buy potatoes and beets and cabbage, an extraordinary undertaking while buzzing on psilly. (Will the grocery clerk realize that we are on an astral plane ready for takeoff?) At the market, we parked in front of the display window plastered with butcher paper signs advertising chicken thighs and dog food. I remained in the car with Pinto Bean John.

Through the window, we spotted a bizarre granny character—white hair, mini dress, and white go-go boots. She must have been at least 70 years old. Pushing her cart was a beefy Hispanic dude with a dour countenance who was a head taller and decades younger than swingin' granny. We sensed his menacing vibe. Juan Corona entered my thoughts, the Mexican serial killer who had recently been convicted of snuffing 25 migrant workers not too far from where we were now parked.

"Who the fuck are they?" we thought or said aloud. Why is she wearing go-go boots? Is he her slave or her keeper? We couldn't keep our eyes off them, too entranced to converse, feeling that if we voiced our concerns, they might come true.

Eventually, the phantastic couple checked out. Their car was parked right next to ours. Granny got in the passenger side. We didn't dare look. The mood in our car had slipped into the bad vibes zone. Out of the corner of my eye, I saw Beefy put their groceries—Drano? Organ meat? Bleach?—in the trunk then walk between our cars. He loomed over John's open window, slowly revealed a pistol, cocked it, and without uttering a word, stuck the barrel a few inches into our car. We looked straight ahead, frozen in our seats while our oblivious cohorts were still inside the store, examining the cabbage.

Was this a dream?

The scene seemed to last at least a minute, a long time to hold your breath when you're tripping. Remaining silent, Beefy un-cocked the pistol, walked around behind his car, got in and drove away with Granny. John and I remained frozen. Speechless. Had we just escaped anonymous assassination? Was it the drugs? A few minutes later, our crew returned to the car.

"Man, did you see that old lady with white boots and that creepy guy she was with?" one asked. "He gave us the skunk eye. I think he caught us laughing at them." They were in a trippy mood while John and I remained silent. How to explain what had just happened? How to properly convey the drug enhanced terror that had, for a few minutes, gripped us. After a long pause, the psycho dam burst, and we spewed a garbled recitation of the pistol encounter. An unexpected brush with violence gives you something to talk about.

The borscht was delicious.

♪ ♪ ♪

After this psychedelic cartoon of all-American adventure—westward migration, immigrants, rednecks, dreams, guns, mind expansion and a drug deal—it was time for me to move on. No money. No job. I decided to return to Lawrence because it was closer than Minneapolis or Chicago, and there were plenty of friendly couches. On the zephyr from Oakland to Denver, I ate a little hash. The combination of hash and zephyr makes you wonder who's driving the train. At the Denver Greyhound station I scrounged bus fare by trading a little hash to an understanding couple.

THE JOURNAL OF EXTINCT INVERTEBRATES

Shipping Department of Allen Press –
Lawrence, KS, Fall, 1971

I BLEW INTO LAWRENCE ON THE GREYHOUND, near penniless save for my shrinking ounce of hash, and in need of any kind of a job. Brian let me crash on his uncomfortable couch and in return, he smoked my hash. The revered couch-for-hash trade. He was now living with Sally in an aged frame house, his VW Bus parked on a slight incline in front, still ready to be jump-started. We attempted to write a song, *Drowning in a Sea of Toast*, but only got as far as the title. (Toast was the cornerstone of our diet.) Brian showed me how to play *Know You Rider* ala Jorma Kaukonen. The guitar lick in "A" is such a great lick. Our recording session in the moldy basement produced little more than a picture.

But I needed money to afford toast. What menial labor could I find without having to cut my hair, shave off my beard or get up insanely early? A drummer friend had a job at a print shop that produced scientific and academic journals near downtown Lawrence. They needed someone in the shipping department. Although overqualified on paper, during the interview I mentioned that I needed to make ends meet while I decided which master's degree to pursue. A guy pursuing his academic dream needs to put sprouts on the table. The guy who hired me sensed I was hornswoggling him, but he was a frustrated writer who had married the shop owner's daughter.

He was now a businessman, not a writer, often in a surly mood because he could see the writing on the wall, and it wasn't his. Writers aren't a happy lot. They're either blocked, threatening to give up because the world sucks, or they're convinced that no one can get what they're getting at.

The job required me to construct shipping boxes, then cram them full of periodicals like *The Journal of Extinct Vertebrates*. My summer job as a mover had rendered me proficient with the tape dispenser used for making boxes. You may be familiar with the sound this sepia-tinted, insanely sticky tape makes when jerked from its roll, then pressed against the terrible ridge of teeth that will severe the piece from the mother roll with one quick pull. This was the first time I had a job where I could use skills learned on a previous job. Looking back, several of my jobs, had a tape theme.

This print company was only a couple of blocks away from the roach-infested residence on Connecticut Street that I now shared with a disparate collection of ex-student radicals, feminists and an ex-SDS leader. Each was in a transitory phase, deciding whether to blow up the system or join it as the Vietnam war dragged on, creating a vibe of resignation that occurs when people realize they're growing up and it's time for plan B—or for any plan at all. The past spring had seen a change of tactics by the antiwar movement, away from humongous marches and more toward blocking traffic and disrupting shit. There wasn't much to disrupt in Lawrence.

My bedroom held the sum of my possessions: a sleeping bag that I unrolled on top of a mattress that had been left on the floor by the last tenant, a dresser of unknown origin, a backpack of clothing, and my guitar. The minimalism of Van Gogh's bedroom. I thought this was romantic. Just off a long year on the road culminating in a madcap hashish deal and now I'm just recharging the old batteries. Laying low.

I had been guitaring with an intense, time-filling conviction since departing Lawrence two years before. Now, every lunch hour I raced home from the shipping department to continue my exploration of the country blues guitar. Never had I been as invested or intrigued by a non-sports endeavor. I was discovering the music from which rock & roll sprang: the thru line from Robert Johnson to Muddy Waters to Mick and Keith. I had a tablature instruction book of songs by the country and ragtime blues legends— Blind Blake, Mississippi John Hurt, Charlie Patton, Blind Boy Fuller, Blind

Lemon Jefferson. These guys all used the guitar to make money. A job. A life. I had worn glasses since the seventh grade and my prescription had steadily increased. Maybe one day I could become Blind Bain?

Learning to play guitar—and no guitarist ever stops learning—you feel your progress, how your fingers do things they couldn't last week, how your digits and eyes and mind become a team that creates a note, a chord, a song. Especially at the beginning, you can sense your skills plateauing then lurching forward. Even sitting on a chair with a guitar in your hands, you become more in tune with your instrument. (Keith Richards sleeps with his guitar I read.) I learned to break things down and play them slowly before trying to play at the speed or the singular rhythm of the old masters. I still recall the liberating feeling of being able to bounce my thumb between the bass strings while my other fingers pinched and picked the trebles. By now I was certain that I would play guitar for the rest of my life and that nothing would ever be more important to me. Time has confirmed this.

A passionate avocation provokes a love of life's possibilities and a sense of optimism. You can't be fired. You set your own hours. There's no dress code. You're the boss. In the name of unfettered idealism, I couldn't allow my life to be centered around a job that did not leave me as fulfilled and satisfied as the guitar did. That was the bar I set. It was a youthful fantasy, but I never strayed too far from that idealism.

Me, Brian, Joe, gin bottle

♫   ♫   ♫

The print shop allowed me a generous Christmas break so I made the trip back to Blodgett Street for a dose of family life and the standard issue Christmas check from my father, whose continued exasperation about my lack of career plans would have been comical in a sitcom but less so in reality. He muted his exasperation in my presence, but fathers and sons sense what the other is thinking.

"You can't live like this forever," he might say, but I knew that he really wanted to use stronger words: that I was behaving as a foolish idealist—an idiot—and why the hell did I even go to college.

"I'm not concerned with forever, Dad. This is how I'm living *now*."

"How are you going to support yourself?"

"I'll figure it out."

"The ham is ready to be carved," said my mother.

These little blow ups didn't last long and were quickly swept under the rug. According to Roger Day Bain Sr., financial security was what any sensible person pursued. He grew up during the Great Depression, which he often mentioned. This trope was a reminder that I couldn't grasp what real austerity was. To me, the depression conjured a landscape washed in gray, filled with grim, dour folk selling pencils on the street corner, all the men wearing newsboy caps. I never asked my parents to sit down and detail what it was *really* like. As you are growing up, the inquisitive spirit is more confined to your own life, not your provider's. In any case, the depression didn't seem a romantic period, like the sixties and seventies have become to modern generations.

As our family sat around the small pine dinner table in our kitchen—we had no dining room—the table talk was a mix of politics, how delicious the ham was, why was the six pack of Coca-Cola bottles purchased this morning now empty, and maybe something about world hunger from my mom, who was involved in various study groups at her Episcopal church. We never had one of those movie scenes where the father screams at the hippie son to get a haircut and a real job as the son flips over the mashed potatoes and lights a joint, the mother starts crying, the dog starts barking, fade to black. My dad had even sprouted a mustache for the first time in his life. In the early 1970s, the mustache was a slight nod to letting your freak flag fly. Was this his show of father/son solidarity or simply a fashion statement? I imagine it was a bit of both.

Neither of my parents attended college and their assumption was that I, the golden boy, the college grad, the number one son, would quickly find his groove in some type of meaningful, well-paying career. Parents sleep easier when their children are financially secure. (My brother was twelve years younger. My sisters were four and eight years my junior; all were too young to have fretful financial issues.) I loved my parents, knew they wished the best for me, and wished not for them lose sleep, but I didn't want to live my life in reaction to their hopes for me. I simply sought to be true to myself, a form of selfishness, I supposed, but not of spite. From my perspective, I'd found a pretty good groove, though it had nothing to do with how much money I could make. It was about how little I could spend and still get by; how much time I had to pursue Robert Johnson licks and what might be around the corner. My plans were momentary.

LINDA

Christmas, 1971

I MET TWENTY-YEAR-OLD LINDA WHEN SHE WAS ON A DATE with my friend Steve, recently back from Nam. They had gone on a couple dates in Carbondale, where they both attended Southern Illinois University. Steve wanted Linda to fix me up with one of her friends, which I wasn't keen on. I considered blind dates to be a last resort for awkward college freshmen. I was relieved that her friends were all busy that night. I tagged along anyway, at Steve's insistence. I had never been a third wheel like this, but we were loose. Life was all one big party. Maybe I'd run into the lady of my dreams at the Quiet Knight on Belmont Avenue in Chicago, where we were headed to catch the Siegal-Schwall Blues Band.

Linda's family had recently moved to the suburbs from the near north side of Chicago. The old neighborhood. I got only a glancing look at her when Steve and I entered Linda's family home in Morton Grove. Gulp. She's a dish, I thought. Why does Steve have all the luck?

"She says her father is like Archie Bunker," Steve had told me on the drive up. Archie was the anti-liberal, anti-hippie, somewhat lovable bigot on the hit TV show, *All in The Family*. Linda attempted a formal introduction.

"Dad," she called from the top of the stairs that led down to the family room. He sprawled in his recliner, continuing to watch television. A half-hearted grunt in our direction was all he could offer, before turning back to the cooking show on TV. He knew vermin when it was in his house. His daughter was leaving for a night out with sissies who have hair like girls. They wouldn't have put up with this in the old neighborhood.

Linda was adorable, with thick dark hair down to her waist, brown eyes, and inviting smile, although I didn't want to dwell on that because Steve was her date. I wondered if her friends looked like her. I wondered if maybe there's a girl for me? I had been so busy adventuring that I hadn't considered the possibility of a true relationship. True romance. As the evening progressed, the Ral Donner song, *The Girl of My Best Friend*, began rattling around in my idea factory. Ral was an Elvis sound-a-like with a couple of hits on Chicago radio. Later, Linda confessed that she thought I was weird because I railed against Coca-Cola, a corporation that was "pushing sugar to the masses."

A few days later, Steve and I rode down to Carbondale, situated near the bottom of Illinois, a hotbed of youthful impiety, the burn-out capital of the Midwest, if not the entire nation. Too many downers, too many Quaaludes, too much acid, too much Mad Dog 20-20, too many totaled cars, dropped classes, misplaced car keys, wallets, dogs, and dreams. Many were from the Chicago area, dragging their feet toward adulthood and some type of career, and still taking a class or two to advance toward that goal. In this exact time, in this exact place, success was measured by louche idleness, not a job.

Steve was taking the semester off and was here for partying purposes. He asked Linda if we could crash at her rental house. When we hit town, she was hurrying off to class, studying to become a teacher I learned. We tossed our sleeping bags onto the bare wooden living room floor then Steve took me to the Student Union, the nerve center of campus debauchery, where friends ran into one another to find out that night's plans or whether Wrench got arrested for drunk driving or Will got his dogs back from the pound or Suzie dropped out and returned to Chicago.

At a small party a couple of nights later, I casually followed Linda from the living room to the kitchen to the porch. There was no denying we were drawn to each other. That spark that precedes combustion. We shared popcorn back at her house then she bade me goodnight, leaving me with kernel hulls in my gums and another hard night on the floor. What a move on her part, it was like saying, "Not so fast, mister." An overwhelming sense of inevitability, one that may occur but once in a lifetime, crept over me. It was a moment of magic. We both knew. We were in separate rooms in an otherwise empty house. We both knew.

The next night again found us alone in her house.. We kissed in the living room then drifted into her bedroom to share her single mattress on the floor. It was a tight fit, but we didn't need much space. You can sleep intertwined or on top of each other at first—and it works.

Steve took our coupling in stride. He saw it coming. No hard feelings. Not as if I had won and he lost. It was simply a matter of the cosmos weighing in. A couple of days later, he left for Mexico. We became caretakers of his VW bug and Thunder, his trusty little mutt. Five years later, Steve would be best man at our wedding.

When it was time for me to head back to my Lawrence print shop job, Linda and I promised to see each other soon. Back in Lawrence, I wrote her the only love letters I would ever pen. Both of us knew that this was "it." I called her from a pay phone, telling her how much I needed to be with her, touting a California road trip. I even tried to get her to take a leave of absence from college. This was during my "bad influence" phase. Being more sensible than I, she declined to drop out of school but said that she would hit the road with me when school was out for the summer.

One Saturday morning in early spring, when I was scheduled to box up 5,000 copies of *The Journal of Extinct Invertebrates*, I called my friend Joe, who lived across town.

"Let's head south." It didn't take much to convince Joe, who was "between" jobs. He owned an orange 1956 Buick Special; lots of chrome, three holes on the front quarter panel referred to as ventiports, jazzy yet non-functional ornamentation.

"When do you want to leave?" asked Joe.

"Now."

Packing requires little time when you own nothing. I left word for my frustrated writer boss at the print shop and said I would provide a forwarding address for my final check. During the ride to Carbondale, I wondered if I should have notified Linda that I had quit my job and would soon be at her front door, but she had no phone. I had no doubts that this move was logical because it makes sense to be with the one you love. I had visions of our reunion all the way from Lawrence to Carbondale.

"I'm a little early," I said as she answered the door. "Hope you don't mind, I brought along my wheel man, Joe. He just needs a corner to crawl up in." Rather than freak out, she was delighted. Spontaneity ruled. We even began throwing around names for the kids we would one day have: Horace and Boogie. (The names didn't stick but the kids eventually came.)

A few months passed while Linda attended school and I gave a few guitar lessons. My first completed song came to life here, *Truck Driving Astronaut*. I worked part-time at a failing leather shop to gather a small road stake for the promised California trip.

THE $300 SUMMER

On the road with Linda, 1972

ON OUR LAST NIGHT IN CARBONDALE, WE bedded in sleeping bags on the hardwood floor of our now empty rental house, our backpacks filled with three months of clothing and essentials. We had $300 to last the summer, a miniscule amount for such an undertaking even back then. I now see how hopeful and optimistic we were, and how full of youthful bravado that bordered on foolishness. We would rely on the kindness of friends, strangers, acquaintances, cheap gas, free rides, and our thumbs. We would eat little other than canned tuna, noodles, avocados, cream cheese, peanut butter and jelly, pinto beans, hard rolls, and eggs. We owned no car, paid no rent, bought no clothes, and avoided restaurants except for truck stop apple pie. Let the journey begin.

My romantic sidekick never quite shared my zeal for rootless adventure. She was more cautious and less an acolyte of worldly escapism than I, her tour guide, but she was excited to be going out to California. Prior to this, her only long-distance trip had been one spring break in Fort Lauderdale where she had shared a hotel room with ten sunburned, puking college chums.

For the first leg of our trip, we arranged a ride with a friend who was headed to LA to open a recording studio. He drove a mint condition 1948

Chevrolet, a vintage of the same year I was born, signaling a good vibes trip. He dropped us off in Lawrence for a week of mingling with friends, some of whom Linda now knew, then off to Kansas City to visit a college friend of mine. Rumor had it she had slept with Abbie Hoffman when he spoke at Allen Fieldhouse two weeks before the KU student union got firebombed in 1970. In the morning, Sally the lawyer explained the hitchhiking ordinances before dropping us off at an Interstate 70 exchange. Off to Colorado!

A sign of the times

We stuck out our thumbs and in minutes were picked up by a young guy in a Pontiac. How were we to know he was a borderline sociopath? After about 20 miles, he announced that his goal was to drive to the west coast without being passed by another car. 80 ... 85 ... 90 ... 95...100. Whatever it took, he was determined to be the speed king of I-70. Linda was fretful but shy. She didn't yet know me well enough to protest. I was outwardly nonchalant but inwardly concerned. If we kept our eye off the speedometer and instead enjoyed the monotonous view of western Kansas wheat fields, maybe it wouldn't end in a fiery crash. She looked out her window, I looked out mine. We got to Boulder in record time, congratulated the driver on his feat, and wished him Godspeed. Relief is a very strong emotion.

In Boulder we crashed with my high school friend, Susan, who graciously lent us her bedroom and loaned us her Pinto for a couple of nights of camping in the Rockies. We headed to Rocky Mountain National Park where I looked up a high school basketball friend who now lived in a hovel near Allen's Park. His squalid shack had that vinegary odor that is a combination of campfire smoke, dirty clothes, sweat and dog. Like me, he was a guitar-playing free spirit with no job, a mountain man now, looking barely recognizable compared to his former clean-shaven b-ball jock days. Tom had run out of beer, a no-no in Colorado. I didn't want to drive the borrowed Pinto any more than necessary, so we hitched down to town. Linda remained at the hovel with a raggedy band of mountain hippies who may have once been Girl Scouts or student councilmen. They invited her to join them in eating amanita mushrooms. She declined. By the time we returned, the hovel hippies were tripping, and Linda was wondering what I had gotten her into. This wouldn't be the last time she wondered.

As dusk approached, we rigged a tube tent in the adjoining woods. Then, I suggested we sleep in the meadow for a better view of the shooting stars. In the middle of the night, we heard snorting. "It's a bear," Linda whispered, her mind racing to the worst-case scenario. Feeling a bit of dread, I slowly peeled back the sleeping bag for a look. No bear. Hooves. We were surrounded by horses. Their whinnying and stomping indicated that they were upset with our presence. We grabbed our bags and went back into the woods. Then it began to pour rain. We were drenched in the tube tent—the romance of the road.

Linda contracted an intestinal parasite when we returned to Boulder, probably from eating at the outdoor "free kitchen" by Boulder Creek. Right then she could have bailed. She had nearly been ravaged by a bear that was really a horse and now she was in gastric misery from some microscopic organ-eating pest. But we were in love. Young love tends to mute feelings that later in a relationship would be much more pronounced. She could have said, "I can't take this weirdness and filth and I'm going home." But she didn't. Calling her parents was out of the question. They were willfully ignorant that we were on the road together. She had to gut it out.

For the next leg of our odyssey, I had pre-arranged a ride with another friend headed to the promised land. Dr. Bingo, one of the advisors in my draft evasion caper, was leaving Lawrence for San Francisco to become head pharmacologist at the Haight Ashbury Free Clinic—a counterculture gig with some true gravitas. He was a jovial guy, a good listener, sported a scraggly beard, dressed more like a nerd than a hippie—well-worn cardigan sweaters and plaid shirts—and was known to have the occasional nitrous oxide party tank at his house. I had also briefly helped him in his lab at KU where he tested street drugs with a mass spectrometer. Someone needed to confirm the efficacy of the purple microdot and whether it was laced with strychnine, or whether the DMMDA was actually horse tranquilizer.

Bingo had replaced the back seats of his Chevy van with a pair of wooden doors laid horizontal to form a platform with storage underneath. As we were about to leave, with no explanation, he pulled a package of hot dogs from under the driver seat, removed one hot dog and stuck it halfway down a tiny opening where the platform did not quite meet the walls of the van. Something snatched the hot dog from his fingers.

"I found a baby coyote two days ago outside Lawrence," Dr. Bingo explained. "The mother was dead, and I couldn't leave the pup." That was the scene as we pulled out of Boulder, Linda lying prone on the platform, still suffering from the gastric parasite, a wild, hot dog-eating coyote pup skulking beneath her, This marked the first time Linda cried in front of me.

In a desolate stretch of Wyoming, we stopped on the Interstate shoulder. Feeding time. When the doctor opened the door to offer the pup a delicious hot dog, it bolted through a gap in the doors and into the wild west. Dr. Bingo was distraught. Linda and I were pleased but tried not to show it.

♫ ♫ ♫

I felt the magic when falling asleep at a roadside rest stop, tucked into a sleeping bag under a night sky of endless stars, to wake at first light with a herd of mule deer grazing not a hundred yards away, the crisp morning smell of the high mountain plains hitting the olfactory, my love lying next to me. "This is my life," I thought, overcome with joy and wonder. When we pulled off the road in Nevada and found a solo female hitchhiker at the completely deserted Rye Patch Reservoir, it was just another casually mysterious experience of the road. How did she get to this intersection of nowhere and the sky? The Rye Patch water stunned us with a blinding shade of shimmering blue made more profound by the surrounding washed-out Nevada desert. We dropped off the hitchhiker at some equally destitute location to continue her flight into the unknown, or back to the known.

We made it to San Francisco and crashed for a week with a gal I had met the previous summer. When Dr. Bingo secured an apartment above a tiny French bistro near Clement and 8th Avenue, he invited us to stay the remainder of the summer with him. The space behind the couch served as our bedroom. Every day we wandered the city, often ending up in Golden Gate Park. Our big splurge was pork fried rice at the Moon Café.

A few weeks into our stay we were recruited to be guinea pigs on some newly synthesized MDA type of drug that the Haight Ashbury Free Clinic brain trust had concocted. Dr. Bingo and his bearded associates observed us during our trip like we were a couple of lab rats. The speedy psychedelic drug made us feel very strange and three guys in white coats taking notes didn't help. I can't believe we agreed to it—especially Linda. We survived, minus a brain cell or two.

This was near the end of my psychedelic drug-taking days (except for weed and its derivatives.) Before I had experienced LSD and psilocybin, I rarely pondered my place in the cosmos. Now, I pondered it. I accepted that the tiniest particles of my DNA were of the same life matter as the Milky Way. Everything in the whole shebang was connected. These hallucinogens were catalysts that had changed my mind. Now I felt that my path was to become not only a man of the world but also a man of the galaxies, the solar system and the beyond. I am grateful for the magical point of view that these drugs provided while I was of the right age with the right attitude, and I didn't have to go to work the next day. Experiences that force you to see life in a new perspective can be painful, positive, or frightening. Beliefs tend to calcify when never challenged. Having said this, I would never again ingest a drug recently synthesized by madcap scientists.

We left the Bingo pad for a backpacking trip with a couple of friends, up through the redwoods and Oregon and Washington. Linda's amazingly long, thick hair got infested with head lice at a campground near the Hoh Rainforest in Washington state. More tears. "It'll be fine," I assured her. We went to a pharmacy in Coos Bay, Oregon for some Quell then afterward had blueberry pancakes at a lumberjack café. When we returned to SF it was time to head back to the Midwest.

On the ferry in Washington

We secured a ride to Chicago from a ride notice board in Berkeley and chipped in our remaining money stash for gas. It was probably no more than $15. Our ride dropped us off at an Illinois tollway oasis and we each called a parent to retrieve us. Now it was back to Carbondale for Linda's next year of college. She had survived.

As the years rolled by, Linda would grow less enthused by my career procrastination. *All you need is love*, sang the Beatles. She thought that a little money should have been in the lyrics—but these sentiments wouldn't crystalize for a while.

SHRINKAGE

Outdoor Shop salesman,
JCPenney in Carbondale, IL, 1972

IN THE BEIGE, WINDOWLESS BACKROOM AT THE JCPenney store in Carbondale, *Shrinkage*, a ten-minute training film is being projected onto a portable screen. The film explains how company inventory disappears by carelessness, slippage, breakage, spillage, droppage and the number one reason: theft, by either customers or employees. Although its sensibility seemed geared toward an elementary school audience, *Shrinkage* was required viewing for new hires like me.

"Duncan knew he was breaking the rules when he shoved the merchandise down his pants and left the store without paying." Cut to a close-up of a big bulge in the front of Duncan's pants. Unwitting corporate camp at its finest.

As I continued to pursue my plan for avoiding predictable middle-class consumerism, conformity, and blandness, I had taken a job with a company that was the epitome of those things. The irony may or may not have registered with me. My interviewers did not see a carefree wanderer just off a three-month vagabond. They saw a very presentable young white guy with a fresh haircut, a college degree, a collared shirt and khaki pants, a guy who expressed an eagerness to "make the outdoor shop realize its potential." Hired!

It's funny how guys like me were only a haircut away from respectability. The haircut was really for Linda, not JCPenney. Love requires responsibility and sometimes shorter hair. We needed money for our rent and for next summer's adventure. If that meant a haircut, so be it.

For the first time since my college internship with 3M, I was working for adult men who wore business suits, were married with children, had mortgages, car payments and needed to do whatever necessary to support those commitments. Like them, I was doing what was necessary to support myself. They sought stability, I sought ... what? To avoid becoming one of *them*.

My new domain was located across the parking lot from the main store, surrounded by a chain-link fence, one of mankind's favorite methods of shrinkage prevention. The smell of fertilizer, grass seed, and lawn poison wafted through the rows of outdoor equipment and fauna. The cheerful, accommodating retail salesperson in me bloomed.

"If you need a fast-growing tree, the Silver Maple's the one," I informed a customer, lifting a scrawny sapling up for his review. I had learned this fact from a previous customer. Or, holding up a green plastic bottle of poison: "This'll take care of your dandelion problem." What I really wanted to say was that taming nature with poison was a bad idea but instead I added, "It'll take care of your chickweed, too." I had learned that fact from the label, although I wouldn't have been able to identify chickweed in a weed line-up. This type of retail selling relied more on being polite and attentive than persuasive. Beautifying American lawns was odd work for a counterculture rebel.

I had read Abbie Hoffman's *Woodstock Nation* and *Steal This Book*. The writing was tongue-in-cheek hyperbole but fun to read. "Ripping off Pig Nation" had more of a revolutionary ring to it than stealing from corporate America. Shrinkage without guilt. I wasn't a natural born rip-off artist, either because of Sunday school or because I was simply too chicken to try, but after a few weeks on the job I'd identified an opportunity.

In a pre-computerized world with no security cameras, my ruse was simple: 1) A fictitious customer returns a dead tree. 2) I refund their money because they have decided that they don't want a replacement tree. 3) I dummy up a return payout to this phantom customer, get a friend's signature as "proof" of the transaction, and then pocket the $15 "refund." The scheme netted me about $60 before the cricket on my shoulder said "enough." I took my friendly accomplice, a sandal maker who had signed the bogus return slips, to an all-you-can-eat seafood joint. I had simply transferred money from a national corporation to a local restaurant, reasoned the Abbie Hoffman part of my brain. But it was nothing more than small-time larceny that left me feeling hollow—for about ten minutes.

Right before Christmas, I turned in my notice because the one-week vacation offered was not long enough.

DIGGING A
TEMPORARY HOLE

Landscape Crew for a Nursery in Southern Illinois, 1973

IN THE LATE WINTER. I TALKED MY WAY INTO A JOB at a small landscaping outfit south of Carbondale. They were skeptical about why a "college boy" wanted to work there. Couldn't blame them. I explained my desire to learn about the flora of our beautiful countryside, which was true. I did love the terrain of southern Illinois; the dogwoods, redbuds, bluffs, creeks, and deciduous forests that surrounded Carbondale; the two-lane blacktop roads that snaked through the hollows and skirted the lakes; the songbirds flitting and tittering, the Canadian Geese gliding downward for a graceful landing in a field of corn stubble.

My work partner was named Ethan; he was the guy who knew what he was doing, and who handled the daily job tickets. I was the guy who followed his orders. He was native to the area, maybe five or six years my senior, and a hard worker. He'd been doing this job since he got out of the army.

"Did you serve?" he inquired about a week into the job.

"They thought I was crazy," I answered.

"Are you?"

"Isn't everybody?"

We left it at that.

The job required digging endless holes and planting truckloads of saplings and evergreens. I never went to work without a pair of gloves. Protecting my guitar hands was a lifelong endeavor. Playing guitar was more of a holy mission than an occupation. It struck a chord deeper than a career. As I read about the history of the country blues, I learned that most of my guitar heroes had done field work. This gig was heroic!

When digging a hole, you come face to face with earth. You feel it and smell it and some of it rubs off on you. It gets you dirty. Good dirty. The smell of freshly dug soil and the effort it takes to dig it become simple reminders of earthly existence. My perceptions were romantic because I knew that I would not be required to dig holes, use shovels, and bust through roots my entire life. At least, I didn't think I would. Ethan had a different perspective, offering insights with a theme of "honest dollar for an honest day's work" that revealed pride as well as a chip on his shoulder. Honest work was anything that involved digging, harvesting, stacking, lifting, planting, or building. Honest work provided a moral superiority for those who used their hands and backs to make a living.

We were both Caucasian of a similar age, born into different circumstances. I was working but not of the working class. I didn't consider myself to be of any class but my own. I didn't feel superior to him, just different. Digging holes was our temporary similarity. To each other, we represented a glimpse at a different life.

"You're the first person I've worked with who's a college boy," he sneered (good-naturedly).

"Glad to be your first. Hope I'm not the last."

He laughed.

"Do you ever think of going to college?" I asked.

"You went to college and you're digging holes like me. Why should I waste time on college?" He had me there.

As we spaded the earth and wrestled with eight-foot Arborvitae, we developed an unspoken camaraderie centered around the simple act of making things grow. We were equals barreling down Highway 51, a road mentioned in a bunch of old blues songs, each sharing the same view of the Shawnee National Forest whizzing by.

When our route took us near the miniscule town of Makanda, we stopped at the general store next to Giant City State Park to sip a soda and bullshit with the regulars—who never appeared to be doing much work. It was understood by the regulars that work done at a desk in the city by the college crowd didn't really qualify as work. It was more like luck. A luck that began at birth. Feeling the part of a noble victim, forgotten and overlooked by the ruling class seems a common thread of rural life. I was a curiosity to them—an "other"—but as we talked in close quarters, on their turf, and as I listened to their yarns, I became one of the "good" hippies. The act of honest listening often dampens animosity.

This was one of those jobs that I knew was temporary. And they knew it was temporary. And I knew that they knew.

"You're a college graduate and you're planting shrubs?"

When I gave notice of my departure, it almost felt wistful. I enjoyed the experience. "You're a college graduate and you're planting trees." No, I'm a college graduate who is still eager for what's around the bend.

CAREFREE IN '73

1973

OUR SOUTHERN ILLINOIS LIFE WAS SIMPLE. A form of privileged poverty. We had little money and didn't care. True poverty isn't carefree. The youthful poverty of white middle class kids is. When Linda was done with class for the day, we might jump in a friend's beater and cruise the back roads that weaved through the bluffed woodlands, maybe stopping to ogle the roaring waters of the Devil's Kitchen spillway or hike amidst the stunning wind and rain sculpted sandstone formations at Garden of the Gods, or wedge through the sheer stone walls of Fat Man's Squeeze in Giant City. Or we might pile in a car and drive toward the Mississippi, to Ma Hale's in Grand Tower for the all-you-can-eat buffet featuring endless biscuits, ham, fried chicken, tomato bread pudding, and peach cobbler for less than two bucks. Anyone who ate at Ma Hale's will never forget it.

Music remained a focal point of my life. Listening or playing. Other than exchanging guitar lessons for weed, I never got paid to perform songs like Robert Johnson's *C'mon in My Kitchen* or Mississippi John Hurt's rendition of *Stack 'O Lee*. From the back porch steps of our tiny rental bungalow on Bridge Street, my audience included squirrels, the neighbors or an occasional friend who dropped by. In this house I composed *Murphysboro Blues* and taught it to my good friend, Smock. One time we played it on the lawn of the Murphysboro courthouse, the county seat of Jackson County, drinking cheap wine from a paper bag.

In Giant City State Park

Old blues from the 1920s and 30s played on our turntable. *My Kitchen Man* by Bessie Smith was a favorite, Leroy Carr's *How Long Blues* another, an ideal song to run through your head when you heard a lonesome train whistle at 3 a.m. on a mystical spring night. *How long has that evenin' train been gone?* One time the overnight freight jumped the track and dropped a load of coal. A friend filled his van with the plunder and brought us a month's supply for our coal burning furnace.

On occasion, I went to Merlin's bar in downtown Carbondale and witnessed long guitar solos by dudes with shag haircuts, ecstatically grimacing as their amp stacks throbbed, me taking it in as a musicologist might, noting that this was derivative music several steps removed from the country blues. For one night, I was a short order cook at Merlin's Grill, serving burgers to downed out party kids. I quit because no one knew what they were doing, including me. I was paid in day-old buns.

A genuine short order heaven was Mary Lou's Grill. She was a for-ty-something, gum-chewing, red-lipsticked, diner goddess with a remarkable ability to juggle orders and conversations while in perpetual motion. I saw her disarm a belligerent dude who was either hungover or drunk. The guy was squabbling with another customer when Mary Lou presented him with a free piece of pie to go and told him not to return until Christmas. And she expected a present. The dude left, and the customers cheered when the door shut behind him. My favorite pie was lemon meringue. Or peanut butter. Or cherry.

♫   ♫   ♫

In early June of 1973, we left Carbondale for another western road trip. This time we had $400 to last the summer. Linda's cousin, Joey, was our ride. At Monarch Pass in Colorado, he had to back his Vega down the twisting mountain highway because the carburetor had conked out from the 11,300-foot altitude. Standing on the roadside precipice with a firm grip on my guitar—why leave my guitar in the car if it might tumble down the mountain?—I stopped traffic as the Vega rolled backward for a hundred feet with the engine in neutral. Nice job, Joey! Linda was terrified of mountain roads, something she brought up each time we were on one. "It'll be fine," I told her as the Vega coughed to life.

On our way to Tucson we explored Anasazi ruins, caught sunset at Mesa Verde and slid down Slide Rock in Oak Creek Canyon. As soon as we got to our friends' place in Tucson, we immediately sensed that this might not be a long stay. Their home was tiny. I worked for a couple of days at a sawmill. Linda and I did odd jobs for an elderly desert lady. We travelled to Aqua Prieta where I bought a bottle of mescal. It tasted awful. Linda and I eventually took the train to California and made it to SF before heading back for Linda's final year at SIU.

♫   ♫   ♫

Joe Amari photo of the carefree couple

At this point, I did not consider myself to be an artist. I didn't consider myself to be anything other than a noble fool of sorts. I was past my psychedelic phase, which had consisted of numerous trips, both good and slightly scary, brief glimpses of the universe, eyelid cartoons, transcendental understanding, journeys through my skin to the tiniest sub particles of my ectoplasm, where I connected with everything that has ever lived. My nonchalance at these revelations was my proof that I could "handle it." In one instance, I ingested some windowpane acid an hour before giving a presentation to my *Cases in Persuasion* class at KU. As fifteen to twenty classmates slouched at their desks, I blasted a bootleg copy of Jimi Hendrix playing the national anthem while I had a classmate turn the light switch on and off. As Jimi's feedback concluded, I explained that the song was an American flag morphing into a dagger plunging into Nixon's blue heart. The professor, who had already been intrigued by my theory that everything was bullshit, was captivated by my youthful absurdity, as only an academic ground down by years of struggle with the university establishment could be. He gave me an "A."

GREASY TIMES

Kitchen Maintenance at S.I.U. dorm, 1973-74

"I HATE TO SEE

That evenin' sun go down ..."

I'm wearing an apron, singing out loud this oldest of blues tunes, carefully walking flat-footed on the greasy floor of the industrial-sized kitchen, feeling alright, having just shared a joint in the bushes out back with a couple of work mates. Eddie Mann, a burly black man with a clean-shaven dome, thirty-five years my senior, gives me a little nod of approval as he scrubs out a giant, stainless steel kettle. I am at work in the kitchen of Grinnell Hall at SIU.

Cleaning up after others is often the job of immigrants, minorities, the unqualified, the downtrodden, or, in my case, the carefree idealist escaping convention or what some refer to as reality. But what was Eddie Mann escaping? The poorhouse, I suppose. We were equals on the job. In "real" life, I had a college degree, he had a grade school education. I grew up in the suburbs of Chicago, he grew up in a sharecropper household in the Mississippi delta. I had just begun to learn the songs of Charlie Patton, but Eddie had witnessed the real country blues played at Saturday night fish fries and juke joints. I was a student of the blues. Eddie had lived the blues. I had little dough but didn't consider myself to be poor. Mine was tourist poverty. I could afford to be poor. Eddie knew what real, dirt floor poverty was. Although we each lived paycheck to paycheck, Eddie put a little away every month for what he said was "when the blues pour down like rain." Meanwhile, I was saving for my next stop on my early retirement tour: Colombia, South America.

Colombia sounded exotic and inexpensive, a place where I could try out my high school Spanish. To get there I would be cleaning up the mealtime mess of college kids: handling ketchup and gravy slathered trays, dumping half-eaten mystery meat that glowed with an iridescent sheen onto the conveyor belt, removing bacon grease, scrubbing hundred-gallon soup pots, breathing steamy grease, keeping my balance on grease-slicked floors, dealing with grease in my hair, nose and lungs. And supplying plenty of elbow grease.

The most memorable of the white guy contingent was Dish Washing Moses, technically a college dropout, who looked like a person drawn by R. Crumb: scraggily black hair, kinky beard, kinky body. I forget his real name. Moses had a tic where he constantly rocked forward and backward as he spoke. This gave him the rhythm of a human metronome. He laughed a lot because he thought life to be a joke and was usually relating an outlandish story to illustrate that theory. Like the three days he spent in a spider-infested, underground hole of a jail cell in Popayan, Colombia, because the secret police had found rolling papers on him. I often queried him about his trip to Colombia as I formed my own travel plan.

The mother/son Sparks combo was another faction. They lived in some holler down the two-lane blacktop from Carbondale. Both were certain they were on the path to salvation, consumed by the fundamentalist teachings of their holy roller church. We would often aim friendly taunts at young boy Sparks.

"Do you think that Jesus had hair like Moses (the dishwasher) or yours?" Sparks had close-cropped red hair, the same tint as his plump mother, who viewed us as irredeemable curiosities put in her path by Satan.

"Real funny," replied young Sparks. "You'll find out on judgement day."

The black guys, all adult lifers, consisted of T.C., Mumbles, and Eddie Mann. Eddie regaled me with stories of the Saturday night fish fries back in

Mississippi, of Howlin' Wolf and moonshine. Eddie was a door to a world that had me captivated: the real country blues. I was always egging him on to tell me blues stories.

"Did you ever go to Dockery Plantation? Have you ever seen Charlie Patton?" I might ask.

"When I was a little kid, Charlie came through our plantation," Eddie told me.

"Did you hear him play?"

"Naw. He got chased away by a jealous guy with a big knife." Made no difference to me whether Eddie was telling the truth or spinning yarns.

T.C. stood about 6'5" and weighed 260. He played basketball in high school and could whistle talk: like burp talking but instead you whistle while you speak. He had a razor cut on his bicep from an attempted assassination at a barrelhouse joint. Mumbles, his best friend, was a half-foot shorter, weighed about 120 pounds less, and had bigger feet. Mumbles had no front teeth, never shut up, and was impossible to understand. At first, he appeared a simpleton, mainly because of his missing teeth and poor elocution, but he possessed street smarts and seemed to live a normal, working class, southern Illinois life.

Mumbles laughed a lot and one of his most understandable phrases was, "that's what *I'm* talkin' about." He would always say this at the end of a long exchange of insults with T.C.—involving the proclivities of each other's mother—that ended in uproarious laughter and commotion that might grab the attention of Old Lady Drummitt. She was not a fan of her workers playing the dozens.

Old Lady Drummitt was our direct supervisor. She wasn't that old— maybe twenty years my senior—but Moses tagged her with the old lady prefix. She viewed her staff as shiftless miscreants who needed constant oversight, beneath her in every way. She didn't seem to like those in her employ, and we didn't like her. Only the Sparks' tried to kiss up to her. She wore a white kitchen dress uniform, white hose, and white shoes, like a kitchen version of Nurse Ratchet from *Cuckoo's Nest*. This woman, with her hair tied in a tight bun, was begging to be tested. With dead insects and rodents. With the old salt-sugar mix up. With timecards inflated enough that she smelled a rat. She suspected that someone had a key to the time machine.

Old Lady Drummit often consulted *the manual* to solve problems of behavior or procedure. When the manual wasn't enough, she lodged a complaint with Mr. Gray. Commander Gray, as we called him (not to his face). The Commander was never known to crack a smile or laugh, and you could tell he was not pleased that a bunch of misfits and jokers in a damn dormitory mess hall were now at his command, instead of a Naval destroyer. That's why he took nips from a bottle stashed in his office when he thought no one was looking.

During our fifteen-minute break times, the college contingent went outside in the bushes to smoke weed. The older, local black guys—who could not join in for fear of getting fired, or worse—would get together and talk shit and break balls in a rambunctious way. The Sparks tended to keep to themselves and gossip about members of their congregation or argue about scripture, and on occasion would utter a proclamation involving hellfire and damnation. They eventually gave up trying to save us.

At the end of each mealtime, it was rush hour. As the conveyor belt chugged and clanked with piles of smeared dishes, no longer recognizable food and wadded up napkins, it was almost exhilarating. Or comedic. T.C. would bellow, "Roll, Moses!" Moses, with his pointy, kinky beard and flashing black eyes, grabbed at the plates and sorted them into the proper machine. Mumbles carried on an endless, incomprehensible commentary over the din. Eddie Mann concentrated on the job at hand because he knew he needed the work and was too old to find something else. For a brief while, we were a team with a common goal. We dispatched the mess as one unit. I felt part of something because we relied on each other not to slack.

After seven months, I was ready to feel a part of something bigger than Grinnell Hall. Or Carbondale. Or the United States. I was ready to be a man of the world, not just a man of the kitchen. Time to test my high school Spanish.

MY COLOMBIAN YEAR

Colombia S.A. 1974

THE GRINGO LIFE

LINDA WAS USED TO MY NATURE BY NOW. I had been her guide on months-long cross-country odysseys in the U.S., but Colombia would be a destination new to both of us. She had graduated from SIU and now her travels could be more than summer journeys. Linda's look, born from her pure Sicilian ancestry, didn't scream *gringo*. Her olive skin and dark eyes could have been from almost anywhere—Polynesia? Sardinia? Colombia? I cut my hair, packed my white linen pants—my splurge purchase—and brushed up on my Spanish. In high school Spanish class, my name had been Rogelio. Now in real life, I would be Rogelio.

Colombia beckoned the seekers, a destination for travelers, not tourists. No cruise ships, no package tours for Bob and Betty from Green Bay. It was a notch up from Mexico on the exotic scale. Pablo Escobar and the cocaine explosion had not yet made the country a no-go, but it was still wild and wooly. Guerillas. Drugs. Poverty. Corruption. Outlaws. *La violencia,* a national epidemic of mayhem, had claimed hundreds of thousands of Colombian lives over the previous decades.

Linda on Rodadero Beach

Aerocondor's roundtrip from Miami to the Caribbean port of Barranquilla was just $80. After going through customs, we flagged a taxi and said, Santa Marta, a city 60 miles down the coast. Within minutes our driver had broken most U.S. traffic laws. Tailgate at 60. Drive on the wrong side of the road. Pass on a blind curve. We arrived in Santa Marta with no hotel in mind. A consultation between our cab driver and a few guys on the street, resulted in us travelling a few miles back to Playa Rodadero, a beach resort with a handful of hotels and condos, none higher than eight or nine stories.

The taxi brought us to a whitewashed three-story hotel, La Riviera, one block from the Caribbean. Bordering the hotel was the stop-and-start construction rubble that permeates tropical Latin America: half-completed cinder block walls, stacks of broken tile, piles of brush. The hotel's immediate grounds were orderly, well-kept, and free of refuse. An oasis. A room for two with three meals was $10 a day. A month for $300! A young helper carried our luggage to a corner room on the third floor that faced the hills. "El Matrimonio," he said. The marriage suite. It was a spare but clean room with a balcony overlooking the rubble, jungle mountains rising in the distance. Although not yet married, Linda was now my jungle wife.

Opening and closing doors at La Riviera proved tricky due to the near constant, freakishly powerful airstream that rushed down from the 19,000-foot peak of Sierra Nevada de Santa Marta. We couldn't see Pico Cristobal Colon from the hotel—the highest coastal peak in the world—but felt its presence whenever we engaged a door. The halls reverberated with a near constant whistling sound and the intermittent bang of a door sucked shut. We had arrived at the zone of slamming doors.

The meals were simple and delicious, served with informal elegance on white linen by an ever-changing cast of jovial boys as young as twelve. For breakfast, scrambled eggs with onion and tomato. Lunch and dinner consisted of either a pounded, tasty beef steak or local grilled fish accompanied by rice, beans, salad, fried plantains and starchy roots or breadfruit.

The hotel manager was a small, tightly wound, ex-professional soccer player named Tatin. The second in command was a dark, slender guy named Roberto. Both were Argentinians of Italian heritage. They liked to smoke cigarettes, eat meat, make fun of clueless gringos, and drink many small cups of strong coffee. I soon picked up the afternoon coffee habit with a daily tinto doble or two. This is the life, thought me.

In front of La Riviera with Tatin y Roberto

Our first or second evening, a beach boy hustler struck up a solicitous conversation with us, using his pidgin English while I tried out my high school Spanish, never certain what the other truly meant. We didn't trust him, but how do you take full advantage of life's possibilities without dealing with the occasional guy you don't trust? One of his many offerings was a cheap lobster dinner. "I will take you to the nice lady who makes good longostino just down the beach," A lobster dinner at a beach estate—touted by a hustler—was the type of caper that resonated with me, a man of the world in search of adventure, intrigue, and romance in a far-off land. Linda was trepidatious but hungry for lobster, her favorite shellfish. She had become somewhat accustomed to me dragging her all over the place. As the hustler guided us, frigate birds soared high above, tossing off a pre-historic vibe. Dog barking blended with strains of distant cumbia music providing the perfect soundtrack. I spied animal tracks in the sand. "What are these?" I asked the hustler. "Cocodrillo," he answered.

We arrived at our destination, immediately greeted by an effusive woman, ready to serve. "She's a very nice lady," endorsed the hustler, as he slid off somewhere out of sight. A pile of terracotta roof tiles was strewn by the side of the house. Broken cinder blocks lay scattered about. A stack of rebar rusted in the fading sun. We had reached the intersection of poverty, beauty, and undetermined vibes.

We sat down at a bare table in an open-sided room with a view of the turquoise waters of the Caribbean and instantly began swatting at biting pests. The nice lady saw our plight and crawled under the table, rubbing alcohol on our legs, as Linda and I stared dreamily into each other's eyes. Very romantic. When our legs were momentarily vermin-free, she presented plates of Caribbean spiny lobster ringed by large glops of a mayonnaise-like substance. Thoughts of spoiled potato salad warnings at summertime picnics came rushing back but we dug in. Sort of.

As we finished our meal, leaving most of the glops uneaten, a man in a small truck pulled up. At the same time, the beachboy hustler popped back into the scene, explaining that this man, one of the finest men in Playa Rodadero, was here to offer us a good deal on the purest cocaine in Colombia. We had not mentioned drugs to the hustler. He assumed that because we were young gringos, we had travelled here to get high. There was a street saying in these parts that "all gringos smoke." And most partook in beach snow. But we weren't fans of blow. It caused my heart to race. I explained that we weren't interested and held my breath. With a stone-cold glare, one of the finest men in Rodadero wheeled around, jumped into his truck, and spewed off in a rain of dust and gravel. No threats made but not sure how well the beach hustler fared. A tongue lashing from one of the finest men in Rodadero at least. Had we scored I'm sure the cops would have shaken us down somewhere on the path home.

We paid the very nice lady and began the trek back to the matrimonial suite. On the way, we saw something that looked like a pig-dog lurking in the shadows. I told Tatin about this creature and he said it was an odondo. We'll never know what it really was and never again have I heard of odondos.

♫ ♫ ♫

The first gringo we befriended at La Riviera was a guy named Jim who appeared to be a full-time resident. Lord Jim, as I called him, was in his early thirties, fair haired and fair skinned, and from Philadelphia. Every day he dressed in a crisp white, long sleeve shirt and pressed khakis. He spoke impeccable Spanish and sniffed huge piles of cocaine.

When I eventually asked him what he did to support himself, he answered, "What do you think?" We left it at that. When I inquired about weed, he suggested we meet his friends, Susan and Cilla, who lived a few miles away. Colombian weed was famous. In Carbondale and Lawrence, we called it Colombo. Or just bo. We were now in the birthplace of bo.

Linda and I taxied a short drive into the hills to the small homestead of Susan and Cilla. Our hosts were preoccupied because their baby ocelot had just run away. Chickens scrambled and clucked about the property as their naked, three-year-old daughter rambled underfoot. Because we had been vetted by Lord Jim, Susan and Cilla felt secure in relating their story of exile from the U.S. At some time in the not-too-distant past they had been a part of a Timothy Leary-related commune. Dr. Leary, a Harvard psychologist, had tried to turn on a generation with LSD, resulting in non-stop busts and harassment from the authorities. Somehow due to their Leary connection, Susan and Cilla were wanted by the law back home. They were on the run.

Susan seemed like someone you might run into at a Grateful Dead concert: short curly hair and Granny glasses. Cilla sported a sandy ponytail and not an ounce of fat on his frame. He described how he once rode on horseback from the center of Colombia across the jungle mountains into Peru, where he was forced to eat his horse. Hearing this tale from an outlaw while sitting in his *finca* in the hills beneath the Sierra Nevada so many miles from home gave our trip the purpose I had craved: adventure, mind expansion, and learning the stories of the world. Would I ever eat my horse?

We sampled their weed, remarkably powerful buds, gold and sticky. With a proper buzz on, it was time to be introduced to the pre-Columbian beads of the lost Tayrona tribe. I am sure that we were not the first couple to hear the story. While giving a brief history of the tribe, our hosts showed us a few strands of beads, the ones that they wore around their necks, then a small stash from a leather pouch. The Tayronas had lived right out their back door. "We hear them chant on the wind at night." They described the jungle as a zone of perpetual superstition, inhabited by phantom tribes, magical winds, and spectacled bears "that could rip a tree in two." Cilla held up a necklace with an inch-long amulet of what looked to be a pitted, jade larva. "This is from a time before Columbus." He held up another that was black and looked to be a tiny bird bust. "This is a guacamaya. A parrot."

We bought the jade larva and the guacamaya. In the back of my mind, I began to think that if we could find enough of these little treasures, we might sell them back home. They were like nothing we had ever owned. Ancient. Supernatural. Entire Colombian families made a living harvesting the lapidary riches of the long dead. To possess something created by a stone age culture is a reminder of the timeline we are on. Will someone in the distant future possess one of my guitar picks? Will plastic outlast stone?

There were no national antiquity laws preventing us from buying these beads. It was a thriving trade around Santa Marta. *Väceros* (grave robbers) roamed the mystical jungle mountains looking for graves of the lost tribe. It was their job, their life. It never crossed my mind that we were breaking any law and technically we weren't. I thought of it as like buying arrowheads at a dusty outpost in the American west.

The beads were fashioned from agate, carnelian, jade, jasper, quartz, chert, pottery, gold, soapstone, bone, coral, and a bunch of other minerals and substances that I can no longer recall. Some were trading beads of Venetian glass, now pitted with age, that had found their way to the new world. Some were smooth, perfectly shaped tubes of agate, two to five inches long with a diameter of one-quarter to one-half inch. Each bead had a hole bored through its entire length. Bead boring must have been ritualistic, arduous, and focused. Imagine spending a year of your life using stone-age tools to fashion a bead. *When he died, he had 23 beads to his credit.* The beads may have been a form of currency, so the bead maker was literally making money. Or they may have been fashion pieces or tokens of good fortune. Or they were traded like baseball cards.

Other beads were amulets inspired by the shape of animals: tigers, macaws, ducks and other birds, sea creatures, insects, guzanillos (larvae), and humans—especially chieftains: *Caciques*. Yet others were more stylized: fetuses, spacemen, and space re-entry capsules. Did these shapes prove that something like space travel might have been conceived centuries and hundreds of centuries before its invention? The beads stoked my imagination and suggested the existence of other worlds. Upon returning to the States, I read every piece of anthropology or geology ever written about the Tayrona. The tribe was last seen by Spanish conquistadors in about 1520. When the Spaniards returned twenty years later, the tribe had disappeared. Or been wiped out by European diseases. Or entered another dimension through a secret wormhole in the jungle.

♪ ♪ ♪

I brought a guitar on the trip and wrote *Frijoles*, an ode to pinto beans sung in Spanish with a Slavic march tempo. This became a favorite with little Olgita, an adorable nine-year-old vacationing at La Riviera with her father and drunken uncle. The drunken uncle was normally a sober doctor in Bogota but on vacation he made up for the required sobriety with all-day rum benders. You could sense that this was some sort of ritual the doctor went through on vacation. Like "the cure" in reverse.

"Como esta, hoy?" I would ask him, playing the straight man. His reply: "Borracho." Then he would shake with laughter, and I couldn't help joining in. Every day Olgita and her uncle requested—demanded—that I play *Frijoles*. The song would become a staple of my future band, The Barking Geckos.

Linda with Olgita

♫   ♫   ♫

There was a strange exhilaration to be in a place where danger lurked, and many public services were unreliable. The municipal electricity and water cut out once or twice daily, an accepted fact of life. Vehicles were kept together with spit and a prayer. Spot the bald-tired bus swerving past an abandoned lorry blocking a lane on a blind mountain pass with no guard rails. Drivers practiced anarchy, a constant game of chicken. A truck might get repaired in the middle of the road where it had conked out. The police and secret police were noted more for sowing fear than for justice. Shakedowns were a way of life. And men carried guns. We heard about a taxi driver and a bus driver going opposite ways down a one-lane street in Santa Marta, precipitating an angry shootout that left one of them dead. It happened just before we arrived. Or maybe it was a couple of months back. Or a year ago.

One day we took the bus to Parque de Tayrona, the wildest beach we had ever seen. On the return, an armed brigade of soldiers with sub machine guns stopped our bus, presumably looking for rebels. The locals on the bus told me they feared the soldiers more than they did the guerilla insurgents.

♫　♫　♫

We travelled to Cartagena for a few days of exploration and extreme gastric misery compounded by hotel plumbing that didn't work. We then left for Medellin; the city of Eternal Spring perched in the Andes. On the first morning in our hotel, I picked up a copy of the local daily newspaper, *El Tiempo*. Wow! Heiress Patty Hearst had been kidnapped in Berkeley by the Symbionese Liberation Army, a small group of "revolutionaries" seeking the destruction of Amerika. One of the SLA members was identified as Emily Harris. In the accompanying photo I recognized Emily Schwartz, nee Harris, a girl who had been one year ahead of me at Prospect Elementary school. I had attended grade school with the most famous kidnapper in the western world. One more who had been radicalized by the Vietnam War era. She had reached a point where kidnapping an heiress seemed logical. Learning that my former classmate was now a notorious criminal while I was in a land of desperados seemed fitting.

Our Colombian adventure ended in Medellin. Linda was invaded by a burrowing worm that entered her foot when her espadrille broke as she lurched out of the path of a thief being chased, requiring her to walk barefoot for a few city blocks. Within a few hours, she felt an itch. Over the next day, we watched, in horror, as a small red line just underneath her skin made a determined path from the entry point on her sole toward her ... heart? A doctor suggested options that included poisoning, spraying, freezing, or cutting, and confirmed that the worm would get into her bloodstream and lay eggs. She balked at taking a poison pill in the Andes, so we returned to

Chicago for medical attention, where the doctor called all the other doctors in to look. Linda felt more comfortable taking a big fat poison pill in her hometown. "It'll be fine, honey," I assured her.

THE BEAD BUSINESS

We again journeyed to Colombia several months later, intent on buying more beads to design and sell necklaces. After a week-long stopover on the island of San Andres, we flew to Barranquilla on a plane with duct tape holding the emergency door intact. This would have made a great Colombian advertisement for duct tape: "keeping you safe on your next flight over the ocean." I had roped Linda into yet another uncomfortable caper. As I began to whisper, "It'll be fine," the tape started flapping, accompanied by an ominous, high-pitched howl of wind pressure. The guy across the aisle pulled out a bottle of aguardiente and offered me a sip. Tasted like a blend of sambuca and lighter fluid. Worth a try if you think you're about to die. Upon landing, Linda announced that this would be her last trip Colombia.

♫ ♫ ♫

There was no central marketplace for beads. We looked in small indigenous craft shops. A taxi driver delivered us to a modest home in a Santa Marta neighborhood where a charming couple who looked like they were dressed for dinner or church, showed us strands of jade beads. We were approached on the street by a short man who ushered us to a nearby bench on the waterfront. From one pocket he pulled a snatch of black velvet, within which was a strand of agate beads. He spread the velvet onto the bench then placed the strand on the black cloth. How could we resist this instant pop-up? We bought black velvet for our own displays as soon as we returned home.

Customs at the Barranquilla airport was nerve racking. Young gringos always caused suspicion. Agents rummaged through our luggage, glanced at our beads, and passed us through. They didn't care. They were looking for drugs, not trinkets. Today it may be different.

Once home, we designed a couple dozen necklaces, made business cards, and attempted to sell our Tayrona creations. Women who were attracted to turquoise jewelry—very popular at the time—were often drawn to the beads. We gave our "bead spiel" to family and friends. Anyone we met was fair game. There was no market rate for our creations because no one had seen or heard of Tayrona beads.

We attempted one art fair with little success. Friends bought a few. We sold four or five to ladies who wanted something different. I did a showing at a very large home in Hinsdale one Saturday afternoon while the husband was at the office. After my practiced patter about the history of the Tayrona tribe, I spread our necklace designs onto my swatch of black velvet. The woman was interested but she sighed that her husband had recently purchased a company and put her on a spending leash. Looking around the huge home, I told her I could come back after he sold the company. I was not a hard-sell bead monger.

Our sales effort more than paid for the cost of buying the beads plus airfare, but it was hardly a financial path to the future.

INTERPRETER

A friend, Arvin, was about to open a native craft store in Chicago and needed some native crafts. He knew that I had been to Colombia and spoke passable Spanish. Could I serve as his guide and interpreter in Colombia? All expenses paid! I knew the craft store was just a front for his Chicago weed business but that wasn't my concern. Crafts seemed a safe bet. I said sure. Baskets. Weavings. Whatever. Thus was born my short career as an interpreter. Linda remained in Chicago, keeping her vow of no more Colombia.

Arvin and I stayed one night in Barranquilla's version of a five-star hotel: the staff wore golden brown outfits with epaulettes. Screechy little parrots darted and dived past our balcony, exotic and obnoxious. The faintly sweet smell of rotting vegetation mingled with the odor of bus fumes, the sea and hot cooking oil. It was a humid 90 degrees. I felt as if in a Graham Greene novel.

The next day, we taxied to La Riviera. By now, Arvin had settled on a search for baskets. Tatin knew right where to find baskets because he knew everything. "Usiacurí," he told us. It was situated in the jungle hills between Cartagena and Barranquilla, about a half-day's journey from Rodedero and about 15 or 20 miles from the Caribbean Sea as the condor flies. The town's industry was basket weaving.

Tatin arranged an early morning taxi. The driver left us at the edge of this rustic outpost. We wandered the rutted streets, dodged the free running pigs, and searched for "*familias que hacen bultos.*" Families that make baskets. The first person we asked pointed to a shack of cinder block, corrugated tin, and sticks. We peered in the open front door and saw a stack of baskets. Before we could knock, a squat, middle aged gent smelling of alcohol and bullshit greeted us. The patriarch.

I imagined that gringo clients did not often appear at his craft shack home. He guided us into the main parlor where his family was dutifully weaving. A single, framed picture of Jesus hung on a wall. We looked at the various stacks of baskets and I explained that my client wanted the best price, and we were prepared to traipse to the next basket operation up the hill if necessary.

"No es necesario," the patriarch explained. "We have the best price, and we make the best baskets." This sounded great to us because we preferred to get the transaction underway as soon as possible in order to arrive at the Barranquilla airport before dark.

Midway through the negotiations, a platter of spit-roasted, freshly slaughtered pork was presented to us. This was high class jungle cuisine, a step up from capybara, but my friend flinched at the offering. I explained to the family that he could not partake due to his religion, not his revulsion.

"Who doesn't eat pigs?" asked the patriarch, more puzzled than offended. It can be tricky to turn down a free lunch in the jungle, but I made up for it. This was my job. In the spirit of deal making, I attacked the platter with a gusto that demonstrated my appreciation for their hospitality. Arvin munched some bread.

When the transaction concluded, while Arvin counted baskets with the grandmother and the children, the patriarch motioned for me to join him outside. We walked down a path to a roofless white stone structure on the edge of the village. A bar counter and a wall of empty shelves, save for half a bottle of white rum, suggested that we were in a drinking establishment: or the patriarch's private lair. The patriarch took a generous swig of rum and pounded his chest.

"*Fuerte!*" he proclaimed. I did the same. After several slugs, the "*Fuertes!*" were becoming forceful. His chest pound now included a chest bump. Then another. Another swig, another bump. I began to wonder what the next step would be: a wrestling match? Revolvers at sixteen paces? Did some sort of symbolic struggle conclude each jungle basket negotiation? We were drinking and pounding our chests and shoving each other, all to clinch the deal. I was an interpreter with barely passable Spanish, not a drunken brawler. When he went looking for more rum, I hoofed it back to the craft shack. From behind, I heard the patriarch calling my name. I turned around. He was hoisting a new bottle of rum.

We departed Usiacurí with four giant cardboard boxes filled with cute little baskets that would eventually hold gringo dinner napkins. There was no taxi to take us to the Barranquilla airport. Busses came at irregular intervals, and no one was sure when the next one would arrive. I began imagining that no bus would ever come, but jungle luck was with us. A bus bound for Barranquilla snorted to a stop and we climbed in! A bus helper lashed three of our boxes to the roof and we crammed one into the aisle.

The bus dropped us nearly a half-mile from the airport. The flight was scheduled to leave in two hours. Pushing the boxes—they stood up to my waist—would take too long. We needed to get the baskets onto the late afternoon flight or face the prospect of holing up for the night in some wretched airport hotel with our damn boxes. We managed to flag a cab and the driver roped the boxes onto the roof and into his trunk, with the trunk lid pointing straight up. This took at least fifteen minutes as we helped and paced and felt the creep of anxiety.

"*Andale!*" The driver picked up speed and threaded his way through the bicycles, pedestrians, and old trucks that haphazardly careened along the dusty, pot-holed airport road. And then ... an explosion. A blowout! The driver lost control and we began fishtailing, then spinning a 360. I recall instinctually clutching the back of the front seat as the doors flew open, a blurred vision of the driver flying out of the taxi. When we finally came to a sputtering stop, a street hoard descended like it was the final scene of a B-movie adventure drama, "*The Last Days of Barranquilla.*" My client and I, full of adrenaline, jumped out and spotted our boxes scattered down the road. They were smashed but intact. The cab driver was on all fours but seemed to be missing part of one ear. There was a lot of blood. He crawled and lurched to the driver side door and grasped at the pesos in his ashtray. The mob eyeballed the pesos too, but he kept them at bay with a short, heavy stick stashed under his seat.

"Should we pay him?" asked Arvin, as we surveyed the scene. Because I have always had a soft spot for freshly wounded taxi drivers, I said yes, even though we still had a hundred yards to go to the airport. We each pushed two boxes until we found a cart.

After a frantic search we found the customs office, got shuttled to a few windowless rooms and were then shaken down by a bunch of thug-like, sneering "officials." Pirates in uniform. To secure the necessary paperwork, they demanded a payment greater than the cost of the baskets. We were in a lawless situation, doubtful that the boxes would ever make it back to Chicago, but it was time to let fate take its course and head back to La Riviera to have a beer with Tatín y Roberto. And sleep! All in a day's work as interpreter.

The baskets did make it back to Chicago about three weeks later. I had earned my free trip to Colombia. On my resume, I could now add interpreter/negotiator. One of these baskets would hold napkins on our kitchen table for years to come.

SEEKING THE LOST TRIBE

The business part of our trip was concluded but we had several more days before our flight back to Chicago. Because I was still attempting to sell beads back home, I wanted to see where they came from. During my previous visits to Colombia, I had befriended a guy about my own age, Estaban, who operated an art/antiquity store called La Rana Morada in Playa Rodedero. He shared my curiosity about the archaeology and the mystery of this lost Tayrona tribe. Months ago, we had discussed taking a trip to Parque Nacional de Tayrona. When I had visited the park with Linda, we walked the ferocious beach and marveled at the harsh beauty of the setting but had not attempted the trail to Pueblito, the name given to the ruins site. Estaban and I planned to take the trail that led from the beach into the jungle mountains, presumably ending at Pueblito.

We took an early morning bus from Rodedero to Santa Marta, then another bus ride for an hour toward the Guajira peninsula, land of salt flats and desperados. The bus finally dropped us near the parque. We walked through a vacant parking lot that must have been built for some imagined crowd that never showed up, and spotted a trail that led to the sea. Giant surf, alive with big fish and sharks, pounded the shore. This was not a swimming beach. It was a beautiful wilderness. The rainforest spilled down the mountainside to the crashing waves. Treacherous currents and hulking sea rocks dotted the shoreline. No one else was in sight. Estaban and I were the last two inhabitants of earth. That's how it felt.

This was not like a national park in the U.S. There were no rangers, no trail maps, no restrooms, no gift shop. In 1974, it was empty save for a random vagabond dressed like Robinson Caruso. As the trail left the beach, we came to a small, abandoned, windowless structure that had a sign on it: *Peligroso! Malaria*. We quickened our pace.

The first part of the trail consisted of a series of small hills. Our technique was to carefully run down a hill then have momentum carry us halfway up the next one. At the side of the path, a three-inch wide procession of leaf-cutter ants now accompanied us. I had read about these creatures but never seen them. We gathered a few mangos that grew trailside. A large yellow butterfly landed on my mango, and I expected it to begin talking.

With few words, we walked this prehistoric pathway, passing looted graves that at one time had held the treasures that now captivated us: the beads. About an hour into the walk, we encountered a wiry, barefoot man adorned in shorts and a torn T-shirt. Over one shoulder was slung an old-fashioned rifle that resembled a blunderbuss. Over the other shoulder, a dead capybara. Dinner. He grinned as he passed us. Flies buzzed about the capy's snout.

As we climbed, the trail surface changed from thin, hard packed jungle soil into a carefully laid series of huge, rectangular stones placed a thousand years ago, worn smooth by centuries of barefoot Tayrona traffic. We were walking in the footsteps of the lost tribe. The huge, darkish-green stones served as the roadway. At one location, a tunnel cut into the mountainside precipice. At certain points, tremendous boulders abutted the path. Orchids dangled, providing vivid bursts of purple and white against the monotony of jungle green. Bats darted everywhere; a screeching wildlife cacophony accompanied us.

After a long climb through vine-choked jungle, at the top of a rise, we came to a small level clearing: a stone terrace. Before us lay a scattering of bleached white paving stones, smooth with age. Some had canals fluted along their edges. You could sense that at one time these stones had interconnected. Some were the length of a car. It appeared to be an ancient drainage system. But there was no friendly ranger to fill in the details. No rental headphones to tell "The Story of The Lost Tayrona." At the time of our visit, Pueblito may have gone days without a human presence—other than the spirits.

The Tayrona, sometimes spelled Tairona, had a 2,000-year history in the region. When Spanish conquistadors arrived, the tribe moved from the coast upward into the mountains. Pueblito was one of many settlements with stone terraces and housing platforms. Descendants still lived in the area. Most Americans know of the Mayas and the Aztecs and the Incas, but few have heard of the Tayronas.

We were now many hours from the nearest highway. Estaban and I were weary as we sat down on one of the ancient gutter stones, marveling at their integrity while catching our breath. After a few moments, Estaban stood up to survey our surroundings.

"Mira!" he exclaimed, nodding his head in a downward direction. I pushed myself up off the stone and looked at the trail as it descended the hill. Before us spread the stone foundation of a neatly planned village; terraces, retaining walls, pavement. We had arrived at Pueblito. The path leading down to the village looked exquisite. As my friend stepped onto the path, I agreed to follow in about five minutes, after I caught my breath. I felt wonderfully spent, pleased to experience such pure discovery. Though we had ascended hundreds of feet from the beach, the air was still close and moist.

Alone in this pre-Colombian theater, I heard a snuffling to my left. A very large anteater with serious claws appeared from the green tangle. The giant anteater was feasting on the line of leafcutters that had been with us for hours. He was no more than a few feet away from me but paid me no heed. Meanwhile, I was heeding. One thing you do in the jungle is you heed.

But it all seemed so natural—as if I were accustomed to relaxing in these circumstances. I wondered if I was hallucinating, that maybe life was just a hallucination. I sensed that elusive feeling of everything beginning to make cosmic sense. What was in those mangoes?

A nasty roar snapped me to attention. Just one big roar. I assumed it was a jaguar, the same way I might assume the barking I heard in my backyard growing up was probably from the Wilson's dalmatian. But I was in a mellow sort of mood, the way you get when experiencing the most exotic place you have ever been, while hanging with wild animals and crazy insects and exploring the bleached stone ruins of a phantom culture as time runs through you and you are alive and know that your spirit will always live.

As I headed down the path, I passed enormous avocados growing from tall trees. Estaban lay face up on a flat, three-foot-thick stone, a fluted drain carved outward from its center. It appeared to be a sacrificial stone with a little alley for the stream of sacrificial blood. I sat down on the stone.

"Oída el tigre?" Estaban asked. His eyes were wide. Yes. I'd heard the tiger. I lay down on the stone, staring up through the trees. I wasn't dozing but I wasn't awake. It was 500 years ago. I was pre-Columbian.

A thundering noise violated our surreality. My first thought, I swear to God, was: *It must be some conquistadors crashing through the jungle on their beasts.* What else could it be? Instead, we both looked up to witness a giant, 100-foot ceiba tree that had chosen that precise moment to fall over in our presence. A mighty event. The crashing racket lasted nearly a half-minute, then there was silence. The jungle held its breath. All creatures took momentary pause. The insect drone gave way. The tree may have been standing dead for a hundred years. It may have sprouted when the Tayronas lived here. The tree knew a lot. We were exhilarated.

Our reverie was cut short when a swarthy guy dressed in dirty white pants and holding a machete materialized out of the jungle, like a scene from a 1950s Saturday morning adventure serial. The vibes turned precarious. He explained that there was a shorter path back to the highway, *over that way.* The sun was getting lower in the chattering jungle, growing a darker shade of green. We thanked him for his excellent advice and politely declined his recommendation. He disappeared into the jungle the way he had come. Esteban shook his head "no" and gave me the universal sign of a throat being slit. We began our walk back to the highway as quickly as our tired legs permitted, with frequent looks over the shoulder.

We were now more tired, hungry, thirsty, wise, in-tune, in touch, and omniscient than we had been that morning. In a way, we were different. We hoped to flag down a bus on the darkened jungle road but eventually thumbed a ride in the back of a semi-trailer loaded with empty 50-gallon oil drums, wedging ourselves between a couple of drums, so as not to get crushed. Stars danced through a tear in the tarp roof that flapped as the jungle whizzed by. Back in Santa Marta, we bought buñuelos from a little stand. There was no need to talk. Not now. We would have weeks, years, lifetimes to reflect on our day trip. I wonder if Esteban is still with us and if he ever relates the story of our hike to Pueblito?

♪　♪　♪

After this third Colombian trip, I rejoined Linda in Chicago, where she had been hanging with family and friends while substitute teaching at inner-city schools. We crashed in sleeping bags on the floor of a friend's unheated rear porch on the north side. Twenty feet away, the Ravenswood El rattled by every ten to fifteen minutes until around midnight, when service began to slow. We were lulled to sleep by clatter and screech; sounds of the urban jungle. I thought it to be romantic.

We sold a couple of necklaces at an Evanston art fair then left Chicago for Minneapolis. After a few months, Linda split for a road trip through the South with girlfriends. We weren't exactly "breaking up," just taking some time off. I still wasn't ready to seek a career job. Being next to a giant anteater amidst pre-Columbian ruins had meant more to me than anything I could imagine a job would offer.

Friends from my past were now in careers, wearing neckties to work, getting married, having lunch with office mates, going to grad school, teaching, saving money, buying cars and homes, and generally behaving like responsible middle-class citizens. My work philosophy continued to be: don't let work get in the way of life. In the back of my mind—or the middle—I had confidence that piling up life experience would pay off. As I looked back through the four years since college graduation, I felt that everything was working. Except me.

FAKE JAZZ, LOW PAY, AND BARKING

Guitar Store Manager, McKinney-Mason Stringed
Instruments, Lawrence, KS, 1975-76

AFTER HER SOUTHERN ROAD TRIP, LINDA AND I met up in Lawrence. The guitar was now my focus. A couple of years back in Minneapolis, I bought a Martin D-35 on the cheap from a guy who wasn't a player. I played for hours every day. The guitar had become my vehicle for creativity and relaxation: for providing continuity to life. I looked up Brian, who was now back in Lawrence after a stint learning to build guitars at Mossman Guitars in Winfield, Kansas. Thanks to Brian, I was about to enter guitar nirvana.

Brian, and his new partner, Steve Mason, had met while they were working at Mossman. They left Winfield for Lawrence to start a new venture, McKinney-Mason Stringed Instruments, and they had finagled a small business loan from the government. Their new operation was situated in the front of an old roller rink on New Hampshire Street in downtown Lawrence, a space five times larger than necessary for a retail acoustic instrument shop. The rear of the building became a live music venue—Off the Wall Hall. Knowing of my retail prowess—ha ha—from the Funk & Rose waterbed store, Brian named me guitar store manager. Think of this as a 1975 start up.

Brian booked an amazing variety of musical acts for Off the Wall Hall including Pat Metheny, Ralph Towner and Oregon, Vassar Clemens, New Grass Revival, Paul Winter, Koko Taylor, and Son Seals. He booked Hound Dog Taylor—at the recommendation of Linda and I, who had seen him many times—but the Dog succumbed to cancer a few days before the gig.

When the blues bands played, the after-gig party was at the house Linda and I shared with our friend, Joe. We drank whiskey and jammed into the wee hours with band members. Impromptu music making is where you learn, test boundaries, try new things and create momentary connections that may be the secret to life: experiencing experimental, unplanned joy with other humans.

♫ ♫ ♫

While puffing Marlboros, a red kerchief tied around his neck, his pale face framed by long hair and mutton chop sideburns, Brian spent most waking hours on the phone, dealing with bands, managers, and a growing list of creditors. At any time, he might blast into the shop, pick up a guitar and whip through three or four riffs before taking a phone call. He had replaced the standard five-foot phone cord with a recent innovation—the 50-footer—to better engage in endless deal conversations while pacing around his empire, often getting tangled up or tangling up whoever was in the vicinity.

"You tell him he has to be here by eight o'clock because that's when he's going on ... look, I'm trying to run a club here and people are paying good money to see him at eight ... fuck you, too!" On occasion he napped for a few minutes while sitting in a straight-backed chair. Annie Liebowitz would have had a field day shooting him. .

My job had no benefits other than the very real benefit of being surrounded by guitars. I seldom went five minutes without a guitar in my hands; playing them, talking about them, selling them, smelling them, holding them. I loved selling guitars because I believed in the product. The guitar is a beautiful thing, an instrument that can reproduce the full range of emotion and provide comfort, inspiration—even social change—to so many. When Woody Guthrie scrawled on the top of his guitar, *This Machine Kills*

Fascists, he was unleashing the power of the guitar, the power of music. For me, it's an extension of my soul, a vehicle of expression, a diversion, a palette, something I rely on, a beautiful thing to look at and hold.

Because of Steve and Brian, I learned how to sight down the neck of a guitar, looking for straightness and properly filed fret edges; how to inspect the sound hole to determine if it was a solid top or a laminate; to notice the grain of the wood; to peer into the sound hole and maybe give it a sniff, making sure no dead mouse was desiccating inside. I'd play a chord and let it ring out, adjust the tuning, if necessary, then play more chords and notes up and down the neck, until I truly felt the guitar.

During slow spells at the store, I sat around with two or three guys who were also semi-employed in Brian's realm and began to play what I called "fake jazz". Noodle around till something happens, until some spontaneous gibberish of notes and patterns produces a recognition of truth and beauty, or more likely, utter dissonant weirdness. Free form ad-libbing on the fretboard can easily go off the rails until you realize that there are no rails. If you hit a so-called wrong note, hit another, then another, until a pattern develops. The number of patterns is infinite. No pattern is wrong, but some patterns are more pleasing or delightfully strange than others. Spur-of-the-moment guitar improvisation is an expression of infinity.

I also gave guitar lessons. Back in sixth grade I took piano lessons but my desire to improvise, not read notes, upset my classically trained grandparents. That experience may have been my earliest attempt at fake jazz. I quit after a half-dozen lessons. Few of us look back fondly on forced childhood music lessons. Now I was the teacher of music lessons. With no curriculum or books, I showed my students how to make basic chords, how to hold the guitar, a few favorite licks and whatever they wished to learn. I spent many lessons simply trying to get a student to bend their fingers into an F chord position. If you want to play guitar, especially at the beginning, you better be consumed by the quest, or you will fail. I had no students that had the same mad desire to learn that I had. When, years later, I ran into one I asked if she still played.

"No."

♪ ♪ ♪

The first attempt at using my advertising major occurred when I placed a series of half-baked ads in the *Lawrence Journal World*. Typical copy:

Frankly I Was Shocked ... *at the nose grease on the front window, left there by a guy who peered longingly at a guitar in our showroom, pressing his nose against the window, smearing the plate glass in the process. I saw the nose grease and frankly, I was shocked.*

This was more a burst of louche absurdity than a persuasive advertisement. Mr. Mason wisely demanded that I pull the campaign. I hadn't quite hit my creative stride. In-store signage became a less controversial forum for my promotional musings because they didn't cost anything. I taped a sign on the front door window that read: *No Tights, No Ballet Slippers, No Service.* Another read: *Don't play guitar unless your life depends on it.* Some customers got it, whatever "it" was.

My store manager duties paid about $300 a month and I earned another $100 from guitar instruction—a paltry sum even in 1975 Kansas. But paltry was better than zilch. Linda was waitressing at the Casbah Café in downtown Lawrence and brought home tips and unsold quiche. She also worked in a stained-glass studio on Massachusetts Street and made a dozen beautiful pieces, a few of which are still displayed in our home. We made ends meet at a time in our life when *enough* was plenty, when the future was distant. It sure was fun while it lasted.

My boots they have holes
And I don't have many goals
(from "There's a Dead Mouse Resting on my Conscience")

YIP! YIP! BARK! BARK! HERE COME THE GECKOS.

It was those lazy Lawrence afternoons spent catching a buzz while listening to *Natty Dread*, the recent Bob Marley and the Wailers album, that created the ideal incubation atmosphere for hatching The Barking Geckos. This was not so much a band as it was a concept of absurdity, anarchy, and joy. Singing along to *Bend Down Low* while banging pots, pans, and tambourines, our collective of under-employed, ex-college students eventually realized how fun it would be to put on a show. Wouldn't Off the Wall Hall be the only suitable venue?

A gathering of Geckos

We began as a ragtag aggregation of non-professional music lovers with varying degrees of acumen, pulled together by a lack of inhibition and the absence of demanding employment. We never advanced much beyond that stage, but we became part of Lawrence mythology. Brian and I handled guitars with an ever-changing cast on bass, drums, mandolin, and harmonica, plus a vast array of rhythm shakers that often ended up in the hands of the audience. As many as five Geckettes provided percussion and wonderfully shaky background vocals. Linda was a Geckette and would be the first to admit that singing on key was not her strong suit.

Raggedy improvisations were punctuated with frequent, spontaneous outbursts of joyous barking and yelping. Geckettes roamed the stage yipping profusely between songs, which in turn caused the audience to bark and yip.

Our signature sound was equal parts barking and actual musical arrangements. At times, I had to ask the Geckettes to quit barking and yipping long enough to play songs like *There's A Dead Mouse Resting on my Conscience*, a walking blues that featured the Geckettes *"eeking"* like mice; *Frijoles*, the Slavic march sung in Spanish that I had composed in Colombia; or *Slumped Over in a Corner Booth*, a forlorn love song set to a neo-jazz, off-kilter collection of notes that didn't belong together—a nursery rhyme for adults. The Geckos were a reminder that conformity is not a pillar of freedom. Absurdity is truth. Nonsense makes perfect sense.

We opened for another band—Cole Tuckey on Rye—during the launch of Off the Wall Hall. It wasn't a paying gig because there were too many of us to pay. Our motivation was joy, not dough. Subsequent gigs were often provoked by various whimsical occasions like April Fool's Day, Halloween, and May Day.

The Gecko look was influenced by thrift stores, the Marx Brothers, the *Sgt. Pepper's* and *Beggar's Banquet* album covers, plus a host of mind-altering substances. It was anything goes. When Jaw Harp Joe spent a dollar on a box of fifty aprons at a yard sale, he donated them to the cause. Each Geckette improvised a way to showcase her apron at our next gig, either as an anti-fashion statement or as a giveaway item for the audience—a gaggle of tripping hedonists assembled to witness a myth in the making. I wrote a song that became a video project for a budding KU video artist, now lost for the ages, *Cheap Apron Fashion Show*. Decades later, I can recall the lyrics:

> *Sitting here biding my time*
> *Letting life gently roll by*
> *Even the insects sigh*
> *As summer gets ready to die*
> *I get kinda hungry, so I head to the store*
> *And there on the bulletin board*
> *A poster it mentions a fashion show*
> *A cheap apron fashion show*
> *Oh, Cheap apron fashion show*
> *What I wouldn't give to go*
> *To a cheap apron fashion show*

Geckettes sporting cheap apron garb

For one gig, the Geckettes dressed as nuns in homemade pastel habits. At another, they stood behind ironing boards, playing kazoo and washboard. At another, a bagpipe player led us around the block, a goofy troupe gathering curious potential fans as we advanced through sleepy downtown Lawrence. I often wore pajamas and a pencil thin fake mustache above my lip. Our drummer wore a gas mask—just in case. Brian sported pantaloons tucked into high boots as he meandered about the stage tuning his axe before, during, and after each song. Kurt, on mandolin and guitar, looked like he'd stepped out of *Lawrence of Arabia*. Jaw Harp Joe, who had driven me to Carbondale in his 1956 Orange Buick a few years prior, wore reflecto mirror shades and a towel wrapped high on his head. Others wore fake noses, leopard skin prints, and garish non-matching outfits picked from Salvation Army bins. The audience yipped and yapped and held up signs. Mimes circulated. I gave away fake puke and other novelty gag gifts from the stage. The whole thing was wonderfully life affirming.

Our most noteworthy gig was at the National Surrealist Party Convention in 1976, a brainchild of Firesign Theater founding member, David Ossman and his wife, Tiny. Firesign Theater was an absurdist group that began in the 1960s and had recorded a few well-known comedy albums. I have no idea how Lawrence became the convention site but when Ossman saw the Geckos, he knew we were of the same cloth.

The Surrealist candidate for President was George Papoon, a guy with a brown paper bag over his head. His campaign slogan was "Not Insane." We went on just before the introduction of VP candidate, George Tirebiter. The *real* national candidates in 1976—Nixon had resigned—were eventual winner, Jimmy Carter, and Gerald Ford, whose running mate was the Kansan, Bob Dole, who we referred to as Bob Dull. The Surrealist Party Convention was an antidote to Dullsville. We were in opposite-land, at the far reaches of time and space. A fine place to be.

As an eight-year-old, I had been mesmerized by Elvis. In my teen years the Rolling Stones captivated me. When I discovered the country blues of Robert Johnson and Blind Blake, et al., I was hooked. I now thought of myself as a musician, just like those guys. Not a famous musician or even an "incredible" musician. But a musician, nonetheless. An identity other than class clown; good athlete; middle class college grad; long haired hipster.

'76 Surrealist Convention

NOT A FARM HAND

Lawrence, KS, 1976-79

BALING HAY

WHEN I WAS FIVE YEARS OLD. MY parents took me to Rochelle, Illinois, to visit Aunt Leddy and Uncle Jack, relatives from the Bain side of the family. They had a working farm with a barn and crops and a pump in the kitchen and a harp in the parlor. They had a hen house where I saw a real egg that had just been laid by a real chicken. The egg was warm. It didn't come from the refrigerator. My five-year-old brain thought that farm life was magical. But here in the Kansas hay field, it was a different story.

Jaw Harp Joe had invited me to partake in a ritual of Kansas manhood: baling hay. His gentleman farmer brother owned a hay field that needed tending a few miles from Lawrence. Machines did the cutting and baling, and one version also hurled the bales onto a trailing wagon. Our operation had no hurling apparatus. Joe and I took turns as the human hurlers. One hurled, the other stood on the wagon and stacked.

Sweat stung my eyes. Long sleeves protected my forearms from hay scratch. At first, I tried to silence the natural inclination to grunt while I tossed. After a while, as I heaved each bale, the dripping air was punctuated with my grunts. Why fight it? Animals grunt. I was an animal: a heaving, grunting man of the world. Exhausted. Drained. Spent. I found a new appreciation for water.

Dig deep enough into any midwestern family and you'll find a farmer. My great grandfather, John Bain, emigrated from Scotland to farm the rich soil of Northern Illinois. I could never be a farmer. Nor did I wish to be. But when farm work is done and you have showered and you're sipping a cold beer, you feel pretty good, even if your muscles are twitching a bit. You have done what is often referred to as an honest day's labor.

DE-TASSELING CORN

As July approached in the summer of 1976, word went out that a farmer a few miles outside the Lawrence city limits needed a crew to de-tassel his corn. The job lasted about a week in my memory, but Linda says that we de-tasseled for only one day: the 4th of July, also America's Bicentennial celebration. Farm work doesn't stop because of our nation's two-hundred-year anniversary.

We woke before daybreak and put on long-sleeved shirts to prevent corn rash. The forecast called for—surprise—mid-90s and humid. We were advised to bring two pairs of work gloves because pair number one would most certainly become frayed and ripped before the day was done. (Working through two pairs of gloves in a day is not a guitarist's dream job.)

An American flag affixed to an odd-looking contraption was the first thing that caught your eye at the farm. The flag might have commemorated two hundred years of democracy, or it might have been to honor America getting back on track after Nixon's impeachment, or the end of the Vietnam War. The sight of old glory instigated our crew to belt out a spontaneous rendition of *America the Beautiful,* a song that mentions grain but not corn.

During the singing, I surveyed this contraption, which would serve as our ride for the day. The de-tasseling vehicle resembled an open-air, square framed, motorized chassis on four wheels: the creation of a mad max farmer. A horizontal beam was affixed from the top of this chassis. Hanging from the beam were four carrier platforms on either side of the chassis, like an eight-person corn chariot with a driver. The platforms got us high enough off the ground to better reach the tassels on top of the stalk. Moving through tall rows of corn while standing on your platform, you snatched every damn tassel in sight. The trick was to grip the tassel at its base, bend it a little, yank it off and drop it on the ground. This encouraged pollination. Corn sex. For the pollination to be successful, something like 99 percent of the tassels had to be snapped off. Yes, there were machines that could do this, but they couldn't get every tassel. That required a human, the ultimate machine. Linda and I might have earned $50.

After the farmer called it a day, the smell of raw corn lingered in my nose. Decades later, I can still conjure that smell.

TRIMMING BUDS

The farm job that paid the most was against the law. Open air marijuana cultivation was a burgeoning underground cash crop around Lawrence in the 1970s and I knew some of the growers. One had finagled marijuana seeds from Afghanistan, which, when planted in eastern Kansas soil, resulted in a strain referred to as Afkansastan. Before putting the illegal produce up for sale, the cannabis buds needed a manicure. The longer leaves were trimmed off to make the buds look lovelier. Show Buds. Trimming buds was suitable work for me. It paid $10 an hour in cash—good dough in 1976 when the minimum wage was $1.60.

Wild hemp—ditch weed—grew along roadsides and streams. This stuff couldn't get you high, but it could make you cough. Hemp had been cultivated for its fiber going all the way back to the Jamestown settlement. It was no longer cultivated because of its illegal cousin, marijuana. Scraggly entrepreneurs picked it, dried it, and sold it to unsuspecting buyers or scam artists. But there was resistance, and not only from the constabulary. A sixteen-year-old Lawrence kid became a notorious anti-pot crusader. He went on excursions to find the harmless hemp in order to spray it with a highly toxic weed killer, paraquat, a poison with no known antidote. During one of these forays, he fell into a river and drowned. True story. Had he smoked weed rather than poisoned it, he might be alive today.

Bud trimming was agricultural work that didn't scratch your forearms or make you pass out in the heat. And the smell was quite different from hay or corn; sweeter, more pungent. We used makeup scissors to snip the leaves off the still moist, seedless buds. My trimming buddies included an out of work harmonica player, a future restaurateur, and the girlfriend of a grower. We snipped away in a house on the outskirts of town in north Lawrence, bullshitting, passing the time, slightly paranoid. If you didn't wear gloves the THC would permeate your skin, giving you a bit of a buzz at the end of the workday, like edibles. You had to be careful where you went after work because you sure smelled like weed.

Our goal was to trim the perfect bud; to make what we referred to as "ball bats." Our eight-inch bats were tightly packed with little orange or reddish hairs and a crystalline coating. Like a dusting of fine sugar. Even the non-countercultural observer might marvel at these horticultural wonders, as beautiful as any fruit or vegetable you might see at a produce market in Nice. One day I imagine they'll be judged alongside the pickles and relishes at Annual 4-H Club shows.

Though I never witnessed it—after harvesting and trimming—a near circus-sized tent was pitched at an undisclosed location "in the country" and buyers from California came in to meet with growers from Kansas: an auction with lots of cash changing hands. Afkansistan was a prized commodity.

I trimmed at random times but declined one opportunity. It took place at a ramshackle residence about fifteen miles north of Lawrence, hosted by a grower who a decade later gained renown as a National Geographic photographer. Dozens of deputies from the county sheriff's office swarmed the pastoral gathering. Everyone got caught and fined and had to hire lawyers. I was lucky again.

♪ ♪ ♪

Like many Midwestern college towns, Lawrence was a bubble. Ambition and the fast track were not the prevailing social currency. Making rent, getting along, socializing, dreaming, eating fried brown rice from the Cornucopia Cafe, and being pleasantly comfortable was the vibe. If you had a yearning for something more—more action, money, choices, people—you moved away. I was yearning, but it hadn't dawned on me to move because

I didn't feel stuck—yet. But I was approaching a period of limbo, a period where resourceful loafing and simply trying to make sense of it all might not be enough to satisfy me. My skill set—music, songwriting, and an appreciation of absurdity—did not fit any job description that I had come across. Employers weren't looking for my type and I was still not ready to become their type. But it was becoming clear that even *I* needed money to survive. Would we forever live in a rental house—with roommates—where the toilet leaked and the freezer required weekly defrosting? Hmmmm. A slight shift had begun to occur regarding what I considered to be *enough*. I was beginning to want something more. My life as an easy-going escape artist who played guitar and travelled was beginning to thin.

HAMMER TIME

House framer, Lawrence and vicinity, 1976-77

SINCE GRADUATING FROM COLLEGE, MY EMPLOYMENT HAD been a random collection of jobs with no future. I had become adept at finding these jobs with no future because I had yet to define my future. Was I growing older and wiser, or becoming more predictable in my escape from predictability? I continued my vow to better understand the world and myself by inhabiting different situations, but how many more situations did I need? Stasis had crept in. My goals had not sharpened. Did they even exist? Yet, I was coming to realize— without admitting it to anyone—that perhaps it was beginning to matter what I did to pay the bills.

I accepted an offer to join a crew building houses west of Lawrence. "I am a carpenter," had a nice ring to it. Who doesn't respect a carpenter? I had always perceived carpenters to be crafty, independent spirits who provided an essential skill. Building shelter is a noble pursuit. The most famous person in history was a carpenter! If it was good enough for Jesus, shouldn't it be good enough for me? However, Jesus didn't play the guitar. I would be putting my guitar hands at risk because I needed money. How many cartoons had I seen where a guy hits his thumb with a hammer and it swells to triple the size. N-o-o-o-o!

My "Apprentice Carpenter" gig some ten years previous had been a glorified title for a laborer: I was mostly on wheelbarrow and shovel duty and rarely required to use my hammer. This would be different. The new gig began in the fall and was to continue through the winter, depending on the Kansas weather. I was the only one of our five-man crew without full-fledged, union carpentry skills, but I quickly got up to speed on snapping chalk lines, toenailing studs, measuring, making cuts with a circular saw, and balancing on rafters. This rigorous work made sense to me.

One crew member was my version of the "ideal" carpenter. His name may have been Tom, and he was originally from somewhere back East. He had blonde hair, wire rimmed glasses and was well-spoken, able to discuss music, books, movies and whatever it was that needed discussing. And he was not only a master of carpentry skills but was an expert at reading blueprints. He had studied architecture before quitting the program when his wife became pregnant—unplanned. He had a family to support, and he loved carpentry. College towns are full of folks like Tom—tradesmen with a university degree. If I had wished to become a carpenter—and I'm not sure I did—this was my carpenter role model.

On a gloomy day of freezing rain, we were framing a house close to Topeka. The four-man crew piled into a work van in Lawrence, loaded with compressors, generators and tools, and headed west. Our route took us through fields and woods, past sparse homesteads, dry creek beds: the outskirts of town. Parts of the drive looked as it had to the pioneers in the early 1800s on the leg of the Oregon Trail that ran from Lawrence to Topeka, before the railroads came.

The sleet and freezing drizzle made work a waste of time: it was treacherous, miserable, and ice coated, too slippery to balance on exposed rafters. About mid-morning, we decided to knock off. All four of us nestled into the fully loaded van. It felt good to be out of the ice. I distinctly remember that I began eating a tuna sandwich. (Funny how seemingly inconsequential details seep through the memory bank.) The cavalier way that the crew boss was driving on curvy, ice-glazed, country roads didn't help me enjoy my working-class seafood lunch.

"Hey, man, slow down," we implored as he hit an ice patch, fishtailing a bit. To the driver the icy road was a challenge to be conquered via macho driving skills. Like anyone else, carpenters can be foolish.

Our final fishtail took us right off the road. Skidding in an out-of-control van crammed with machines, tools, and eight hundred human pounds is a gut grabber. You are very quickly in a reality not of your own choosing, akin to a lifetime of carnival rides crammed into a single moment. In a flash, the notion of up and down, backward and forward, left and right becomes jumbled. You are no longer holding your tuna sandwich. You are no longer sitting, or standing, or lying down. For agonizing seconds, your posture is incomprehensible. We slid off the road into a bog below, rolled at least once, and somehow got wedged in the low fork of a scrub tree, several feet off the ground. It was like being shot from a cannon. The momentary cacophony of clattering tools, involuntary exclamations of "oh, shit!" and careening bodies oomph-ing about gave way to silence save for the hum of the still spinning van wheels.

I extracted myself from the wreck and crumpled when my feet touched ground. My right ankle felt mangled. I glanced at it then quickly looked away. Shock and frozen pain set in. Somehow, the rest of the crew was okay. My dazed workmates flagged down a car to notify an ambulance—it probably involved using a pay phone at the nearest gas station. When the ambulance arrived, I was apprehensive about riding in another vehicle full of equipment on an icy road. Ambulances aren't noted for driving slowly but we got to the hospital without mishap. X-rays showed a badly broken right ankle and torn ligaments. This put an end to my days as a carpenter. I would never again get to carry plywood on a rooftop in the wind. The important thing: my hands had survived.

Back home, on crutches, it was too much of a hassle to climb to the second story bedroom I shared with Linda. I now slept on a mattress thrown on the living room floor. Reading and writing became my primary entertainment. No iPhone, no tablet, no computer, no cable satellite channels to compete for my attention. And daytime television gave me a feeling of being in purgatory. In the mid-1970s it was just game shows and soap operas—a form of intellectual torture. I read *Under the Volcano* by Malcolm Lowry. With my dictionary nearby, I learned the meaning of *plinth* and *crenellation*. I tried writing a song based on the novel. Eventually, I kept the chords and melody but changed the refrain from *Underneath the Volcano* to *I Hear a Kansas Rhapsody*. I also read the manuscript of Magellan's circumnavigation scribed by Antonio Pigafetta, who had accompanied Magellan and kept a detailed journal. The journal inspired a song, *Magellan*. A neighbor obsessed with polishing his sedan, provoked my very first short story, *The Adventurous Kansan*, about a guy who daydreams of famous explorers while detailing his ride.

During these reading and writing sessions on the mattress, there was often a poker game in the kitchen, hosted by our roommate, Joe. He was a union laborer but had many "off" days. A collection of his friends—scruffy, underemployed dropouts, kitchen table philosophers and petty gamblers—joined him at the poker table. A ringing phone on the kitchen wall interrupted the game.

"Roger ... phone!" I put down my book and crutched into the kitchen. It was Linda, who had travelled to Chicago for a cousin's wedding. The wedding had reminded Linda of her own situation. After over four years living together, we were still unmarried.

She asked about my ankle, then put it to me something like this: "Are we getting married or what?"

"Or what?" I replied, trying to gain a little time before quickly realizing that this moment had been in the cards since our first night together, and it was now time to do what we both knew was the only thing that made sense. "Yes. Of course. Sure," I quickly added; one of the weakest marriage proposals ever documented.

We had discussed getting married, we had always wanted children, but I considered marriage to be more of an inevitability that didn't require getting down on one knee or petitioning the father-in-law. In my mind, the marriage would just sort of occur in some indeterminate future and all would be good. Like my approach to worthwhile employment.

Since Linda had come into my life, my parents had become less worried about me—especially my mother, who saw Linda as a stabilizing force. And with marriage now looming, they assumed I would grow up and finally get a real job. Linda and I had vaguely kicked around the idea of a laid back, non-traditional little gathering in my parents' backyard: shoes optional. No tuxedos or gowns. Something befitting our lifestyle. *Fugetaboutit!* That was not the deal on the table. Italian girls are married in the Catholic Church, not in a backyard. And after the ceremony, without question, there is a big reception: a traditional Italian wedding.

"We'll be showered with little white envelopes filled with enough money to travel through Europe next summer," Linda reminded me. Sounded good to me, the travel gigolo. So much for my idea of a humble, organic, meaning-ful ceremony untainted by the dogma of organized religion. All it took was the promise of extended travel and I crumbled. Sometimes "selling out" is another name for being reasonable. I knew that a small backyard ceremony could never reward us with enough cash to finance a three-month trip to Europe. That required a guest list of over 300, a list top heavy on Linda's side: a staggering collection of cousins, friends from the old Chicago neighborhood and a few shady characters from her father's days as a Rush Street club own-er, where Sammy Davis Jr. once gave a private after-hours performance for a contingent of wise guys at his joint, The Four Winds.

Meanwhile, back in the kitchen, I hung up the phone. I had carried on this life-changing, intimate conversation surrounded by a bunch of smoking, drinking, braying gamblers shouting *hold!* and *raise!* and *you're bluffing*, with the occasional *motherfucker* thrown in. I casually announced that I would soon be getting married to the kitchen assembly. After a brief round of con-gratulations, the boys resumed their poker hand as I hobbled back to my mattress and Magellan, while experiencing the warm grasp of commitment.

♫ ♫ ♫

We got married in August of 1977 at Saint Martha's Church near Lin-da's folks' house in Morton Grove. I survived the priest's pre-marriage coun-seling, a requirement for non-Catholics. Our reception rocked the Casa Royale in suburban Des Plaines. What a bash! Have you ever attended a wedding where the groom was happily unemployed? My younger brother, a groomsman, managed to spill a platter of mostaccioli and marinara sauce on Linda's dress, Tino the Sicilian street singer serenaded us with his version of *Imma rhine-a-stone-a-cowboy* and we danced on table-tops. I also discovered gin martinis. People got high.

Even after paying for the entire shindig, we had enough dough for a sum-mer in Europe the following year, 1978. We visited relations in England and Sicily, on a mission to discover our roots. We saw the theater in the north Yorkshire village of Middlesbrough where my grandfather had played piano the night my mother was born in 1922 (now turned into an adult movie theater). We spent a few days with Linda's grandmother's elderly cousin in Palermo. They loved that I could eat a lot. *Mangia, mangia*! We spent time in London, Rome, Venice, Taormina, Corfu, Mykonos, and Scotland.

Extended travel is both discovery and escape. How could I possibly look for a job as we meandered through the Valley of the Temples in Agrigento, Sicily, or while sipping ice cold retsina at sunset on the whitewashed steps of our room in Mykonos, where we partied with a Colombian who knew Tatín?

Linda had a teaching gig lined up when we returned. I was still winging it. The cinch of responsibility was beginning to tighten. Eventually, I hired a lawyer and filed a workman's compensation claim for my busted ankle. The driver of the van was deemed negligent. A year or so later I was awarded $6,000 for pain and suffering. It was more money than I had ever earned in a year.

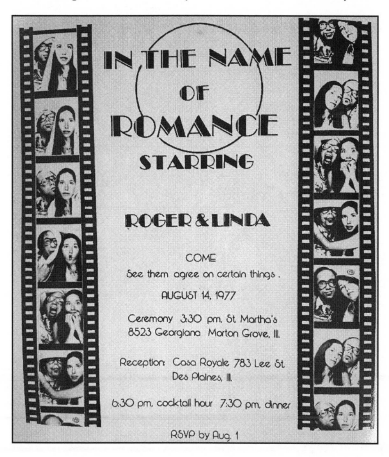

A DABBLING SCRIBBLER

Freelance Writer, Lawrence, KS, 1977-79

BY NOW, I WAS CERTAIN THAT MY career path would involve a creative endeavor. Within each of us lurks something artistic, but this "something" may lie dormant unless partnered with a dose of obsession. Through discipline, obsession's cousin, I had learned to play guitar so that I could write songs. My songwriting, however, required little discipline. Songwriting is rather mystical in that many songs just tumble out of the subconscious. Songs seemed to fall out of me. I might noodle on a guitar riff and construct lyrics to fit the cadence or, overhear a memorable line in a conversation and put a melody to it, or think, gee, shouldn't there be a song about leisure suits? It was fun and fulfilling, as all creations are, but it wasn't a discipline. I didn't slave over melody, lyrics or chord changes like a tin pan alley or Brill Building pro would. There was no time clock, no deadlines, no financial rewards. I had developed a skill that required little discipline but instead was a discovery of something baked into my genetic code: observational humor and an appreciation of absurdity. I was writing songs for myself, my friends, for the cosmos. For those who *get it*.

I had also begun to fancy myself to be a writer in a broader sense—not that I had ever written for the school newspaper or taken a fiction writing course. My longest piece of expository writing to date had been a six-pager titled "The Puritans and the Devil" for an American History class at KU. I got a "C." But language fascinated me. I loved history and literature. I was always reading a book. That was a start, but true writing is best practiced as a routine. There must be an urgency from within that *demands* you to write: vanity? hubris? an obsessive nature? You have no choice but to tell a story and no one else can quite tell it the way you do. Even *you* cannot always get it just right as you try to make sense of the mess that is life. The gap between the story in your head and the one that appears on paper can be elusive. And maddening.

For a few years, I had been sporadically jotting down thoughts and observations in small notebooks, which meant that, if not a writer, I was at least a jotter. But journals have no requirements. Any gibberish, any personal graffiti is acceptable. We all have thoughts but how many are worthy of sharing? The wise sayings: *keep your thoughts to yourself* or, *if you don't have anything nice to say, don't say it*, are sentiments that must be ignored by the writer. (In modern times, social media is proof that many ideas are better left unsaid.) The work is in the rewriting, where you attempt to close that gap between mind and page. Although hesitant to say it aloud, I entertained dreams of becoming one of these rewriters.

Every morning, when Linda left for her job at the Casbah Café or later, when she began teaching first grade, I sat down to write for at least two hours. During these morning sessions I wrote short stories, primarily because it seemed easier to write something short. I attempted that one true sentence technique ala Hemingway. I bought a copy of the *Writer's Digest* and versed myself in the art of the submission. A few of my stories received hand-written rejection slips with words of encouragement from the editor or publisher. Being politely rejected was progress of sorts. Most of the stories were never sent to anyone or seen by anyone but Linda and a close friend or two.

My first writing for payment was when a graphic designer friend hooked me up with the Kansas Arborists Association to write a series of public service newspaper ads. This was not jotting. It required every sentence to have impact and advance the narrative. The campaign won an award. I was a budding arborist influencer.

When I heard that a six-year-old marathon runner in my town of Lawrence, Kansas, was slated to run in the Chicago Marathon, I phoned the *Kansas City Star*, explained that I was making a switch from fiction to journalism and had a great human-interest story of endurance and possibly child abuse. To my amazement, they agreed. They told me they needed five hundred words and some photos, and I had a Sunday supplement cover story.

My next *Star* piece was a self-effacing story about my real-life stint as a babysitter. One of Linda's fellow teachers needed part-time help for a couple of weeks with his one-year-old. I suppose I was an obvious choice. What strapping 30-year-old would announce to the world—in writing—that he was a babysitter? Shouldn't I hide that fact? Shouldn't I be ashamed that it had come to this? It's understandable when you wipe your own kid's ass, which I hadn't yet had the privilege of doing, but to wipe someone else's kid's ass, then to write about it in a renowned Midwestern daily? That showed that I truly didn't give a shit. But if I could write about it, it wasn't so bad.

After managing to place a few more pieces in regional or trade publications, I had entered the world of freelancing. Now, when asked what I did, I could say, "I'm a freelance writer," with a touch of pride.

Can you make a living as a freelance writer? Millions try but only thousands succeed. It depends upon your standard of living. Do you prefer shopping at Nordstrom or The Good Will Store? Does your spouse have a good job or an inheritance? Does your spouse think you're selfish for pursuing a "dream"?

In this age prior to personal computers, a yellow legal pad and a #2 -and-a-half pencil or a ballpoint pen were my writing tools. I sat on the same upholstered chair every day in the same tiny house that we referred to as the cottage, a legal pad on my lap with scattered stacks of other legal pads and loose papers at my feet and on the surrounding furniture. At the end of the writing day, I would straighten the papers into stacks, which Linda referred to as "my piles." These stacks were hard to miss in our miniscule living room.

I considered feature stories to be a form of work. My absurdist vignettes and short stories were for fun. An indulgence. I was entertaining myself, yet

I would have been thrilled to have a story published. I would have loved recognition and maybe 10¢ a word. Looking back, writing was more a cathartic hobby than a commitment. When I signed up for a two-day writer's conference in Eureka Springs, Arkansas, I had hoped to find a bunch of Kerouac or Thomas Wolfe types, but the welcome reception was a gaggle of white-haired ladies trying to place articles in *Reader's Digest*. I bailed without attending a session.

My short stories are still tucked away in a file cabinet in the ex-bedroom that now serves as my "office". A few are entertaining, like the portrayal I did of Linda's family getting ready for church. It was rejected as "too loud" by *Chicago Magazine*. (Of course, that Sunday morning scene in Morton Grove really *was* loud.)

The exercise of daily writing, submitting, and receiving rejection letters forced me to comprehend the vast amount of solitary work, patience, luck, and perseverance that being a writer requires. Can you handle rejection? Being criticized? Are you willing to spend three hours or three days on a paragraph until you're sure that you have *precisely* expressed *exactly* what you wish to say? And what, exactly, were you wishing to say? Are you willing to spend years on a manuscript without knowing whether you can even get a publisher to read it because you have no connections, had never attended an MFA writing program, and had no agent? Locating an agent is just as difficult as finding a willing publisher. No wonder many writers drink. I prefer gin.

MY BRUSH WITH GUANO

Union Laborer in Lawrence, 1978-ish

EIGHT YEARS INTO MY DECADE OF EARLY retirement, you could say that the experiment was running out of gas. Was it time to call it off? In the fall of 1978, upon returning to Lawrence from our three-month European jaunt, I had no job prospects and no specific plans. No road trips were on the horizon; the Geckos had gone dormant; Off the Wall Hall was kaput; friends were departing for new worlds. Linda was busy teaching first grade, her calling. I was still waiting to be called. It wasn't that I was morose or depressed. I don't seem to possess that genetic tendency. I didn't blame anyone for my growing predicament.

As my sixth-grade teacher, Miss Pope, used to say, "You made your bed. Now lie in it." Or something like that. But how could I uncover that elusive "something more" that I had been looking for? And where to earn my next buck? Would taking yet another short term, going nowhere job add to my understanding of life, of myself? How much more was there for me to understand?

♬ ♬ ♬

Most days, after two or three hours of writing, I walked a few blocks to a friend's house to drink coffee, blow dope, discuss music, play guitar, and awkwardly listen to the daily argument between the friend and his wife as she departed for her full-time job as a dental assistant. She worked. He loafed. She always slammed the door upon departing. Joe joined our loafers' coffee klatch when he wasn't working as a laborer. He encouraged me to check out the local laborer's union.

"Just go down to the union hall and sign up," he said. The $10/hr. pay was better than any other menial job I could find. It wasn't quite as laid back as trimming buds but also wasn't illegal.

I followed Joe's advice. First thing every morning, I moseyed down to the hall and sat for a half-hour at the far end of the room in a state of hopeful dread, reminiscent of my days waiting for a loop at the caddy shack. When the clock over the office window hit 8:00 and I had not been summoned, I left for the day. Having no job was not my fault, honey, it was the lack of work in my new profession: union laborer (who wrote short stories on the side.)

I finally landed a union gig at the aging Sunflower Ammunition Plant, south of DeSoto, Kansas. During WWII, the Korean War and the Vietnam War, Sunflower had been buzzing with thousands of workers who manufactured propellant for the large bore guns America had used to obliterate whoever and whatever needed obliterating. Now, during a brief lull in the obliteration, the plant was being updated due to a switch to nitroguanidine as the propellant. The Vietnam War had ended a few years prior, but things were heating up in the Middle East and the Cold War with Russia was in full tilt, and who knew when we would need tons of nitroguanidine? I was now working for the war industry.

My voluminous foreman didn't much care if we *was doin' anything, as long as it looked like we wasn't just sittin' on our damn asses doin' nothin'.* Here was a man who had reached his station in life. He had a deeply sunburned neck. He fished on the weekends to "get away from the wife." He spoke of jerky and bacon with reverence.

My first task had that familiar ring to it: carry out some busy work until the foreman thinks of something better for me to do. I was to remove rust from the inside of a two-story powder propellant tank being readied for a load of bat guano, the key ingredient in nitroguanidine. I crawled through a small hatch on the side of the tank armed with my tools: a portable lamp and a bag of steel wool. The air was hot and still in my guano tank. The metallic scent of rust permeated the darkness. From this lonely outpost, I wondered: is the foreman the only person on earth who knows I'm inside this rusty tank? What if signals get crossed and I'm inside while tons of bat guano rain down from above? Every few years there is a story of someone who drowns in animal waste. **Union Laborer Smothered by Bat Guano!** To lessen the chance of this fate, I did most of my rust rubbing within a few yards of the escape hatch. If the entire inside of the tank were to be truly cleaned, it would require ladders, scaffolding, light rigs, power grinders and a crew: way more than one dude with steel wool. The union had most likely negotiated for X number of jobs with management, whether it was necessary work or busy work. Not for the first time in my life, I was busy doing busy work.

After a few days of this miserable, seemingly pointless undertaking, the foreman decided that there were better ways to keep me busy. Grab a shovel, he said. It's time to mix mud. Mud is job site slang for concrete mortar. The routine: dump bag after bag of dry cement into a wheelbarrow, hold it steady for the guy with the water hose and when it's wet enough, take a shovel, and mix it all up into a fine, sticky consistency; then grab the barrow handles and wheel the heavy load to where the masons were laying. This work was done on scaffolding a couple of stories above ground. Using every ounce of my strength, I guided countless wheelbarrows full of mud over rickety, cement encrusted, two-by-twelve boards while way above ground.

Our crew included a few guys about my age who lived in small Kansas towns: guys you might meet in a Larry McMurtry novel; hell-raisers six or seven years into life after high school, dues-paying members of the laborer's union. College was for smart-ass pansies like me, and they detected a whiff of college whenever I opened my mouth. I could have affected a country boy accent "in order to relate," but thought better of it. Decals on their cars touted popular brands of motor oil and carburetors. Their baseball hats showcased the names of automotive or heavy equipment companies like Peterbilt, Penske, and Caterpillar. After work, they bee-lined to their vehicles, opened the backseat cooler, popped open a beer, fired up their engines, and raced down the dusty road from the plant to the highway and off to a tavern where they knew everyone. I was never invited to join in the fun as we barely ever spoke and my guess is, they assumed I thought that I was too good for them. To me, it wasn't a matter of being too good. I could simply tell where I was not wanted.

Another guy on the crew was named Boots. He was black, about fifty-two, or maybe sixty-five, didn't have a half-ounce of fat on him and spoke in a high, excited voice. *Mutherfucker* was usually the first or second word out of his mouth. One Saturday, after a heavy snowfall, Boots happened to drive by my house while I was shoveling the driveway. He stopped and yelled at me. "Don't go bustin' yo ass too hard now or you'll suffer a mutherfuckin' heart attack. I mean that shit." And then he drove off. I still remember the advice, and though I've read similar guidance many times since in well-meaning newspaper columns, none has had the resonance of Boots' warning.

♪   ♪   ♪

My favorite work assignment was trash duty. It meant I would be on my own, wandering all over the ammo dump and hurling trash into the company pickup. It was easy to look busy doing this. If I came across a big hunk of something that I wasn't sure was trash, I could walk around asking, "Is this trash?" That took up time and allowed whoever I was asking to feel important.

The trash heap was about a half mile down a dirt road from the main job site. During these moments by myself, I belted out a favorite song from my freshman year in high school: *The Surfin' Bird* by the Trashmen. I was now the real thing—a trashman. One day at the dump, I saw a coyote skulking around the garbage heap, looking for varmints. Through the windshield, I watched him chase something that was too small for me to make out. A mouse, I thought. Watching the coyote chase the mouse around the trash heap of this resurrected ammo dump in Kansas seemed like a life lesson. The coyote was working hard to catch the mouse. The mouse was working hard to get away from the coyote. I was hardly working.

Most days, I took my lunch break in my car and ate yogurt while reading

Conrad's *Heart of Darkness* or *Jungle Wife*, an account of a city gal who married a Jaguar hunter and lived in the Brazilian jungle. For the record, each book inspired a song, *Hearts Beating in the Darkness* and *Honeymoon with the Geckos*.

I had done the math and at $10 an hour I'd make $20,000 if I worked for fifty weeks. This sounded like a lot of money. But the gig lasted only several months and I never returned to the union hall.

I BELIEVE IN SANTA

Gibson's Department Store Lawrence, KS, 1978

AS I BUZZED THROUGH A VARIETY OF inconsequential jobs, my decade of exploration now resembled the road to nowhere. An undercurrent of frustration, not noticeable to others, took root. Pretending to be a laborer had kept the wolf from my door for a few months, but it was now time for me to look at a future that spanned more than a few months. The need for a paycheck, however, forced me to continue my masquerade, my act. At least I would be in disguise on my new job at Gibson's Department Store, where I was hired to be Santa Claus, a job that is often a last refuge of the serially under-employed.

The first time I peered into the Gibson's lunchroom mirror as a white whiskered Santa, I had to laugh. Sardonic laughter. It had come to *this*. My intention was to write a feature story for the *Kansas City Star*: "Santa Like Me." Then I could explain to any who wondered that I was simply doing background research. By the end of the gig, however, I realized that writing about the quirky things that kids said and did— the angle that a *Star* piece required—would force me to tamp down my own feelings about this mythical, pipe smoking dude who had become a symbol of capitalism. Santa doesn't ask kids what they need. He asks what they want. Needs are fine but wants are what matters if GDP levels are to continue upward. Santa was the be-whiskered, Coca-Cola drinking Pope of capitalism. The newspaper would never publish my true thoughts: that impersonating this beloved icon—for money—was a low point of my job cavalcade.

The thing was, I liked kids. I had always enjoyed entertaining the younger siblings or offspring of friends with my passable Donald Duck voice, or goofy skip-walking or Three Stooges gyrations. I liked the unfiltered honesty of children, their wide-eyed wonder, and their nutty sense of humor. Kids didn't need to know how I felt about mindless consumption.

My Dad revealed—confessed might be a better word—that many years prior, he had applied for a Santa position at Carson's in Chicago. He was down to his last few hundred dollars with a wife and three kids: a situation even more desperate than mine. But a job came through and he never had to put on the red suit. When I joked that I would now be realizing his missed Santa experience, I assumed that Dad might commiserate.

"You'll be fired by Christmas," he said.

My suit and hat were made of stiff red felt-like material, cruel to the touch. The fake beard became a form of torture, causing a brutal rash to break out on my increasingly ulcerous upper lip, requiring gobs of Vaseline. Beneath the hideous whiskers, my philtrum glowed the color of Rudolph's nose. My aviator style glasses were a dead giveaway of my fakery, and I had no money or inclination to invest in wire frames. My brown sideburns stood out against my white wig and beard. I was a cheesy Santa in a cheesy department store, who bellowed "Yo Ho Ho" (and a bottle of rum) instead of "Ho Ho Ho," who jigged around his throne when things were slow, as if victimized by Saint Vitus' Dance disorder. I was a madcap Santa ready for action.

One who has never portrayed Santa might believe the job to be fun. Was it fun to have a strange kid wet their pants on your red lap? Was it fun having a two-hundred-pound woman plop down on your quivering knees and request that a husband come down her chimney? Was it fun to breathe so many germs? Was it fun to have 80-year-old male twins on your lap, each sporting sunglasses, each chomping an unlit cigar? Scenes from a Diane Arbus fever dream.

Why am I here?

How did I get here?

When can I get out of here?

I tried not to lose patience with kids who screamed, "You're not real!" or "You're fake!" or "You're just a man dressed up!" In those situations, using the power of Santa, I threatened them with coal. Bituminous not anthracite. I gave them no choice. The coal threat usually worked.

Santa is often put on the spot, like when a diminutive girl, about eight, confessed her nasty habit to me.

"You know what?" she asked.

"What? Tell Santa." I replied, in my best concerned Santa voice.

"I smoke."

"Oh. I see."

"And my best friend, Lisa—but she doesn't like me that much—she smokes, too."

"You know smoking is bad for you, don't you?"

"Yes."

"Okay. Promise Santa you won't smoke anymore."

"I promise."

♫ ♫ ♫

Ratting out Santa to a little believer is one of childhood's perverse pleasures, often done by a kid who has recently discovered the earth-shattering truth themselves. An eight-year-old girl—I always asked their ages—gushed that she'd seen me on TV the previous night and I looked great. She brimmed with enthusiasm and good cheer. Then she spied an older girlfriend who was loitering in front of the popcorn machine. They whispered for a few minutes, she returned and told me that my stomach was a pillow, and my boots weren't real. The older kid had wised her up. Her belief system had turned on a dime.

"Please say a prayer for Santa," I whispered.

One afternoon, David, a six-year-old kid who lived next door to me in real life, entered Gibson's with a babysitter. I had often observed his loud, bratty behavior. He glanced toward me and hustled away, as if he had seen the bogeyman.

"Come here, David," I called. "Have you been good?" This put the fear of God/Santa in him. He scurried away. He had not been good—and Santa knew his name.

Life was profoundly different after work in my regular clothes. None of the kids recognized me or even noticed me. Ten minutes before, they were staring and waving at me and telling me their youthful consumer dreams. Now I was just another adult. I visited Linda's class dressed in street clothes— kids loved to meet the teacher's husband—and restrained myself from bellowing ho-ho-ho. At Dillon's supermarket, when I saw two little girls in a shopping cart, my first thought was to saunter up and ask them what they wanted for Christmas. Posing this question to random kids—when not in Santa drag —is a bad idea.

I talked to more children than I had at any time since I was a young child, and it gave me a sense of what my elementary school teacher wife went through daily. As expected, dad's prediction came true: I was dismissed on Christmas Eve. Gibsons told me I could keep the suit. It still rests in our attic in a black plastic garbage bag, next to a bin of Christmas tree lights.

Have you been good?

THE HUMILITY OF A F-STOP CHARLATAN

Camera Salesman at Gibson's, 1979

THE GENERAL MANAGER OF GIBSON'S HAD BEEN impressed with my rendition of Santa. We hadn't often interacted, but many times I noticed him glancing my way from across the store. He had travelling eyes and always seemed to be skulking about, a master of the art of the sideways glance. At the end of the holiday season, while the rash on my upper lip was still healing, he offered me the position of retail camera consultant, a fancy name for a clerk. I had no choice but to take the job.

Being in this cheesy department store *without* my red disguise was freaky at first. My hair was of respectable length, suitably groomed for the position and in compliance with company policy. The man of the world, the jungle explorer, the leader of the Barking Geckos, now wore khaki slacks and a collared shirt as he stood behind the glass display case of cameras in a small, Kansas department store.

I arranged the merchandise, Windex-ed the glass countertop, cheerfully greeted curious customers and did my best to stay engaged and polite. No camera sales training was provided but I was now an "expert." My acting skills came in handy: I acted like I knew about cameras. Having hung around a few professional photographers—and Linda had a Cannon SLR—I sounded like I knew more than I did. The Gibson's clientele was likely to own an Instamatic or some other point and shoot camera. My job was to encourage an upgrade, like a single lens reflex, a more expensive alternative. There were some nice cameras under the glass counter, and I sort of liked selling them.

"Just look through the viewfinder, hold your breath, and squeeze. Make your f-stop adjustments *before* you look through the viewfinder and squeeze. Frame the scene in your mind first, then squeeze."

Customers came to my domain eating free popcorn from the rickety machine by the front door. The slightly acrid, chemical corn smell was impossible to escape. In the farthest reaches of the store, you could still smell it. This low-grade, overly salted popcorn stuck in every oral crevice, provided negative nutrition, and left you craving a sugary soda. One day I took a seat in the lunchroom as a cashier on break gazed into the mirror affixed to the inside of the cupboard above the sink. She was inspecting her gum lines for kernels. She paid me no notice, and kept right on inspecting, like I wasn't there. Maybe I wasn't?

This job was just one more chapter in my act, which was what my succession of jobs had become. An act, with me in the starring role. Most of those who I worked alongside did not seem to consider their jobs to be an act. Drudgery, perhaps. The price one must pay during earthly existence, maybe? The fatalists vs. me, the existentialist. But few of the fatalists had college degrees.

The way I rationalized my situation: would I rather be behind this counter, or at a desk, or digging a hole, or operating a machine or tromping around in a warehouse? Or discovering a cure for torpor? These thoughts swirled, the thoughts of an overqualified wise guy in a fix of his own design, each meal tasting like humble pie. Even more terrifying—maybe I was not so overqualified after all. Maybe I had gone so far out on that limb that I couldn't get back? Back to what? Conformity? The thing that at the beginning of the decade I had resolved to avoid. No. I wasn't looking to conform. I wanted fulfillment. Not from Santa Claus or guano or washing pots and pans but from something that was my destiny. My early retirement experiment officially ran its course behind the camera counter. I was all amped up with no place to go. Clerking was not my destiny. Perhaps something involving music?

Four years prior, I had written a song for the Geckos about a clerk from Toledo, Ohio, who gets high with a friend after ingesting a mackerel. Couldn't I, the clerk, write a song for Gibson's? My notion was that a jingle should reflect the personality of the business: in this case something bland, innocuous; a musical cliché. As my inspiration, I used a John's Bargain Store jingle that I had heard countless times while growing up. What I remember of my vapid jingle lyrics honoring Gibson's:

Courtesy, convenience, value galore
You get a whole lot more than you bargained for
At Gibson's Department Store

The music consisted of a guitar track recorded on a small portable cassette. It had that *recorded underwater* sound.

When I explained my creation to the General Manager, he accepted my cassette tape with an air of reluctance, gave me a sideways glance, and without a shred of enthusiasm, agreed to send it to the home office. Maybe all the way up to old Mr. Gibson himself. However, the jingle went nowhere. Who knew if the manager even listened to it, much less Mr. Gibson? It was just a demo, and the GM wasn't a creative director. How could I expect him to comprehend what it could be when produced with a budget in a recording studio? I would come to learn that evaluating advertising creative—especially an unfinished version—is best done by someone with experience. Or at least, an imagination. The explanation I finally got a month later from the GM—who barely seemed to remember that I had given him the cassette demo in the first place—was that Gibson's was a newspaper advertiser and didn't have radio advertising in the budget. I had fantasized that maybe Gibson's could become my account and radio would pave the way to an uptick in sales and a new career for me. A career in advertising: new thinking on my part.

Had I only been smart enough to use their official slogan in the lyrics—"Where you buy the best for less."—maybe I would have had a better shot? I should have thumbed through the pages of Herbert Gibson's autobiography, *This Man Gibson*, which was required to be on the shelves of the book aisle.

187

Advertising lurked somewhere in my future. I was resigned to overlook its role in encouraging people to buy things they don't need. Creating a little jingle was hardly like authoring *The Capitalist Manifesto*. But for now, I was still a clerk, surrounded by co-workers going nowhere but to the popcorn machine; middle aged check-out counter women with high school degrees married to stoic, tobacco-chewing husbands in bib overalls who waited for them in their pickup trucks at the end of the shift. A low hum of quiet desperation seemed to fill the store, including my own.

♫ ♫ ♫

Time goes by very slowly in a small-town discount department store. You can stare at the clock for two minutes and realize that only one has passed. You can fantasize that you are a pirate on the Spanish Main. Then the manager walks by and gives you a sideways glance to let you know he's checking up on you without having to look straight at you. The sideways glance is meant to keep you off balance and in line. You can't pull one over on the manager. He senses that you'd make trouble if given the chance. He has your number. He knows you don't eat mashed potatoes every night like he does. Picture him still wearing his cheap suit at the dinner table, his wife trying to think of conversation that doesn't have to do with the damn store.

"We need some new napkin rings," she tells her husband, who murmurs, "okay" as he downs a glass of milk for his ulcer. Of course, I am fantasizing, but he *did* have my number.

Clerking at JC Penny years ago had been a lark for me. Clerking at Gibson's had no lark factor. It was sobering, like I had caught a glimpse of a dystopian future, like I was in an Alfred Hitchcock movie: *The Clerk Who Knew Too Much*.

The Gibson's type of department store is gone from the American landscape, swallowed up by the Big Boxes. Gibson's was founded during the Great Depression and had grown to over six hundred stores by the time I worked there. It was pretty much kaput by the 1990s. Rumor has it that Mister Gibson turned down a franchise request from Sam Walton, who soon went on to start Wal-Mart. There may still be a store with the Gibson's name on it—I swear I spotted one in Kerrville, Texas while visiting my cousin sometime around 2010.

THANKS MISTER BANKS

Lawrence & Chicago, 1979

WHILE EATING HOSTESS CUPCAKES IN MY NEIGHBOR'S knotty pine basement, circa 1959, we watched Ernie Banks tell Jack Brickhouse on WGN TV's *The Lead Off Man* how happy he was to be at "beautiful Wrigley Field...Let's play two today," proclaimed Ernie. We didn't know Ernie's salary or where he lived or if he was married or his favorite restaurant or even if he had kids. We just knew he loved to play baseball, like we did. Ernie was one of us, playing a game that he loved.

And when Jack Brickhouse recited—with enthusiasm—the "happy totals" on that semi-rare occasion when the Cubs were victorious, us kids saw a guy who was on cloud 9 because the Cubs had won a game. Maybe being an adult would be okay? Jack showed us that you can still be enthusiastic as an adult.

♪ ♪ ♪

Flash forward to 1979. I had been writing songs for a half-dozen years when I decided to write an Ernie Banks song. Five years had passed since he had been inducted into the Baseball Hall of Fame and I thought my boyhood baseball hero warranted a song. *Thanks Mister Banks* would be a tribute to baseball, youth, Ernie Banks, and the Chicago Cubs. After jamming on it a few times with my music mates, I knew I had to record it. A record.

Sound recording was an expensive endeavor in 1979, done mainly by popular artists signed to record labels. Putting out a 45 RPM vinyl record was an uncommon undertaking for someone like me, an unheard of nobody. But my $6,000 workman's comp settlement from the broken ankle incident had finally arrived and was burning a hole in my pocket. I deserved to make a record. At least, that was my reasoning. Linda, my pragmatic partner, suggested that $6,000 would make a nice down payment on a house, but she knew my heart was in making the record. If it had been her ankle, we would have bought a house.

With my current playing partners, I recorded the song at Exceptions Studio in Topeka. Two guitars, bass, drums, background vocals. A giant leap upward from my Gibson's demo. We all were pleased with the recording. Now what to do? I had no connections in a business built on connections.

One of my dad's high school friends, George Hooker, was a cameraman at WGN-TV. "Get it to Hooker," dad told me. This television cameraman was my distant connection to the music business. Not much of a connection at all. I took a cassette tape to WGN-TV studios. Hooker listened and was impressed enough to get it to midday WGN radio personality Roy Leonard and his huge audience. Roy liked the song and said he would air it. I was ecstatic. I dropped off a reel-to-reel copy for him.

One day I was in Clarendon Hills at our next-door neighbor's, explaining to them what I was trying to do with the record and my potential new career path. In mid-explanation, my mother came running to the neighbor's back door and screamed, "turn on WGN (radio). They're playing your song!" I caught the last half of the song and tried to act nonchalant when Roy gave me an on-air plug, marking the first time my name was uttered on Chicago radio. Roy played it again the next day. He referred to it as a "professional" recording.

Although WGN was the biggest radio station in the Midwest, I told Roy not to play *Thanks Mister Banks* again until I could press a record. I didn't want Chicagoland to get all jazzed up about something that was not yet for sale. A bonehead request by me. A huge mistake. In hindsight, I should have kept my mouth shut. Radio airplay—repetition—is what popularizes a song.

To get onto radio playlists and into stores I needed a distributor. Linda's girlfriend's husband knew a promo guy who worked for one of the bigger record distributors in Chicago. I got his number and set up a meeting. The promo guy was impressed that Roy Leonard had played the song and suggested that I press 10,000 45s. Wow! He must have thought I had a potential hit! Could I catapult from the grind of dead-end jobs to stardom? How seductive is the fantasy of mass recognition.

The promo man gave me the name of a record pressing plant. I hoped he knew what he was talking about. Oh, he must know. He's a genuine Chicago record promoter. He could have told me to press a million. It wasn't *his* settlement money from a work injury. He also explained—strictly off the record—the importance of cash payments to those who might be helpful. The next day, after this none too subtle hint, I returned and greased his palm with a couple of fifty-dollar bills. His sporadic sniffling gave me pause, making me think that my hundred dollars might go up his nose. But I reasoned that this was the music business I'd heard so much about. Shady guys, payola, and drugs. I didn't trust him but saw no alternative.

A 45 needs a flip side so I went back to Lawrence and recorded *Weather Girl*, an atmospheric song about a guy who falls in love with the weather girl on TV. My parents loved it, which meant a lot to me. This tune eventually got a nice long write up from the Arts & Entertainment Editor of the *Kansas City Star*. "Lawrence lyricist strikes a chord for satire, pathos." A friend designed artwork for the Barking Gecko label, and everything was ready. I sent both song masters to the pressing plant with the label design. When I got the test pressing, I sent one to Roy, who said he would premiere it on opening day, a couple of months after those initial two airings.

Sure enough, I was invited to Roy's live broadcast before the game. His guests that day were Ernie Banks and the Cubs' nine-time all-star third baseman, Ron Santo. I sensed that something big could happen. When Roy spun the record, I sat in an adjoining booth, watching through the glass. Ten seconds into the tune, Ernie stood up and began dancing. The song had moved him right out of his seat, waving his arms and bopping around.

When the song ended, Ernie said, "disco ... disco," which it wasn't. I was not a fan of disco and was a bit puzzled that the subject of my song could have been so wrong about his own tribute record. But disco was the current craze, so this may have been Ernie's way of saying he liked it. He was smiling. (He was always smiling.) What a thrill to watch my boyhood baseball hero dancing to my song in the broadcast booth of one of the biggest radio stations in North America on Cubs opening day!

I was ushered around the building and introduced to various WGN executives, each with white hair, a reddish face and a large, uncluttered desk adorned by a few pictures taken at golf outings. If you were casting for a white guy executive spoof movie, this is where you would go—WGN. I was handed a box seat ticket and off I went to Wrigley. I have no recollection of the game or who won or who I sat next to. All I recall is that it wasn't snowing, as it is is at many Cubs home openers.

With Ernie on Opening Day 1979

The following week, when I called Roy Leonard to ask about more airplay, he explained that he liked the original mix on the tape better than the 45. He wouldn't be playing it again. What? Hadn't he read the recent article about me in the *Clarendon Hills Doings*? Didn't he know that Billboard magazine *almost* wrote an article about me? His reasoning sounded jive to me. As I came to learn more, I suspected it may have been a performing rights situation. I had registered the record with BMI and WGN did not pay a BMI license fee. Playing a tape was okay but not an official, licensed record. In fact, WGN hardly ever played music. They were a talk station. My "in" was with a station that was all talk, no music.

I made the rounds at Chicago radio stations, slipping an awkward $50 to a couple of program directors, learning that I was lousy at payola. Most stations played it once or twice and that was it. To them, Ernie was old news. A record had no chance at serious airplay unless it was on the Billboard Hot 100. A couple of months later, the shady promo guy told me that it had been played for three weeks on morning drive at the Number One station in Rockford, Illinois. If any records were sold in Rockford, I never saw the revenue.

Later in the season I found out that the Cubs PR department had been trying to contact me so that I could sing the song live at Wrigley during some sort of Ernie Banks day. When this news reached me, the date long past, I called them from Lawrence and politely expressed my exasperation at this missed opportunity.

Near the end of the baseball season, the Cubs did invite me for a private audience with Ernie at Wrigley Field on a day the team was out of town. Ernie and I strolled beneath the silent grandstands accompanied by a reporter from the *Gary Tribune* who was interviewing Ernie. She seemed completely oblivious as to who I was or what I was doing there. It was hard to tell if Ernie had given much thought to his song. It was often difficult to tell *what* he was thinking other than how beautiful Wrigley Field was. Oh well. It had become obvious that this record would not be my financial salvation.

Of the ten thousand 45s pressed, I sold a few hundred, gave away hundreds of promo copies, and still have a few hundred in the basement. The others may be for sale in a vinyl store on a parallel planet. But my major disappointment was that my tribute to Ernie seemed to have no effect on him. He never asked for a copy of the record, or for my autograph—ha ha.

The Ernie in my mind might have said, "Thanks Mister Bain." I did get *his* autograph—on the brim of a Cub hat that faded after a few years.

Calling the radio stations and making the rounds provided a glimpse of something that could be in my future. I knew the record was good. Everybody liked it. But in the business world, "good" doesn't matter as much as timing and connections. And great is better than good. The entire experience provided an interesting diversion from my disparate assortment of jobs during the 1970s, but it was unique in one way: I lost money on the job.

Photo by Joe Amari

III. SEARCHING FOR MEANINGFUL EMPLOYMENT

IS THE AD BUSINESS WORTHY OF ME?

Lawrence, KS, 1979-80

POTENTIAL MAY BE A DESIRED TRAIT IN TWO-YEAR-OLD thoroughbreds, eleven-year-old baseball players and twenty-two-year-old college grads, but it's less admirable when you're a thirty-year-old who's never held the same lousy job for more than a few months or weeks. As my youthful bravado buckled beneath the weight of creeping pragmatism, I thought, "why not advertising?" After all, that was my degree. And pedigree.

Linda had become increasingly annoyed at my cavalier, "everything will work out fine," attitude. She needed something from me other than potential. How would we support the kids we'd talked of having unless I had a real job? And would it hurt to please my parents? How bad could this job thing be? This newly imagined future might entail a necktie and office hours. Why not advertising? I surmised, stroking my chin, pipe dreaming myself as a peddler of toothpaste and paint. Couldn't I become a worthy member of the persuasion industry? Couldn't I become a member of this gang that both reflected and instigated popular culture with words and images and music and sex and humor and puffery, this industry that greased the skids of capitalism?

I wasn't sure.

My dad was now selling ad space for a group of midwestern agricultural trade publications, including *The Prairie Farmer,* the trade bible for Illinois farmers. A couple of times while in college, I had joined him and a few of his work cronies at Riccardo's, a well-known advertising and media watering hole in Chicago. As I listened to their adult tales, I sensed that they were good at their jobs but could see they also had time for a few laughs. In fact, they laughed a lot. They drank, too. That's what advertising people did at the time. Booze lubricated the industry. These guys seemed to have the freedom to come and go as they pleased. They were in the bright lights, in the boozy glamour of the big city. All I had to do now was sell my soul to the company store.

It was tough to envision myself "selling space" for life. Or writing ads to convince consumer-citizens that breakfast cereal drenched in sugar was the best way to begin the day. My dad was skeptical, too, but he set up an interview for me with an ad agency in Kansas City. I didn't own a proper interview suit, but I located a tie to match my one pair of presentable slacks.

Sure enough, I quickly learned that potential alone doesn't cut it. My interview was with an agency dude twenty years my senior. I showed him a *Thanks Mister Banks* 45 as proof of my creative prowess. He smiled.

"Potential is fine for kids right out of college. If we need a writer, we want experience in a specific industry."

"I have experience writing about trees," I told him and showed the Kansas Arborist Association campaign, already knowing that this interview was going nowhere fast.

"We don't have a tree account," he replied. Writing to sell soap or cars didn't quite have the panache I was looking for. If I landed an ad job, I might have to write about deodorant. That was enough to make me sweat.

The interview was nothing more than a perfunctory favor to my father. It took at most twenty minutes. There was no job here for me. Yet my interviewer confessed an admiration for what I was doing. Freelancing. Winging it. He admitted resignedly that if he were to do it all over again, he'd rather write stage plays than ad copy. Who knows, maybe that was the first time he had expressed that sentiment aloud? Exit stage left. I said thank you and goodbye to the man who would never become a playwright.

♪   ♪   ♪

The next day, I telephoned a pledge brother from freshman year at KU who was now a successful ad agency hotshot working on the burgeoning Wal-Mart account.

"You haven't turned into one of those assholes, have you?" I asked, instantly regretting my condescending attitude.

"No, I haven't," he said. But I'd blown it. Looking back, it wouldn't have killed me to be polite. This was a true personal connection. I'd let my bravado slam a door just as it was creaking open. At that moment, I realized that swallowing some of my idealism would be the price I'd have to pay to enter adulthood. How to join a world I had been avoiding.

EVEN TROPICAL FISH NEED ADVERTISING

Ad Space Sales for TV Movie News, Eastern, KS, 1980

"CLOSERS WANTED FOR FAST PACED ADVERTISING SALES position. Hollywood! The entertainment industry! Television stars! Big $$ potential. Complete training. Exclusive territories available now! Make your own hours!"

As I scanned the want ads, both my gut and my brain told me that this was a boiler room operation aimed at people who had run out of options, people who had no leverage, desperate souls who couldn't find a more traditional ad sales gig—or any kind of gig. Desperados such as myself. *The Bossman.*

The ad turned out to be for a rag called *TV Movie News,* a weekly publication of network television schedules, a few local display ads, and a horoscope for those who didn't want to fork out the dough for *TV Guide*. It was pamphlet size, printed on rough newsprint in black and white and stuffed into grocery bags at small town grocery stores. This was at a time when satellite-delivered cable television channels had not fully emerged to swell the schedule. Cable was primarily a rural medium that afforded better picture quality to folks who lived close to cows. CNN was still a glint in Ted Turner's eye. MTV had not yet hatched. ESPN was a miniscule upstart.

I pounced.

EVEN TROPICAL FISH NEED ADVERTISING

♪ ♪ ♪

It's showtime! The chumps who have responded to this week's ad straggle into the cheap motel conference room somewhere between Lawrence and Manhattan, Kansas. We sample the weak coffee and stale donuts. We listen to the pitch delivered by a slick but homespun territory manager who exudes an air of frank casualness, who spouts homilies of sales evangelism designed to simultaneously tear down and uplift the marks seated before him. He glances at his watch (part of the act) then scans the room.

"The secret to getting ahead is getting started. Let's get started." I look around to see if any fellow chumps are rolling their eyes or pretending to upchuck. None are.

"How much money did you make last week?" the pitchmeister asks a go-getter in the first row.

"Not enough," replies the go-getter.

"It's never enough," says the man with the answers. "If you want to get ahead you can never have enough. That's why you're all here today." He holds up a limp copy of *TV Movie News*. "This beautiful little publication can change your life if you just let it. All you have to do is believe. This piece of paper is a vessel to channel belief in yourself." In the last row, I was squirming.

The evangelical aspect of the presentation had similarities to the Billy Graham rally I had attended at Oakland Coliseum. Slick. Simple. Requiring a lot of faith. The Travelaide salesmen from my 3M job ten years prior were at least backed by a big corporate name. I had no idea who or what was behind this operation.

"Now, I'm going to let you in on a little secret. (Pause.) Winners aren't born. (Pause.) Winners create themselves. Winners are born of their own desire. Hold up your hand if you think you're a winner." Arms shoot up. Never had I been around so many winners. I raise my hand just enough, so I won't be called upon, so I won't have to point out that winners wouldn't be in this beige, stale donut hell.

He goes on to explain the mechanics of the deal: 500 copies of *TV Movie News* are stuffed weekly into 500 grocery bags at the busiest grocery store in town. Each weekly edition had room for two pages of ads.

"You can sell two full pages and call it a week, or you can sell eight quarter pages. You'll be offering targeted advertising to local businesses. Their ad will be seen only by people who shop in their own hometown. It's a beautiful thing."

Now it was time for him to introduce a *TV Movie News* superhero: a shining example of small-town sales acumen, a guy who had made "over $60,000" last year doing this exact sales job. I imagined that this icon of success, in his rumpled suit, probably relayed his tale at several of these meetings each week. He revealed his technique.

"It's simple. I don't take 'no' for an answer. 'No' doesn't exist in my book. Start with a full page. Remind them that a full-page is impossible to miss. If they don't want a full page, I get them to commit to a half. Or even a quarter page. You don't leave without the order. A quarter page is only 200 bucks for a month. Their ad will be in 2,000 grocery bags, right here in their hometown, where it matters the most."

Was it my cynical mind or was I simply utilizing my education and experience to surmise that this form of bag-stuffer advertising was probably a waste of money? That it would require the hard sell. The hard sell comes in handy when you are selling something that's hard to sell. The little businesses that we were to target most likely didn't have an advertising budget.

This guy went on and on. He was a breed apart. He was happy to sell anything to anyone, anywhere, anytime. I both admired and pitied this sales archetype. He was someone that I knew I could never be. But I thought I might as well take a crack at it, my first door-to-door sales gig since my brief outing as a Fuller Brush man some ten years prior.

After hearing from the sixty-thousand-dollar man, we were invited to be closers. And we could start right away.

"Start this afternoon if you want. Start now!" Choice territories were offered to each of us. Territories that had been vacated by the last guy who went went back to school, or whose wife got sick, or who was just a loser who took "no" for an answer, or who got in his car and left Kansas forever.

The closest available territory I could find was 85 miles away from our home in Lawrence: Manhattan, Kansas, the heartland. To me, the middle of nowhere. If I could make it in Manhattan, I could make it anywhere.

My first day on the job I walked into a pet store, feeling like a pest as I followed the owner who was servicing the tropical fish tanks. I tried to get him to bite as he netted an expired Plecostomus.

"You've got a nice store," I told him. "Don't be shy about reminding people." When he gave in and agreed to a half-page, I felt sorry for both of us. We settled on promoting 10 percent off all Neon Tetras and Zebras. As he wrote the check, I thought, "Your ad will be at the bottom of 500 grocery bags this week—unless the clerks forget to stuff them, or they put ten at a time into 50 bags, or the thing gets thrown away before it's even read, and no one sees it at all." If the ad didn't work, at least the *TV Movie News* would make a great bird cage liner.

Landing the tropical fish account called for a celebration, in this case, an incongruous lunch at a Chinese restaurant with walls of knotty pine on the outskirts of Manhattan. I joined several sad sacks at the counter and ordered the egg foo young. As I finished my lunch, the woman owner left her position behind the counter and walked swiftly to the front door and locked it. "Is she afraid someone is about to bolt?" I wondered.

In a dramatic whisper, her pointer finger pressed vertically across her lips, she told the puzzled diners "Lock doh. Niggey." The soldiers from Ft. Reilly were about to get off duty and she apparently didn't like the black ones, so she locked the door.

When one minority aims an epithet against another minority, what's a white guy to do? I was touched by a feeling of shame. Maybe I had this all wrong? Maybe the soldiers were rowdy jerks and she meant to say negro, but it came out as niggey in her Chinglish accent? Is Chinglish an epithet? The Chinese woman had undoubtedly been subject to an assortment of barbs, taunts or worse. That is the American way. Hey, that is pretty much the human way. Who knows this better than a minority? Would the world be a better place had I counseled her instead of giving her a half-hearted pitch for the *TV Movie News,* which is what I did? She brusquely turned me down. Thank God because I was ready for the drive back to Lawrence.

This miserable gig lasted two weeks and I received one commission check for $400. Was this my fate? The absolute bottom of the ad sales chain. No cocktails. No glamour. No money. My soul sulked. There had to be a better way.

I'M THE CABLE TV
MARKETING MAN

Lawrence, KS, 1980

1979 HAD BEEN FINANCIALLY FUTILE FOR ME. The *TV Movie News* gig was too depressing to continue, and my *Thanks Mister Banks* record was a commercial dud, earning nothing other than the occasional request from a random Ernie Banks fan who had managed to track me down and send me five dollars for a couple of 45s. During the past year or two, I had placed the occasional freelance magazine feature, landed a few low-paying music gigs, and worked the odd afternoon trimming buds or baling hay. None of these gigs paid enough.

They say you never grow old in a college town. You're always within spitting distance of the latest young crop of idealists. Just hang in there. If people knew you or knew of you, you soon qualified as an "old-timer," a designa-

204

tion a friend of mine used to denote those who had rattled around Lawrence long enough that when they walked down Massachusetts Street, they could nod or say howdy to a person or two.

An old-timer acquaintance named Dave Clark had recently been promoted from the director of locally originated programming to general manager of the Lawrence cable television franchise. A real job! He suggested I visit him at Sunflower Cablevision and have a look at the operation. It sounded interesting to me, although Linda and I weren't cable subscribers. We still jiggled rabbit ears and used tin foil to improve reception on our 12-inch black and white television that was mostly turned off.

Sunflower Cablevision was situated just down the street from a compound of stark white grain elevators that hulked above the banks of the Kansas River. I had walked past the single story, cinder block building many times without giving it a thought until Dave led me on the five-minute tour. He was especially proud of the video editing suite and the soundstage. I sensed that he had free reign to do whatever he wished so I spontaneously suggested we do a video of my song: *There's A Dead Mouse Resting on My Conscience.* Dave agreed.

Yes! I had found a collaborator to create video mischief. The next weekend, Dave shot and edited an exceedingly low budget video. The cast: me in a red silk robe and Brian in a second-hand mouse outfit, shivering in a snowbank near Dave's house. I have no recollection where we located the mouse outfit.

He'll surely freeze you know the snow's up to his knees

This zero-budget video ran on Sunflower's Cable Channel 6 lineup of locally originated programming. Unsuspecting cable customers witnessed the dead mouse. I had found a way to invade the living rooms of Lawrence with Gecko level absurdity and nonsense.

Another Sunflower employee, Randy Mason, used *Thanks Mister Banks* and another song of mine, *Truck Driving Astronaut*, for quirky video features on his half-hour, Channel 6 music show, *Bringin' It All Back Home*. I pondered the possibilities of this new world of video and cable. Had I serendipitously stumbled into an operation receptive to my brand of laissez faire humor? A form of humor where anything goes if it's stupid enough, because stupid is good when done right. I could feel something opening before me as I thought of ways to harness video's capabilities. A switch had been turned on. Could I get paid for this? First, I needed an angle that would permit me to become a more established part of the Sunflower operation. I began to see the world through the lens of the video camera. While thumbing through the *Lawrence Daily Journal World,* a real estate ad provided a catalyst.

I knew nothing about real estate but thought there *must* be a livelier way to showcase a home than a black and white newspaper ad. We were now in the video age. That's where home sales belonged. A show of real estate listings could never run out of content ideas. It was time to pitch Dave on my hastily brainstormed real estate show concept.

The premise was simple: locate a forward-thinking realtor who wants to be on cable TV, place the budding star in front of a listing and have him or her explain the home's virtues to the camera. Dave got it right away.

"Go out and sell it," he said. Say no more. I phoned a local real estate broker I'd seen in the paper and told him I wanted to put him on TV. He hardly let me finish my pitch. He was dying to be on camera. We made a deal, and I took it back to Dave. Thus was born *The Gill Tour of Homes.*

My commission kept us in shoelaces and guitar strings but wasn't enough to live on. And Linda the teacher was pregnant. What would we do with a baby and me without a job? This was a level of responsibility that I hadn't experienced. Time for another pitch to Dave: hire me to be Sunflower's dedicated ad salesperson. Hell, I had actual ad sales experience. Hadn't I recently spent two weeks pounding the pavement for *TV Movie News* in Manhattan, Kansas? And hadn't I just created and sold *The Gill Tour of Homes*? Dave agreed. Advertising Sales Manager had a nice ring to it.

Armed with a title, a business card, and a slim salary I began to sell advertising time on KU and Lawrence High football and basketball replays and a few other shows like *Fearless Football Forecasters,* where a cigar smoking curmudgeon nicknamed the Old Jayhawk, and a bespectacled sports nerd, Rich Bailey, exchanged prognostications for the big game with a few other local rah-rah boys. I wrote and recorded a low budget theme song for the show and now I was the singing Ad Sales Manager.

♪ ♪ ♪

For the next thirty years, excluding a two-week stint, I would never again be unemployed. In that time, I would do both what I loved and what I *had to* do.

♪ ♪ ♪

Employment counselors will tell you that the best job you have is the one you're currently in because you have an opportunity to improve your situation by assuming more responsibility or being at the right place at the right time to get a promotion. After a month or two, following this tenet, I sought more responsibilities, more prestige, and a heftier title. I suggested to Dave that he name me Marketing Director, although I had no first-hand knowledge of what a marketing director did. I argued that it would be a good move for him because he could now refer to me as *his* Director of Marketing. Dave saw the benefits of such a move and soon adopted my suggestion. I was hustling my way upward.

And there was more good news when Randy Mason suggested a Barking Gecko reunion on Halloween weekend at the Lawrence Opera House—all to be captured on video—for a special edition of *Bringing It All Back Home.* With Randy's help, I gathered a new incarnation of Geckos. This version of the Geckettes could sing in tune and didn't need to bark as much. Linda was not a Geckette for this performance. She had given birth to Janina a couple of months prior to the show—thanks God for Sunflower's maternity insurance—and was busy mothering. I wouldn't describe her as happy with me on the evenings I practiced but she knew the show must go on.

The Halloween extravaganza began with a cheesy movie projected above the cavernous stage (I can't recall if it was *Invasion of the Saucer Men* or *Party Crashers*) followed by Lawrence native, John Andrews—yes, that John Andrews, last seen with George Funk in Minneapolis—opening the show with an earnest rendition of the second verse of the national anthem. I was carried on stage on a stretcher as the drums pounded out a middle eastern tattoo. We played two sets: a night of musical madness.

The Gospel according to the Geckettes

In a matter of months, I had become Marketing Director and re-formed the Geckos. What a job! Right after I was hired, I received an offer from the promotion department of the Chicago Tribune, where I had applied months before. The Tribune job paid more and was with a major company, but with Linda six months pregnant, moving to Chicago seemed daunting. Falling into this free-wheeling video laboratory at Sunflower was something I couldn't pass up.

THE CABLE TV JUGGERNAUT

I had joined an exploding industry. Local programming was but one aspect of cable TV. New channels beamed in from satellites were the real game changers. What began as a way to improve rural television reception had evolved into a new, multichannel medium—a programming frontier. It's not that the public had been clamoring for more viewing options, but now that technology had made it possible, the game was on. CNN, ESPN, and MTV all began within a year either side of me joining Sunflower Cable. This was supply side—not demand side—programming. This was programming that we all could have done without and went on our merry way. But what it really tapped into was America's increasing desire for distraction. Broadcast television, and before that, radio, had been a unifying cultural factor as nearly the entire nation tuned in to the same program at the same time. When Lucy gave birth to Little Ricky on *I Love Lucy* in 1953, 71% of the country tuned in. (A great rating today might be 10%.) Cable television would eventually help divide us—and not just politically. As shared national viewing began to slide, something more precious took a tumble: a shared frame of reference. Cable TV allowed you to watch your own favorite channel while the spouse was in the next room, watching something on a different set. More channels instigated an increase in the number of television sets in a home. (Now referred to as screens, not sets.) With so many programming options, why watch any one program? Just flip the channel. A burgeoning population of couch potatoes relished having more channels to view as their attention spans diminished, their waistlines ballooned, and they had a new line item on the monthly budget—paying to watch television.

At Sunflower, we named our new channel capacity the "extended service package." I promoted it with a video skit where I cross-dressed as a heavily rouged woman named Rogene. With my mumbling, grunting husband, Bull, we learned about the new channel package from the slightly crazed customer service rep, Lincoln Pinkie. Bull (Mary) and Lincoln Pinkie (Rusty) were both Sunflower customer service reps in real life. Wait! This was real life. Just another cross-dressing day of absurdist marketing at Sunflower Cablevision. Just another day where I shaped the job to my whims.

♪ ♪ ♪

The launch of MTV in 1981 was a cable milestone. Inspired by MTV videos and cable industry publications, I wrote a theme song that was my comment on the cable business. *I'm The Cable TV Marketing Man* became my singing resume, a self-mocking satire that poked fun at the industry. Dave directed the video.

Videos on MTV often featured either backlit venetian blinds or smoke. For this low budget opus, we settled on smoke from a dry ice machine. Scene: Me sitting behind my desk, in a coat and tie, rocking back and forth to the beat while perusing *The Multichannel News*—an industry broadsheet—as the Geckettes, posing as subscribers, sashayed in and sang: "*How many channels can there possibly be?*" I promptly hopped onto my desk, stretched out on my side (in a repose I'd borrowed from Groucho Marx) and lip synced through the dry ice vapors:

> *You are in luck because you've asked the right man,*
> *Pull up your set and let me lay out my plan*
> *I can improve your video tan,*
> *Cuz I'm the Cable TV marketing man.*
> *Cable TV*
> *For you and for me*
> *How many channels can there possibly be? (The Geckettes)*

I'm The Cable TV Marketing Man played at a few national cable sales and marketing conferences, including HBO's, and was often shown in Chicago on WTTW's *Image Union*. It became the centerpiece of *The Barking Gecko Video Review: Not for Chowderheads*, a hodgepodge of my songs and skits woven into a half hour program produced by Gerry Cullen for Topeka public television's KTWU. Topeka! I'd hit the small time. To a practicing absurdist, Topeka was not only the capitol of Kansas; it was the capitol of mockery, the squarest, most bible-belt-y town in the lower 48: at least to my sardonic sensibility it was. For one music video—*I Doktor*—Gerry snuck us into Topeka's NBC affiliate station after the last newscast on a Sunday and used their equipment to shoot what at the time was probably the single most bizarre music video ever shot in the Sunflower State.

I Doktor with his patients, Ardys and Mary

I had found a way to flex my own creativity from within the system. It is hard to describe the joy one feels doing this.

Although on my real job I created newspaper and billboard ads, strategized with Dave, reviewed the new subscriber numbers, supervised a pair of customer service reps—Bull and Lincoln Pinkie—and attended meetings and seminars, in my mind I was more of a satirical version of a marketing director. I was playing a role in my own screenplay.

Real life video warrior

MEETING THE MOGUL

A year after Turner Broadcasting launched CNN in 1981, Dave sent me to a local ad seminar at Turner headquarters in Atlanta. At lunch break on the first day, Ted Turner loped in. A combination of Rhett Butler's southern swagger—with the same mustache—and PT Barnum's gift of promotion, he was cable's shining star, the conqueror who had cracked the stranglehold of the broadcast triumvirate of NBC, CBS, and ABC. He was the culprit who introduced the 24-hour news cycle that has relentlessly engaged our culture ever since. The empire-juggling mogul wore a sport coat and carelessly knotted necktie. Here was the big cheese about to lunch with the plebes. Every seminar attendee stole an awestruck glance his way. My fellow seminar attendees seemed hesitant to sit with Ted, so I glided into the seat next to him and introduced myself.

"Hi, Ted. I'm the cable tv marketing man from Sunflower Cablevision." He gave me a nod and we shook hands while remaining seated. Our discussion turned to international news, specifically the recent nuclear sabre rattling between President Reagan and Moscow. Ted wolfed down his sandwich, bits of lunchmeat flying out of his mouth as he voiced his apprehension: if things didn't cool down soon, we could get blasted into the Stone Age by a nuclear firestorm. He told me that he had just returned from a trip to Cuba where he'd met with Fidel Castro. He said that Fidel was mighty nervous too, which in turn had stoked his own nervousness. He and Castro had been nervous together. That made me nervous.

After polishing off his pickle, Ted lit up a cigar, a gift from Fidel, and told me with a wave and a puff that Castro had cut a CNN promo—"This is Fidel Castro and you're watching CNN"—but it couldn't air because of the guaranteed backlash from Miami Cubans who would cancel their cable subscriptions. Even renegade Ted had parameters. After discussing the impending nuclear holocaust with the mogul, I managed to get in some sort of pitch regarding my own creative prowess, but Ted professed that he was too high up the chain for my ilk.

My lunch with Ted

THE ONE AND ONLY JOHNNY A

And now, John Andrews re-enters the picture. I had witnessed the crowd reactiion when he sang the second verse of the national anthem to open for the Geckos at the Opera House. His performance provoked plenty of barking and yelping. He could often be seen zipping through downtown Lawrence on his Italian motor scooter, wearing a navy blazer, sporting a bow tie, a briefcase full of sheet music wedged between his black oxfords on the scooter floor, his dark hair shining with pomade. He demanded attention. He was unusual and like many unusuals, had faced a lifetime of disparagement and ridicule. But he craved performing and was always looking for gigs. While belting out German lieder, John reached for the high "C" and always hit it. Every year he trekked to Chicago to audition for the Chicago Lyric Opera Company and every year he was politely turned down. They weren't sure what to do with him, but I was. His itch to perform could be turned into a marketing asset.

It is an understatement to say that John was an unlikely fit for MTV. But the unlikely grabs your attention. Why not harness John's magic to promote MTV? All satellite channels reserved two-minute slots each hour for local cable systems to use for local advertising or promotion. In a cosmic marketing juxtaposition, this over-the-top opera tenor, "The Fabulous Johnny A," appeared in full costume during these two-minute breaks as:

- A rockabilly hep cat with swingin' hair
- A pilgrim down by the river for Thanksgiving
- An Easter bunny performing with a saxophonist
- A vampire thrashing out of his casket for Halloween
- A prancing marching band leader for a 4th of July Parade in an alley

**John, accompanied by portable tape player,
opens for the Geckos**

The spots were unforgettable. I suppose not everyone *got it*, especially Sunflower's owner, Dolph Simons, who was a very straightforward, old school, newspaper guy. The few times I went into Dolph's office he seemed wary of my presence. His demeanor said, "Who is this goof that somehow is working for me?" He was more comfortable with local politicians or university dignitaries. But we were always cordial, and he never asked Dave to get rid of me. That I know of.

DIP HEAD AND THE BOYS

A key cohort in on-the-job absurdity was Rusty Laushman (aka Lincoln Pinkie), a talented, serious actor making ends meet as a cable customer service rep. At work, we engaged in constant running banter, mocking the cable industry, rock stars (the TV in our office was always tuned to MTV), Sunflower staff members, and anything else we could wrap our minds around. Of the many video skits that we performed together, one gained national notoriety: *Dip Head*. It was insti-

214

gated when Rusty came to work with a shaved head. He had just snared the lead role in the KU Theater Department's, *Nosferatu* (Dracula). This creepy vampire, based on the 1920s movie, was hairless. For reasons unknown, I imagined how hilarious it would be to smear peanut butter onto Rusty's shaved dome. After scripting a concept for the peanut butter head, I swept into Dave's office.

"We've got to produce *Dip Head!*" It went without saying that Dave would direct.

Within a day, we'd bought the supplies necessary for the skit: a sheet of plywood—in the center of which Dave jig-sawed a hole—peanut butter, parsley, radishes, marshmallows, and a bag appropriately titled, Dip Chips. We placed the plywood on a couple of sawhorses, arranged tablecloths to create the appearance of a buffet table and spread the parsley and radishes around the hole. Rusty climbed beneath the table and sat on the floor with only his head emerging through the hole. We then smeared his head with a thick layer of creamy peanut butter—everything but his face. Finally, Dave and I studded Dip Head with marshmallows. Who wouldn't want a chip full of this?

The skit begins with Rusty facing away from the camera. A guy in a summer suit—me, seen from the shoulders down—grabs a chip and samples the dip, proclaiming it to be marvelous. Rusty then swivels his peanut butter-smeared head to the camera and announces, "Hi. I'm Dip Head," quickly rattling off his available flavors, including Chocolate Clam, creamy garlic and Hungarian Surprise, where he can be purchased (discount barns) and what occasions he's good for (chamber mixers, stag parties, bar mitzvahs). As Dip Head rotates his gaze away from the camera, the announcer tells viewers of Dip Head's trio of personalities (effervescent, cynical, and obnoxious).

The total budget including plywood and food props was less than $25.00. A few years after I departed Sunflower, *Dip Head* ended up on the #1 television program in the USA, *America's Funniest Home Videos*. I had submitted it on a lark. Rusty, Linda, and I were flown to Hollywood (Dave should have been included) and were lodged in that pink hotel on the strip. They gave us flowers and a dressing room with our name on it. We even received an on-air shout out from host, Bob Sagett, as the camera cut to Rusty and I mugging in the front row of the audience. Tens of millions saw *Dip Head*.

After some four-and-a-half years at Sunflower Cablevision, I felt that I had reached the limits of what I could achieve at a local cable system. That bit about never growing old in a college town was wearing thin. The time had come to grow. For quite a while, Linda had been anxious to leave Lawrence and return to Chicago. *If mama ain't happy, ain't nobody happy.* Atlanta, Denver, and New York City were all cable industry hot spots. I could have job-hunted in one of those cities, but our families were in Chicago, and I needed time with my mother, who was four years into her hopeless war with breast cancer. We now had a six-month old son, Anthony. Janina was approaching three. They needed grandparents, uncles, and aunts at their birthday parties. They needed some spoiling, cheek pinching and candy. And I looked forward to the delicious Sicilian cooking of Linda's folks. Because of my mother's declining condition, a veil of melancholy accompanied our eventual return. The anticipated move would be bittersweet.

Dave and I congratulate each other

Sunflower Cablevision allowed me to experiment with both my marketing sense as well as my sense of nitwittery. On my parallel planet, *anything* that I did was marketing. Where else could I put on a leisure suit, grab a camera crew, and go window shopping for cocktail sausages on main street? Or write and produce *The Fool Special*, a half hour special about fools, hosted by Simpson Samson, a bearded host with a passable English accent and an uncanny resemblance to the Marketing Director? This is what I had been looking for: a creative way to make a living on my terms. That job at the Chicago Tribune might have been better for my financial career. Who knows? But there would have been no *Dip Head, Cable TV Marketing Man, The Fabulous Johnny A*, or the final incarnation of The Barking Geckos. At Sunflower, I had not been hampered by bureaucracy or a traditional *this is the way things are done* environment. Dave gave me freedom to do what I was good at, the mark of a good boss. He was also a collaborator and a friend. A career path was coming into focus. As the move took shape, I returned to the cavernous KU library to pour over the *Chicago Tribune* help wanted section. Previously, the want ads had steered me to a bunch of "get-by" jobs. Now I was relying on these little ads—from which my dad had at one time had earned a living—for something more substantial—in Chicago.

**Rusty and I blabbing through another
episode of *Only On Cable***

THE YEAR OF
MY BROWN SUIT

Centel Videopath Program Manager, Chicago, 1984-85

THE WANT ADS CAME THROUGH. I LANDED a job as program manager at Centel Videopath in Chicago. For a few months, we lived with Linda's folks in the suburb of Morton Grove. It was tight quarters, but I was guaranteed a great Italian dinner every night! After a non-stop search, we rented a house in the northwest suburb of Des Plaines, a few miles from Centel headquarters.

The very name, Centel, reminded me of a catchall generic company name, akin to Acme. Would I, too, need to become generic? The Videopath was a microwave link that interconnected all the cable systems in Chicago. In theory this allowed a video program to be distributed simultaneously to the entire network. My job was to locate producers, advertisers, or organizations willing to pay for a crack at this new system. Accountants came up with the way to price the delivery system.

I knew that Centel was not an incubator for the creative tomfoolery I had experienced at Sunflower Cablevision. I would be slathering no one's head with peanut butter on this job. I would be working in a corporation, in an unremarkable building, in a quiet office of cubicles where everyone wore business attire. Engineers, technicians, accountants, regulatory lawyers, administrative assistants, and pole climbing linesmen comprised most of Centel's workforce. The title of VP was bestowed upon those who had demonstrated sufficient allegiance to company culture. Nepotism was an open secret. The President of one division was married to the daughter of the Chairman of the Board. A web of friends and family permeated the staff. Young managers on an upward path always had a mentor higher up in the company. Without a mentor, you were never going to become an assistant vice president. To gain a mentor, you had to impress the mentor with a thought process that mirrored the mentor's own. No boat rockers.

Creativity at Centel was displayed on spreadsheets or financial statements by that guy in accounting who came up with a variation on revenue recognition or net working capital ratios, or by the engineer who devised a new tandem switch for destination routing, or by the Executive VP who laid out a new reporting flowchart. And for the first time since my 3M summer internship, I was expected to come to work (on time) each day wearing a coat and tie. Business attire, as it was referred to. Throughout the previous ten years, my work apparel had been a combination of jeans, boots, sneakers, khakis, aprons, work shirts, collared shirts, and that cheesy Santa Claus outfit. Now I had to display a modicum of sartorial splendor.

At a minimum, I needed at least three suits to rotate through the week. I already owned a tan, summer weight number and one other now forgotten garment. For my third suit, I went shopping at Irv's Men's Warehouse, an outlet store for suits. Irv's lighting was a bit dim, either to cut down on the electric bill—after all, this was a discount emporium—or because the merchandise was better viewed in crepuscular lighting. I needed a different color than the two suits I already owned. The only one I could find in my size and price range was a cheap brown number made of some indestructible material that claimed to be wool but felt more like thick burlap. The wool must have been sheared from a scrawny, low-grade sheep. In terms of quality, it was not much better than my Santa Claus outfit. I had a sinking feeling as I tried it on. To say that the suit was vapid would be an understatement. Its hue was like chewing tobacco or dog doo. It had no give. It didn't drape. It was stiff and could almost stand up on its own. It was the opposite of fashionable. The suit might have been banned in Italy. When I looked in the mirror, I felt embarrassed. When I wore brown shoes and my brown suit to work, it felt like being in a Frank Zappa song. Was I now The Man in The Brown

Flannel Suit? This nasty garment symbolized the oppression of my new job. My twenty-one-year-old self would have freaked out knowing that one day I would become one of the brown suit boys.

Successful corporate workers must fit in so well that they stand out. I was not a success at either fitting in or standing out. Every third day, I felt mirthless while clad in brown, but I had two kids. I had rent, obligations and now a cheap, brown suit. On my after-work dash to the car, I tore off my suit jacket and loosened my tie. Upon arrival home, the kids were often hiding behind the draperies as I wondered aloud where they might be. When they could no longer stand it, they came bounding out. I was surprised every time. They didn't seem to mind the suit. This daily little drama reminded me why I was in a brown suit: to support a family you do what must be done. Even if you are in existential hell.

My first client was a hair restorative product that ran a direct response infomercial over the Videopath. I got free samples—my first perk—and tried it on my own bald pate for about a week with little result except a fine sheen of fuzzy, miniscule peach hairs that required a magnifying glass to detect.

My big assignment was to bring the wildly popular and controversial radio personality, Steve Dahl, and his partner, Garry Meier, to cable. Steve & Garry were pioneers of the "shock jock" school of radio and now they wanted to be on TV. This transition from radio to TV is often a flop, but the line I had to hew was that a successful Steve & Garry show over the Videopath could help fulfill cable's promise of new programming frontiers: good for fans, for cable, for advertisers, for Steve & Garry. Or it could be good for nothing.

My first meeting with Mr. Dahl's agent was at The Palm steakhouse, a power lunch spot in downtown Chicago. We sat at a booth, the agent called over the waitress, leered through his impossibly thick glasses that, because of reverse magnification, made his eyes look tiny, called her "honey," and immediately ordered the largest steak on the menu. He also had a sinus condition that provoked seemingly random snorts as he spoke. I hadn't had time to look at a menu, but his rapid-fire ordering let me know that he was in control, a player, a decisive big shot who knew exactly what he wanted. I ordered the chopped salad.

He referred to me as "pal" or "bud," assuming that I was a corporate straight man, a bean counter with no imagination who he could bend to his will, one who couldn't comprehend the potential genius of the proposed television show. He knew nothing of *Dip Head*, *The Fabulous Johnny A* or *The Barking Geckos*. He snorted and hacked away at his bloody steak, occasionally looking up at his lunch partner, a bald guy with glasses in a suit. (I couldn't bring myself to wear the brown one that day.)

"You guys need Steve and Garry," he said between chews. "They'll be the biggest thing to ever hit local cable."

"And Steve and Garry need Videopath to even have a show," I countered, stabbing a piece of leaf lettuce with my fork.

"You're a monster," he said, pushing away his plate. He had used that phrase several times and I gleaned that being designated "a monster," was a cynical mix of sarcasm and irony bestowed upon those who he deemed worthy of praise, no matter how faint. Or to those whom he was mocking.

I was a monster caught in a vortex of local cable companies run by people who knew nothing of television programming, a precarious microwave delivery system and a shock jock's agent wolfing down a bloody steak—quite an introduction to Chicago business. Negotiating something to please all these parties was a long shot but somehow, after several months of cajoling the most conservative cable GMs, we reached an agreement. As it turned out, my conjecture was correct: the show went nowhere, often literally, because the Videopath conked out half of the time, bringing the show to a dead halt as calls came in that it wasn't airing (cablecasting) in Tinley Park or Palatine or LaGrange, resulting in Mr. Dahl demanding my head as I lurked about the shadowy periphery of the studio where the live show emanated. Added to that: it was on a different channel in each cable system and fans often couldn't find which one; much of the Steve & Garry radio schtick didn't translate well to TV; and the cable operators hated it. No one was happy.

♪ ♪ ♪

After about a year on the job, the VP called me into his office and told me that "we need to cut costs." Panic time. No matter how little I liked it, I *needed* the job. I began to blather about how tough it was out there, the idio-syncrasies of the microwave, and any excuse I could conjure up as he nodded in awkward agreement, then said, "You're being transferred to the brand-new advertising sales department of Centel Cable division." Gasp. For a few moments I felt like I'd been falling off a cliff before being plucked from the air, seconds prior to splatting on the rocks. I thanked him but realized that I had now come full circle in two years. Once again, I would be in the local ca-ble business. In the western suburban hinterlands. The new position didn't require business attire. The brown suit could spend the rest of its days where it belonged—hidden from the world, hanging in a closet.

ALMOST A
TELEVISION STAR

Chicago, 1985/86

DURING MY BROWN-SUITED STINT AT VIDEOPATH, I was fixated on finding opportunities to continue the creative madness that I had experienced at Sunflower Cablevision. Good luck. Chicago's local broadcast TV production was now primarily news, news, and more news, because news made money. Local stations (other than PBS outlet WTTW) were in the creative doldrums compared to the experimentation of earlier decades when Chicago was leading the way with new forms of television for the new medium. The *Dave Garroway Show* had originated in Chicago on Friday nights in the early 1950s: "30 minutes of music, songs and chatter." The show moved to mornings and became what is now NBC's *Today Show*. Chicago had been an incubator of kids shows like *Kukla, Fran and Ollie*, an ad-libbed masterpiece featuring Fran the human interacting with Kukla and Ollie the puppets. It soon caught on with adults. *Ding Dong School* was an early attempt at educational programming for kids. There was Hugh Hefner's *Playboy's Penthouse*, with guests like Lenny Bruce and Nat King Cole; Studs Terkel's *Studs' place*, set in a neighborhood tavern. And of course, *Bozo's Circus*.

Although this era was now a historical footnote, hope springs eternal in the mind of a practicing absurdist. I sent my Sunflower video demo that included *Dip Head* and *Cable Marketing Man* to David Finney, program director of NBC-5 Chicago. He took my call a week later. He liked my stuff. We arranged a meeting. He had a few ideas. Had I found a practicing absurdist? Had I lucked into a collaborator? Could I partake in some renaissance of Chicago video creativity?

Dave's first idea involved Republic serials from the 1940s and 50s. Very campy stuff. Most of these episodes were scripted to leave you dying to find out what calamity was about to happen to the hero or heroine. My host name: Cliff Hanger. The program director thought I would be a good host because of my willingness to be a nitwit. (I still have a clip of Cliff singing *Volaré*, holding the *r-r-r* for an interminably long time, while wearing hotpants and of course a drawn-on pencil thin mustache.) When the station was unable to finalize a license agreement with the Republic people, the whole project got scrapped. Cliff would never be able to leap into the homes of stoned night owls.

Next, Mr. Finney had the idea of producing an irreverent, early morning news show, more akin to a loosey-goosey morning radio sensibility. This was some crazy thinking in 1985, a time when local TV broadcast news reeked of forced jocularity. Most news/weather/sports teams kidded around, laughing at their own inanity while rarely being humorous or profound. For my audition, I wore a sport coat, sat on a chair, and thumbed through articles from that day's newspapers, making deadpan comments, like, "the recent heavy rainfall caused a sewage overflow up in Winnetka, actually improving the water quality of Lake Michigan." For the weather segment I would look out of the top floor window of the Merchandise Mart building and describe that day's meteorology and whatever else crossed my sightline.

When the station selected *me* from a pool of eleven contestants—stand-up comics, actors, and radio personalities—I was momentarily enveloped in a bubble of anxious hope. I contacted a big shot entertainment lawyer (whose biggest client was Oprah) and began to imagine my new life as a TV personality. The meeting at the law office was surreal and awkward. The beautiful assistant he pawned me off to couldn't figure out where I came from. What is a Sunflower Cablevision?

The next step was to produce a thirty-minute pilot. I had to sit on a couch and have a serious conversation with some teenage kid plagued by agoraphobia. Somewhere along the line, the entire conceit of the show seemed to have slipped backward toward normal. Was I still supposed to be zany and rye, or "just the facts, man" straightforward? My goal had never been to host a straight show yet here I was. I began the interview by asking the kid, "If you have agoraphobia, how did you even come to the studio?" He told me it had been tough. Now both of us had anxiety. I flummoxed my way through a few more minutes of interview persiflage—do you have pets?—and it was a wrap.

The pilot wasn't what I had envisioned during my deadpan zany audition. I was now a hesitant host, like an actor who hasn't found their motivation. Look, I wasn't trained to be a cog in the news wheel. I had hoped to make fun of that guy. Literally the next day, as the show concept was coming undone, the station got a replacement GM, shuttled in from out East, who immediately suspended all new local production spending for six months. There would be no wacky early morning show. I wouldn't have to wake up at 2:30 every morning, allowing me to grasp a silver lining of sorts. Going to bed at 7pm with the kids running around, demanding my attention, had never seemed realistic. And it wasn't.

Six months later came the most elaborate opportunity of all—a kids' series. Never had I considered a career as television host for kids, but I was game for anything that might get me out of the oppressive world of cable ad sales. (Of course, I wasn't really oppressed other than psychically and spiritually and whatever else goes into a self-image.) David Finney, the would-be Svengali of off the wall local TV, presented me with the concept: a down home, backyard, Johnny Carson-style show featuring a kid and an adult as co-hosts. I, he explained with glee, would be the adult host, Big Guy. My co-host was Little Guy, a ten-year-old aspiring actor the station had located. My brainstorm was to dress both "guys" in matching powder blue tuxedos and Wayne Newton-style pompadour wigs. Pencil thin mustaches completed our look. (Putting a mustache on a kid is an easy laugh.) As I recall, I turned in the script handwritten on yellow legal paper. I was the co-host while also portraying all of the other characters: Corny Geezer, the world's oldest man; a nameless, demented bandleader who showcased a ridiculous level of enthusiasim; Spud the singing potato; and Ms. Behaveyourself, a female etiquette expert. We settled on the title, A Couple of Wize Guys. Had to spell it wize because of a Joe Piscopo/Danny DeVito movie out at the time, Wise Guys.

I had never worked with a production budget on this scale. At Sunflower Cable, we had spent $25 out of our own pockets to produce *Dip Head*. The *Wize Guys* budget, supported by a seasoned broadcast crew, must have been a thousand times more. We taped over two days at Chicago's NBC studio in front of an audience of elementary school kids and nuns from a nearby Catholic school. Before going on as *Ms. Behaveyourself*—an expert on health, safety, and manners—I muffled my laughter. Was this a dream? I was playing hooky from my cable day job, wearing a dress, and blowing on a kazoo while singing *Elmo the Smelly Elephant* in front of nuns. I was pretending to be a kids' TV host.

Spud gets interviewed

The edited pilot created a major buzz at the station. Our goal was to garner an order for thirteen episodes that would air at NBC owned stations across the country. Once again, I fiercely imagined abandoning a world where

I wouldn't have to wear a brown suit. Where I could instead dress as a potato.

Before I could hand in my day job walking papers the dream shattered. The head of national programming in New York sent a five-page memo to Mr. Finney nixing the show—apparently the longest memo ever received from New York. "Too much schtick" was the theme of the memo. Yes, it was schtick-y. Mighty schtick-y. Possibly the schtick-iest thing aired all year in Chicago. Within the year, Pee Wee Herman launched a kids' show that was even higher budget schtick. Schtick will never die. Our pilot aired a couple of times in Chicago to little fanfare. Why promote a show that'd been canceled before it began?

In show business, failure and success are inches apart. Talent, connections, and determination are important factors, but timing trumps everything. The exact right person must see your work or hear your pitch at exactly the right time. Persistence is more easily practiced when you're young enough or selfish enough to pursue dreams at all costs. I was neither. I didn't own the rights to the show so I couldn't shop it elsewhere. I wasn't connected enough to know where to go or whom to see. I never even had a goal of becoming a kids' TV star. To me, *Wize Guys* was just another opportunity to practice the art of the preposterous, to do something nutty. As my mother-in-law often said, "you're a nut."

I wish my mother could have seen *A Couple of Wize Guys*. She had died the previous year. She would have loved it. I have no recollection of my father's reaction but I'm certain he was relieved that his son wouldn't be wearing a dress or a wig to work. My kids watched a tape of the show about a hundred times.

The night I found out that I would not be a wacky kids' TV star, Linda and I attended a Tina Turner concert. Tina was great. Linda was sad. I was devastated. For the first time in my life, I had sensed that my creative endeavors could find a wider audience. That, yes, it was possible to get paid for being exactly who I was. These months of near misses at NBC had at first given me hope—a way out of the mundanity of my day job. Instead, there was a rejection memo from some guy in New York I would never meet. The hope was gone for now. I tried to drown my disappointment in Tina's wiggling, jiggling, and screaming but I couldn't shake the thought of what might have been.

THE LOCAL CABLE
BLUES AGAIN

West Chicago, IL, 1986-90

FOR THE NEXT FIVE YEARS, I ROAMED the career wilderness, a creative mind stuck inside the body of an ad salesman. Life seemed good, and yet ... was this how it was going to be? I had a decent job, but when you're not doing what you know you *can* be doing and *should* be doing, it becomes an existential drag.

After the initial rush of relief that I still had a Centel paycheck, the thought that I was again in local cable muted my joy. At Videopath, I was often in the city, dealing with a higher level of folks in the worlds of advertising and entertainment. At Centel Cable, I would be working in a squat, unglamorous office plaza positioned in front of a supposedly cleaned-up Kerr Magee hazardous waste dump in the suburban backwater of West Chicago. Rumors circulated of local children born with prehensile tails. The weeds out back seemed to give off an iridescent sheen.

Soon I was named the advertising sales manager of a department of five, not because of my achievements or performance, but because the previous manager had abruptly decided to move to a different state and the company needed the position filled NOW! before the next corporate staff meeting. I was the only possible candidate. The one salesperson in this group of five was a young guy in his first sales job who often wore a black dress shirt with a pink tie and usually had a toothpick jutting out of the side of his jaw. The others were production roadies and an admin assistant. I recalled the words of an older cousin of mine who was quite successful in the financial world. He had opined that for a successful career, one must be in management by age forty. I'm not sure if my current position qualified as his definition of "management." My title proclaimed "manager" but strategic decision making occurred at a higher level: the real management.

In the ensuing years, my crew grew to about twenty in sales, production, and administration. Some I hired and some were placed in the department by the powers that be. Centel often shuttled people around their various departments and divisions, like I had been shuttled from Videopath.

Each Wednesday morning, I held a department meeting and brought coffee cakes to encourage attendance. (Free food is the greatest inducement of all time.) Biting into a delicious slice of raspberry coffee cake, scanning my surroundings, my thoughts centered around the notion that I could go along with this for now, for a paycheck, but this would not be my *life's work*.

Half of the group were professional and diligent. The other half, a mix that included a grifter, a certifiable lunatic, one or two basket cases, a few moochers, suburban hillbillies, and those who hadn't yet achieved—and maybe never would—the acumen or experience to sell in the "big leagues." I enjoyed the staff when they weren't squabbling or displaying their emotional baggage or trying to con me. My main duty was solving problems.

"The ink cartridge on the fax machine is leaking."

"Sorry I'm late. My dog had explosive diarrhea this morning."

"Harold says we're running the wrong spot and he won't pay."

"Can we give fifty bonus spots to Biggers Chevrolet?"

"My last commission check was way off."

"I liked the cheese coffee cake that you brought last time better."

Local cable advertising was still a hot new commodity, especially with auto dealers, who all wished to be in their own commercials, get the lowest possible rates and often not pay the bill until ten minutes before it went to collection. Negotiating with these guys on their turf, in their domain, never sure when they would pay after they had beaten you down, was a form of hell. In fact, when a car dealer check came in, it was a cause for celebration. Like a miracle had occurred.

For most of our mom-and-pop clients, the five hundred or two thousand dollars for a month of advertising was coming out of their own pockets. It had better work! But as long as they saw their own commercial while watching TV, or if their neighbor did, the advertising was working. A much different gauge than the cost-per-thousand and cost-per-point analytics of broadcast advertising. The big leagues.

I now found myself in a generic office with a hazardous waste dump out back, working a job that held little interest for me. Has this ever happened to you? After all those years not even wanting a *real* job, I was now the boss. In most careers, boss-hood is a necessary step up the ladder but being the boss had never been a goal of mine—not counting my freshman year in college when I was *The Bossman*. A boss dude is one thing, being the boss, quite another. Bossman was now the boss. And *the man*. When I heard salesperson Patty refer to me as her boss, my mind went YIKES!

MY OTHER LIFE

Chicagoland, 1986-90

AS MUCH AS I DESIRED, I WAS in no position to quit the cable ad sales world. Not with two young kids and our recently purchased Victorian-era home, where we faced a forever remodeling project. During this local cable lustrum, I had turned forty, one of those age milestones that may or may not mean anything. Linda threw a backyard surprise birthday party for me, hired a belly dancer, and gave me a conga drum. The cops showed up at midnight, called by a neighbor who wasn't invited. No arrests were made.

I was also dealing with the recent death of my mother, as well as a father who needed tending to in his grief. Few events are as bewildering as the death of your mother. During the first disorienting waves of loss, work is the last thing on your mind, yet at the same time, it provides a lifeline of distraction.

Once again, I was saddled with the situation of making this tenet work for me: the best job is the one you have right now. Why engage in the hassle of sending out resumes or going to interviews? You already have a job. Own it.

Steve Jobs stated, "We're here to put a dent in the universe. Otherwise, why even be here?" He also said that great work is done by those who love what they do. Of course, Steve was making millions, a surefire way to love what you do. When put through this filter, how could I do great work or dent the universe? I carried out my duties as outlined in the company manual, but I didn't wake up champing at the bit to get to work. There was no end game here. I was going through the motions but leaving my soul out of the equation. Our economic system is about making money, not making people feel good.

Imagine an economy where every worker was employed doing precisely what he or she enjoyed, doing work for which they were perfectly suited. I was not contributing to this economy of satisfaction. Didn't I owe it to myself and the universe to seek something different?

Still, there is more to life than your job. There is your family. At the end of the workday, I looked forward to getting home, where the family waited, similar to my father's nightly homecoming. "Daddy's home!" And every night at bedtime, I mesmerized Anthony and Janina with the never-ending, improvised tale of The Magic Pig, who had people hands and people feet, who wore a top hat and carried a cane, and who was able to perform feats of magic. These tales were as therapeutic for me as they were enchanting to the kids. The Tales of the Magic Pig helped to mitigate my temporary career situation. Moonlighting and music also kept me sane. A side hustle to the rescue, where my identity wasn't the boss of a small cable ad sales department but instead a creative being.

A clinical psychologist commissioned me to write a movie short based on "Present Moment Thinking" for AT&T. My script featured an anthropomorphic, wise-cracking mind. Then, John Cleese's training film company, Video Arts, hired me for a few freelance projects. I wrote one trade publication ad that compared humor to dynamite: *In the wrong hands, it can blow up in your face.* I also auditioned to be a smarmy HBO game show host and didn't get the part. I scripted all the continuity for *WGN's Bozo 25th Anniversary Special*. I even tried to interest the Hormel company in staging a Spam-O-Rama, a live event celebration of all things Spam. I paid an art director/illustrator to create some presentation boards but never got the chance to pitch the concept. A polite voice from Spam headquarters called to inform me that it was too "left field." They didn't get it. Hormel might have enjoyed the Spam theme party we staged at our home, featuring Spam Wellington and a game of pass the Spam where about thirty friends formed a circle and passed a can of Spam while chanting Pass me Spam/I want Spam/Give me Spam as I pounded my conga drum while wearing a Pith helmet.

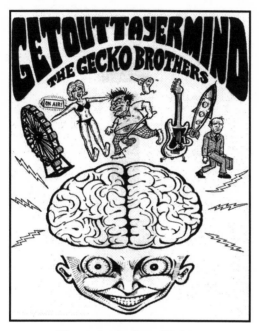

Illustration by Steve Krakow

Of most significance was embarking on a ten-year recording collaboration with ex-Barking Gecko, Mitch Rosenow, an ace engineer and musician who lived in the KC area. We recorded in his basement studio, a sonic laboratory with Mitch, the mad scientist, at the helm. Over the years, we had more than a dozen sessions resulting in over twenty tunes produced and tweaked with Mitch's sonic touch. We referred to the collection as, *Getouttayermind*, one of the tune titles. Sure, we talked about notoriety for the tunes but mainly we were trying to please each other. Very un-pop. A few tunes got a couple of spins on various Chicago radio stations and the nationally syndicated *Dr. Demen-*

to Show. These humorous, preposterous, esoteric songs represented my little dent in the universe, a balm to the soul, a wonderful elixir for a guy stuck in a job going nowhere. Making music was my lifeline. I was also doing live gigs with percussionist, Tom Mohbat, at a few gin mills in Chicago. We always tore through a ten-minute version of *Frijoles.*

GOODBYE, DAD

Clarendon Hills, IL, 1990

IN EARLY 1990, MY DAD PASSED AWAY from pancreatic cancer. Six months from diagnosis to grave. One measure of a life is how others think of us when we are gone. Roger Sr. was the salesman that everybody loved. The all-around good guy, the guy you enjoyed having a drink with or telling a joke to. This wasn't the death of a salesman; it was the death of a good guy. If I can be as fondly remembered as my father, I will have achieved something.

At least my dad had lived long enough to see me get a normal job and make a decent living. During the past decade, his worries about me had disappeared. I had become a version of him. Your father's career can have a profound impact upon your own. My dad didn't seem passionate about his job but appeared to be happy. I recall when he would take a weekend phone call from a work associate on our single house telephone. It might have been a client from John Deere or Monsanto Chemical or an ad agency guy. The calls were often jocular. Whatever it was they were discussing seemed humorous. Whoever these guys were at the other end of the line—I eventually met some of them—they had a good time talking to my dad. The whole family eavesdropped because we all loved to see him enjoying himself.

My career was now unfolding in the same broad category as my father's—advertising—although we were of different generations. My formative years were in the boom of the 1960s, a decade of Kennedys, hippies, psychedelics, and an unpopular war. He grew up during the Great Depression and was seventeen when his father, Jehiel, died. Losing your father at a young age while jobs and money were scarce was something I could only imagine. He disdained debt. Paying bills on time was a religion to him. The delinquency of my own college loans (finally paid) must have gnawed at him. So much of what I had done must have freaked him out. His entire life, he sought security. He had listened to FDR's radio chats as a kid and frequently declared Roosevelt to be the greatest American president. I had practiced a form of insecurity, made possible in part by the secure home I grew up in. I was a writer, performer, musician, and a traveler. My Dad never wrote anything longer than a sales report and his only demonstration of musical prowess was the ability to whistle. (He was a terrific whistler and claimed some distant Bain relative won a whistling contest!) He preferred the comforts of home, travelled little in the first fifty years of his life other than business trips to Peoria or Moline, or Bailey's Harbor, Wisconsin, where he took the family every summer for a week or two, giving his kids a bank of memories that remain dear and filled with the happiness of seeing your parents happy.

A couple of times, my dad had mentioned that he and a cohort had kicked around the idea of starting their own ad sales rep firm. I believe that the reason he didn't follow through was because he had a mortgage, four kids, and my mom, who like most of the moms on Blodgett Street, didn't have a job. (Other than the non-stop work required to run a household of six.) Striking out on his own with a new venture would be a financial risk. He was risk averse. Most of my risks had been at an early age, cloaked in the fiery idealism of youth when not as much was on the line. At present, Linda had a teaching career, guaranteeing that no matter what I did or didn't do, we would have at least one paycheck. My dad didn't have this cushion. He was the sole breadwinner, a more precarious position from which to launch new ventures. There are endless conversations we all wished we had had with those we have lost. I would have liked to dig deeper about that "almost" venture he never tried. I would have liked to better express just how much he meant to me.

With my dad (on left) at his retirement

The day before my dad's funeral, without hesitation, I accepted an offer to be the local ad sales manager of the Greater Chicago Cable Interconnect. The office was on Michigan Avenue and required that I wear a business suit. I know Dad would have been proud. I was pleased to be leaving the suburban backwater for the bright lights.

Though I had not always taken their advice, there was no one I wished to please more than my parents. Now, neither would be around to see how I "turned out."

DOOMED AGAIN

Local Ad Sales Manager –
Greater Chicagoland Cable Interconnect, 1990-91

FROM MY 9TH FLOOR OFFICE PERCH ON Michigan Avenue, a prime view of the WrigleyBuilding clock and the Chicago River stretching before me, I loosened my tie a smidge, hung my suit coat over the chair back and gazed at the brash cityscape of sturdy and magnificent structures. An iron worker balanced untethered on the skeleton of a new building rising from the city floor. The Chicago River snaked through a forest of taillights, concrete, glass, little ant people and heavy metal buildings. My view.

My kingdom: At least it felt like that for a fleeting moment before I had to pick up the telephone to make something happen on my new job as Chicago Sales Manager for the Greater Chicagoland Cable Interconnect.

Although I had little idea how to succeed at this job, it felt good to be back in the daily hubbub of the city for the first time since age sixteen, when I had worked at the garage on Federal Street. I just needed to hang on until something else might happen, some other unknown opportunity that might seep up through a crack in the sidewalk. Within my view lurked hundreds of millions of ad dollars poised to lubricate our economy, dollars to persuade us

238

what we must buy next. And millions in sales commissions to be earned by the torrent of hustling ad salespeople, well-dressed, eager, ready to be your best friend, if only for the length of the meeting. What was in it for me, the fake salesman, the creator trapped in the clothes of a salesman? Yes, I could look the part while hoping that selling ads would not be my career.

How had I even arrived at this place, with this view, if not for my ability to sell? The entire industry of advertising is predicated on selling. That awful or ingenious commercial you saw last night on television was the result of someone selling a concept. I could sell myself and I felt very comfortable selling my own concepts, but I cared little for selling units of time within television programs that I thought to be mundane or superfluous. The ability to persuade is a profound asset. Who hasn't marveled at the person who can sell *anything*, the one who can sell tanning beds in the desert? The combination of reasoning, logic, humor, and emotion that skillful salespeople utilize is one attribute that sets humans apart from monkeys, who are more inclined to scream or throw shit at each other.

Apart from the fact that I didn't think of myself as a salesman, a bigger challenge faced me. What I was supposed to sell was an administrative, technical mess. The Chicago cable market—my sole responsibility—was disdained by ad agency media buyers. Buying a 30 second interconnect spot required a dozen video tapes of the commercial—one for each cable company. Agency buyers, accustomed to a single tape and invoice from their broadcast vendors, would receive a dozen invoices from me, creating twelve times the hassle. And unlike broadcast, the cable channels had no local ratings. Ratings are the backbone of every television ad negotiation. I had no backbone. Few agency media buyers wished to make their hectic job more difficult by taking on this muddle. They often told me, right before hanging up the phone, "We'll look at placing a cable buy in Chicago when you guys make it easier to buy."

About eight months into the gig, I began hearing that "Chicago's numbers have to pick up." That was an understatement because there were barely any numbers at all, mainly a list of possibilities that I detailed each week to my immediate boss, who in turn relayed them to the big boss out East. The few deals I had managed to conclude didn't cover my salary.

Once each month, I woke up in the dark and took the early train into the city for a 7:00 a.m. breakfast meeting with the boss brigade who flew in from points East. After an hour hearing about how well everybody but me was doing, the breakfast meeting ended at exactly 8:00 a.m. so as not to diminish the time we should be out hustling and schmoozing and making it happen. Seasoned ad sales pros knew all the media planners and buyers at all the agencies, knew when the annual budgets came up and when an account switched agencies, knew who was flirting with who and who was about to be fired and where the head buyer for McDonald's liked to eat lunch. (It wasn't McDonald's.) I didn't really belong here. These were all nice people, but I had different aspirations.

Thank God for lunch, a daily respite from the grind, the reward for a productive morning or an escape from a fruitless one. There were hundreds of lunch spots in downtown Chicago, each with its own dynamic, each attracting a different work segment. Where to eat today, who to eat with, who was eating with whom? There was the power lunch; the relaxing lunch; the expense account lunch; the solo lunch; the awkward lunch with a potential client who seemed inattentive; the "let's get together because we haven't seen each other in ages" lunch. Lunch was the best excuse not to work for an hour.

The lunch vibe had changed from the alcohol-fueled lunches of my dad's heyday. We rarely boozed. Most days I ate with co-workers at Blackies, noted for their garbage salad, or the Wendy's salad bar or a little joint behind the Tribune Tower that served Cajun food. For this brief lunchtime interlude, you could put aside your work persona and reveal your off-the-clock self. You'd learn that your co-worker was a scuba diver, ran marathons, and voted for Dukakis. They'd learn that you weren't really an ad salesperson, that you were a pre-Columbian bead trader and Blind Blake aficionado. How melancholy those last couple of French fries could feel, dipping the final fry in ketchup, signaling the end of the meal. When the fries were done, it was time to wrap it up. The beautiful excuse had come to an end.

Back at the office, where business is conducted via land line telephone, Andrew has his sleeves rolled up and is talking on the phone. The guy we nicknamed Crackers is also on the phone with a determined look. Kim and Ivy and Jim are on their phones. You better get on the phone, whispers your salesman conscience. With a ping of trepidation, you peruse the pink "while you were out" call slips on your desk; you see that no one has returned your calls. When the pink slips provide no guidance for the shape of the afternoon, you begin cold calling. The phone receiver feels like 500 pounds of dead weight as you lift the receiver from its cradle with the left hand and begin punching the dial pad with your right index finger, the same finger that Moe used on Larry's eyes, the finger used by catchers to call for a fastball, the finger used to declare that "We're number one!" In this instance, you use the finger to punch in the number of your drummer, Tommy, to see if he wants to play tonight. Let's see. It's one fifteen and in seven hours you'll be toking a joint, sipping wine and playing *Here Come Mister Upscale* in Tommy's west side studio above a glove factory. At least you're on the phone looking like a diligent prospector

In 1990, there were no computers to help you look occupied. No screens to absorb your thoughtful gaze. The only computer in the office was a large terminal that only one secretary knew how to operate. And one day at lunch, you learned that this secretary had spent four years living in the wilds of Alaska and this changed your impression of her and somehow gave you a little hope.

♫　♫　♫

The commute. Every Monday through Friday morning, after three prunes and a cup of coffee, I tucked the morning Tribune under my arm and left the house by 7:02 a.m., fast walking the eight blocks to the Arlington Heights Metra station to catch the 7:16. If you are any good at this, you arrive no more than one minute before the train pulls into the station, then, you join the crush and grab your seat. In the pre-digital age, most commuters read newspapers, books, or work-related documents while on the train.

Real commuters often stand at the exact same spot on the station platform and board the exact same train car every day. Over the months, or years, you find yourself sitting next to someone with whom you get into a conversation. Maybe the next week or the next month you recognize each other until finally, this ex-stranger begins to save a seat for you. A commuter friendship. Could be a person of the opposite sex. Someone who you share a ride with and slowly divulge your dreams to and maybe even partake in some flirtatious banter, a person that exists, for you, only on the train, who upon hitting the station, dissolves into the crowd, leaving behind a faint trail of her perfume, different than your wife's. Poison?

Upon arrival in the city, depending on the season, a bus or the water taxi completed the journey. The morning bus is not a happy place. Everyone is headed to the office mines. Not much laughter on the morning bus. There were no bus friendships.

The water taxi provided a brief relief from the madness. The moment the train jerked to a halt at Northwestern (now Ogilvie) Station, a horde, including me, poured out of each car. I jockeyed for position in the vestibule, jumped off the train steps onto the platform and zig-zagged through the crowd, fast-walked through the atrium and down a long station corridor that expelled me outside for two seconds, then bounded down very steep steps to the yellow taxi boat docked at the Chicago River. With luck, I would catch it right before departure. Without luck, I had to wait fifteen minutes for the next one. Once in my water taxi seat, for the next six minutes I felt like a tourist in this city of big, architecturally significant shoulders as we passed beneath skyscrapers and art deco bridges, as we glided over the graveyard of 844 souls who perished in the Eastland disaster in 1915 between LaSalle and Clark, as we pulled in beneath the finely detailed, gleaming white Wrigley building wrapped in glazed terra cotta.

At the end of the workday, I bolted out of the office by 5:05, doing my best to avoid getting collared into last-minute conversations. Depending on how the elevators were running, I could reach the bus stop on Lower Wacker Drive in front of the Billy Goat Tavern in three minutes. If the bus hadn't arrived within two minutes, I searched for a taxi. If I couldn't flag a cab within two minutes, I began to fast walk about a dozen long city blocks to the station to catch the express train. If I missed the express, it meant waiting twenty minutes for the next train, a local. I was in a procession of business-attired leaf cutter ants in the urban jungle. If my red-light timing was bad, I broke into a trot.

This twenty-minute obstacle course left me flushed and almost panting. Plopping down on the first available seat and cracking open a book, I felt a sense of accomplishment, especially when I made the entire journey without stopping. Yet another edition of The Commuter Olympics.

♪   ♪   ♪

But the job had its perks. At an industry cocktail party, I ran into a friend who worked for VH-1. After a few drinks, she invited me to a live taping of Keith Richards and The Expensive Winos at PBS affiliate, WTTW on the northwest side.

On the day of the taping, Linda contracted stomach flu but was going to give it a try anyway. After all, it was Keith! Sadly, on the way to the show, we had to turn the car around and return Linda home to deal with her ailment. After dropping her off, I didn't have time to think about anything other than threading through expressway traffic and getting to WTTW.

The studio held about 200 standing fans. A low-key, pre-concert buzz filled the room. We were the chosen ones. This wasn't a stadium show with 30,000 *anybodys* in attendance. This was a hyper exclusive event to witness a legend. I wormed my way to the very front, pressed against the stage. The anticipation vibes were intense. Fans talked to whoever was within earshot.

"Right now, I'd rather see the Winos than the Stones," was a common sentiment.

"I heard they were drinking whiskey at the Four Seasons last night."

"Keith always drinks his dinner."

"Wonder if he'll end up at Buddy Guy's tonight?" We had all reverted to our teenage rock fanatic selves, ready to worship at the altar of Keef.

A small camera tethered to a cable zipped behind me. The director was practicing a shot that would swoop over the crowd, right up to the Winos. Just before the band appeared, I heard my name over the studio public address system.

"Bain! Move to the back. Your bald head is in my shot." I knew the woman who was directing. I moved about twenty feet back. Still a great spot to see the band smash through *Take It So Hard* and about ten other tunes including *Time Is on My Side,* sung by Sara Dash.

The set ended and I headed for the stage door where my VH-1 friend had told me to meet her. As I made my way to the backstage door, I said hello to Winos drummer, Steve Jordan and sax legend, Bobby Keys.

"Great set, guys!" What else could I say? The rock royalty was looking for the buffet. Because of the small, private nature of the show there wasn't much security. I walked in. Backstage was a non-descript, dark-ish room with drapes on the walls and a few, dimmed overhead lights. The gathering was just me, my friend, the President of VH-1 and a guitar maker with a custom guitar for Keith to autograph. We were all equals as we waited for Keith.

I had just informed the president of VH-1 that I liked rock better before music videos took over when a hush settled over the room, a barely discernible change in atmosphere like the pressure drop that precedes a tornado. From the shadows, Keith materialized and noiselessly glided our way. He simply appeared, as if waved in by an unseen wand. I swear I detected an aura surrounding him. He seemed in good spirits but how would I know? Had he just smoked hash? Had he just looked at his bank account? Had he just eaten a plate of bangers and mash? In any case, there was no pretense. I could tell that he had done this meet and greet hundreds of times. It was the retail part of his job. He was polite, gracious, at once all-knowing and oblivious. Of course, he had a cigarette going. It crossed my mind to ask Keith for a cigarette. I no longer smoked but I could frame it or something.

I hadn't pondered what I might say to Keith. Do I tell him of my recurring dream where we are jamming together? That in the dream he is always impressed with my style? Except when I forget how to play and can't seem to hit the right licks and he leaves and I wake up?

What do you say to someone who had captivated you since sophomore year in high school? A prepared question would seem hokey, and I wished to present my least hokey self to the world weary riff master.

I settled on blurting out, "Hey, Keith. My wife got sick and she's going to die because she didn't get to see the show and meet you."

Without missing a beat, Keith said, "What you want from me mate? Ta' pay for her funeral?" He was busting my balls.

"That won't be necessary," I chuckled, "but could you tell her to get well soon?" I offered up my event invitation postcard. An assistant who had slipped into the room handed Keith a sharpie and he scribbled, "To Linda. Get well soon," and signed his name. We all posed for a quick photo with Keith and for reasons known only to God and Elvis, I never hunted down a copy. What I remember most was the handshake. Keith's hands were incredibly soft.

♪ ♪ ♪

"Chicago sales need to pick up or we'll have to let you go." For the past six months I had been hearing this from my boss and his boss. It was a numbers game, and my numbers were lackluster. If you've ever suffered from lackluster numbers, you know the feeling. The cure for this malady was surgical. NCA eliminated my position. I had lasted fourteen months in what I always knew was a dead-end job for me. The irony was that I had just closed a deal with a large department store, a store that would close in a couple of decades for the same reason: lackluster numbers. I wangled a small exit commission.

I was now out of work with two young kids and a mortgage. Being fired can be the worst day of your life. However, I would soon feel that, for me, this was a mighty good day. I was put out of my misery. And at least I had met Keith.

IV. MY DREAM JOB

ROGER BAIN
COMMUNICATIONS

Arlington Heights, IL, 1992-2010

FOR A WEEK OR TWO, I TESTED the job interview circuit, trying to get in with the Weather Channel or Turner Broadcasting. Would these time-selling jobs make me happy? Should I even care about happiness? A job is to make money. If it makes you happy, that's a bonus, I supposed. With each perfunctory interview, though, I grew more certain that I didn't want to sell someone else's time for the rest of my life. I wanted to sell my own time, to write and produce, to communicate and strategize, to do something that motivated me.

From age 12, I had worked alongside a vast spectrum of personalities, backgrounds, and economic classes, providing insight into the messy splendor of the human condition: an ideal background for practicing the art of persuasion. Throw in what I had learned about media and audience research, and that I was practiced in the art of performance. My path finally come into focus. It now seemed inevitable.

Throughout the past ten years, I had encountered many small ad agencies, often headed by a slick salesman, not a creative ace. Why not take a crack at this small agency thing using creative as a tool? Why not become a self-employed persuader? A solo artist. No dress code. No office politics. My own hours. I could even chaperone our kids' school outings to the Field Museum or the Lincoln Park Zoo. We had health insurance and a base income from Linda the second-grade teacher, so my move wasn't as daring as it might have been.

Linda knew it was the only move that might allow me fulfillment. Her career path had been my opposite. She worked a variety of jobs in her teens and early twenties, but from a young age she knew that her destiny was to be an elementary school teacher. She even recalls the third-grade teacher who inspired her. You can't do much if you're unsure what it is you want to do. It might have taken me 30 years, but now—finally—I knew.

All I needed was a client.

THE BIRTH OF A BUSINESS

Mail Boxes Etc.

I phoned the ad committee chairperson for Mail Boxes Etc. They were a new franchise group with over forty stores in the Chicago area. During my last job I had pitched cable advertising to them. Now I was pitching myself. Positivity and certainty are clutch tools of persuasion. Their current consultant slunk off to a corner and knew that he had no chance. I walked out of the meeting with my first account.

Songwriting would be my primary ad weapon.

My first creation was a sixty second music bed with a "singing logo" end tag, the words *mail boxes etcetera* sung as a seven-note melody. I hired an upright bass player I had met at Buddy Guy's club and used my gigging partner, Tom Mohbat, on drums. Tommy also ran Bad Dog sound studios. Kept the track simple. Bass and drums. I sang the seven-note melody and overdubbed it a few times for punch. Authentic. Real music. I could have voiced the spots myself but wisely decided to hire Fred Winston, a successful radio personality who was now "between gigs." Fred's recognizable pipes gave the spots credibility.

The client dug the spots. The commercial sounded maddeningly memorable on air. Radio reps descended upon me, and I got to experience buying ad time rather than selling it. Over the ten-year span I kept the account, I wrote and recorded two-dozen different variations with a bunch of different singers and announcers. One of the tenets of my production strategy was to make it my own. If I could ably write it, sing it, voice it, and produce it, why not?

I soon learned that when you are a solo ad agent for a local franchise group, the corporation is rarely your ally. They are jealous of your personal and geographical closeness to the franchisees. You are not their "guy." They are certain that you will not do things by the book—their book. Corporate marketing departments want to control budgets, marketing calendars, ad messaging and media selection. They looked at me as a heretic. The lone wolf. The outsider. The disrupter. Damn right I was.

I had been working out of my basement when I lucked into office space in the city at a small agency headed by ex-Big Agency heavyweights. In exchange for space, I agreed to pose as the agency's in-house retail/cable expert. I even wrote a song for a prospective banking client of theirs, which I performed in the somber, walnut paneled conference room of LaSalle National Bank. I wore a suit as I serenaded bankers; maybe the only time I have played guitar in business attire. Look out folks, here comes the *Singing Biznessman*!

"Whatever you do, whatever account you go after, use your music skills," the owner of the agency, Powell Johns, told me over a glass of wine one day at lunch. That stuck with me for the rest of my career. I had expected that somehow my songwriting and guitar playing would make me money. This was the way. I used songwriting and music in every single advertising endeavor. Without music, I couldn't have done it.

BERLAND'S HOUSE OF TOOLS AND TOOL TV

A family run operation that I dubbed "the most amazing tool store on the planet," Berland's House of Tools was a freak of retail nature. Humongous stores with nothing but tools and accessories for 47 different building trades. No lawn chairs. No paint. No lamp shades or blinds. Just tools. The Lombard store was pushing 30,000 square feet. Dwight Sherman was gradually taking over for his father, Dave, who had founded the business. A family outfit has a different vibe than a corporation with franchisees. You deal directly with the decision maker, the string puller, the check writer. You probably won't get blindsided by some new edict or policy. You look upon each other as humans, not entities.

My initial pitch offered two creative ideas. One was based upon testimonials from Berland's customers. It was solid and safe. The other idea featured cavemen, "the world's first users of tools." I aimed to demonstrate a direct line from those Stone Age cats using crude tools to Berland's, where today's cavemen roamed the aisles. I suggested that Berland's was "where tools have evolved." There was no contest. Let's go with the caveman! I worked with a phenomenal illustrator, John Eggert, to create a series of full color, direct mail and newspaper inserts featuring cavemen using modern power tools. Absurd juxtaposition is a proven attention grabber and illustration is one of the best methods for depicting fantastical situations or worlds. This won a Chicago Art Director's award.

John Eggert Illustration

(A couple of decades later a large insurance company used cave people in their ad campaigns, winning universal acclaim. This same company then featured the gecko in their ads. Hmmm. Was someone following my career? Or had I pre-supposed modern advertising trends?)

For the Berland's television creative, I licensed footage from a 1930s educational film in faded black and white that depicted a couple of cavemen in their eureka moment—inventing the wheel. I voiced these first TV spots in a desperate, high camp tone, like a voice lifted from a 1940s newsreel announcer on diet pills: "Twenty-three thousand years ago, man's only tools were sticks and stones ... Today, man has Berland's!" I also wrote the song, *A Rock, a Stone, a Stick, and a Bone*, that became a music video I directed with Second City cast members as the cave people.

Me as a caveman

I thought of ways to target the Berland's male audience. How about the men's room? An overlooked ad medium, thought I. No one was doing men's room advertising when I negotiated the space above the urinals at the Kane County Cougars minor league baseball stadium. When a guy is holding his sausage, he is more susceptible to an eye level marketing message. I deduced this without the aid of professional research. It just seemed like a wonderful idea. "Grab Your Next Tool at Berland's" became a campaign that lasted many years. Yes, the posters featured cavemen.

If you listened to the top-rated Jonathan Brandmeier *showgram* on Chicago's WLUP during the late 1990s, you might have caught an episode of *Name That Tool*. For this live bit, Dwight turned on power tools in the studio as Johnny B solicited listeners to guess what tool was making that racket. Guess correctly and you got the tool. Wonderfully absurd radio. The phone lines lit up! Great for Berland's, great for the station and fun for the listeners. This is the kind of magic that radio can create. If you're in your car listening and Dwight, without identifying it, turns on a hammer drill and you, the driver, are sure it's a recip saw, how are you going to call into Johnny? You pull over your car on the Kennedy because it takes two hands to work your new phone.

Johnny referred to Dwight as "The Toolman," giving me an idea for *I'm a Toolman,* the Berland's anthem. *If I have my miter box, standing in my thick wool socks, I feel so fine.* Johnny aired the song every time we played *Name That Tool* and usually a couple of times in the days leading up to the appearance.

At this time, the ad industry had not yet perfected the creepy art of stalking. It hadn't yet learned every detail of your life, every place you've shopped, travelled, or used your credit card, which political party you preferred, or how long you'd lingered on a website. Websites did not yet define our daily lives. Though my tools didn't include algorithms or metadata, I still needed to find the best way to target tool users in the Chicago area. What if there was a television show *about* power tools? Most viewers of such a show would likely be tool users and if it aired only in the Chicago market, every viewer could be a potential Berland's customer. No media waste! Since such a show didn't exist, I would have to produce it. And Dwight, who knew everything about tools and the tool industry, who had a special way with customers, who was a natural, low-key salesman, would be the host. Thus emerged a television program that gave me creative freedom like my days at Sunflower Cablevision.

As Tool TV came of age on the Chicago airwaves from the mid 90s through mid-2000s, viewers tuned in to useful tool information from Dwight the Toolman, interspersed with whatever I could think of to have fun while selling tools: a half hour of infotainment. We showcased the latest tools at construction job sites, workshops, warehouses, and frequently from the aisles of a Berland's store. In between these straightforward presentations swirled tool songs, music videos, nonsense skits featuring cavemen and cave-women, and recurring characters like The Hammerheads, Stan the Caveman, various tool babes (what a different era), Shifty the Musical Saw Maestro,

Nigel the Nail, The Drill Sergeant, Keyless Chuck, the Tool Nut Widow, a psychiatrist, The Three Tools (Stooges take-off) and for our holiday extravaganzas, endless variations of Santa, his wives, and the party elves. Berland's sold copies of Tool Tunes and The Songs of Tool TV, compilations of my tool-related recordings. The hammerhead outfits are still resting in my attic.

Hammerheads on the March

Absurdity, information, and power tools proved a winning combination. Sales at Berland's took off like a cordless autofeed screwgun. Dwight the Toolman became a regional celebrity and well over a decade after the last airing, people still remember Tool TV. Kudos to ace editor and collaborator, Paul May, audio maestro, Chuck Kawal, and scenic designer/costumer Laura Darner plus too many shooters and audio folks and production assistants to mention. I love production people!

GLORIA JEAN'S GOURMET COFFEES

The songwriting muse came to me one day as I passed Gloria Jean's Gourmet Coffees in Woodfield Mall. That smell! The fresh ground coffee aroma was intoxicating. Gloria had some nice beans. After singing it a few times a cappella at home, I went back to the mall with Linda.

"Is the manager in?" I asked the woman behind the counter. She summoned him from the back room and after a brief introduction, I sang him the song, snapping my fingers to the beat. *Gloria Jean's coffee beans are the prettiest beans I've ever seen.* My presentation outfit that day was cut off jean shorts and a t-shirt. He liked the song.

"Thank you," I said. "Who do I talk to about producing this?" He gave me the number of Gloria's husband and I eventually made contact, produced the song, *Gloria Jean's Beans*, and got the account. I had loved good, fresh ground coffee ever since going to Colombia years ago and now I was cashing in on this love.

KANE COUNTY COUGARS

My men's room urinal advertising campaign with Berland's introduced me to the management of the Kane County Cougars Class A Minor League baseball team.

"You guys need a theme song," I told them. I believed that every organization needed one. Cougars' management was aware of my *Thanks Mister Banks* record and the general manager, Wild Bill Larsen, liked the song idea.

For the *Cougars Swing* recording session, I recruited my son, Anthony, then about eleven years old, and two of his friends to the studio. The song's chorus was inspired by the chatter I had first heard in Little League.

Hey batter
Hey batter
Hey batter
Swing!

The kids shouted the word *swing*, giving the tune a nice, authentic hook. Swinging kids, they were.

Cougars' games were noted for between innings entertainment—base running dogs, marching bands and the Dynamite Lady blowing herself up at home plate. It was like a cross between a county fair and a church picnic planned by someone who had hit the bong. Somehow, a baseball game was sandwiched in between the shenanigans. When Wild Bill offered me an opportunity to assist in the game day wackiness, I agreed. From atop the visitor's dugout, in a lounge-y, opera-gone-wrong voice, my character crooned *Happy Birthday* to a preselected birthday kid. My outfit: a gauche yellow leisure suit, shiny white patent leather stacked heel shoes (purchased at a sidewalk sale in Lawrence for $1), and a John Deere polyester hat pulled below my eyebrows, the brim bent upward: an outfit reprised from skits performed with Rusty at Sunflower Cable. I presented a melting, still delicious Dairy Queen cake to the birthday kid. (A cake I would soon sing about.) Thankfully, I was never recognized.

Recently I had written and recorded, *What's Wrong with Being Bald and Wearing Glasses*? What if we give the first thousand bald guys with glasses free admission to a Cougars game? Take me out to the bald game. Wild Bill was all in. Sweating patrons streamed into the park on the day of the promotion. It was 106 degrees. Ticket takers made snap judgment calls as to which hairlines were deemed worthy of free admission. Good natured arguments broke out as to the definition of baldness. Guys with full hair heads claimed to be bald and were rebuffed. Women with thinning hair were given free entrance. Cougars' employees scurried around the park directing the most obviously bald to go down to the field. Bald guys rushed the field and formed lines down the first and third base lines where I directed them in an improvised can-can dance while the song cranked over the P.A.

News crews from a half-dozen local and national TV outlets showed up to cover the bald game. The local ABC sports anchor interviewed me while I was surrounded by Cougars players wearing bald wigs. It was hot, dripping chaos all in the name of marketing, promotion, and the absurdity of life, a textbook example of promotional anarchy.

I next wanted to stage a mass sit-in on Whoopee Cushions with 5,000 people but it never panned out. My advocate Wild Bill had moved on to a different team, but oh it would have made an unforgettable sound.

THE NEXT STEP

By now, I had named my business Roger Bain Communications. That title confused some into thinking I was a long-distance phone service provider. I could have been Roger Bain Advertising or Roger Bain Productions but communicating was the essence of what I did. I reasoned, spoke, calculated, presented, composed, sang, and wrote. Advertising was a byproduct of all that. My new logo featured a straight on view of the top half of my glasses' frames and my bald head; self-effacing humor that focused on the brain region, that primary source of communication.

I had clients, an identity, and now I needed to "hang my shingle" at a real office. In a stroke of luck, I found something in my price range an eight-minute walk from my home. The current tenant offering the sublet was involved in real estate and Dairy Queen franchising and needed something larger. He would even throw in his desk. The desk was the clincher. I had never owned an office desk. I agreed to the sublet. He saw that I was in advertising and suggested I contact the local DQ Ad Committee, writing down the name of a guy named John whose company had franchising rights to northeast Illinois.

COURTING THE QUEEN

Part I: The Big Meeting

I phoned the guy named John and before I could finish outlining my experience, he stated, "We need new blood." I told him that my blood was in that category. The two of us then proceeded to have one of those animated conversations where you're both coming up with a new idea every thirty seconds and they're all good and it becomes obvious you're on the same marketing wavelength and the timing is perfect.

John wanted to give the local DQ ad program a kick in the ass. I would be the kicker. He arranged an introductory meeting with the Chicagoland/Northwest Indiana Dairy Queen franchise ad committee. The local group was dissatisfied with the current advertising from their national agency and appeared eager to try something new, but they were skeptical that Corporate would allow me to have the account. Wait a minute, thought I. Corporate? What? This was the first time I realized that it would not be the ad committee's decision to engage me. I had been speaking with committee members, franchisees, not decision makers.

After some behind the scenes negotiating between John, the ad committee, and Corporate, the IDQ (International Dairy Queen) team begrudgingly decided to "allow" me to make a presentation at the big annual franchise meeting for Chicagoland/Northwest Indiana Dairy Queen. In attendance would be franchisees from 155 stores, a slew of folks from DQ's corporate marketing department, and a half dozen account, media, and creative department representatives from the current DQ ad agency, Campbell Mithun.

Campbell Mithun and International Dairy Queen were both headquartered in Minneapolis. This client/agency relationship was as tight as it gets: two corporations holding hands. Representatives from each company sat on the other's boards—a lot for me to overcome if I was going to get a piece of the account. The franchisees would have to exercise some newfound power instead of acquiescing to whatever the corporation dictated. My partner in crime, John, was wildly enthused at the new path he was spearheading. I looked forward to the opportunity with a mix of confidence and the anxiety of the unknown.

At least 150 people crowded into the large, generic meeting room at the Holiday Inn in the far south Chicago suburb of Matteson to witness this real-life David vs. Goliath showdown: a gigantic national ad agency with thousands of employees versus a solo ad agent. Six besuited C-M soldiers were prepared to do battle with me.

First up, the big agency boys. The Campbell Mithun suits gave their stunningly blasé presentation with pie charts and flow charts and stiff shirts and weak humor—basically the same presentation the franchisees had seen for years. They mailed it in. The room had little reaction. How much does a

DQ operator want to hear about gross ratings points and cost per thousand?

Now it was my turn. John introduced me. "Here's a guy with a different approach. I think we should hear what he has to say." Showtime! I strode up to the microphone with my guitar slung over my shoulder. I was wearing slacks and a shirt, the only presenter not in business attire. The audience of franchisees was also casually attired. I was dressed like they were. Major franchise drama was unfolding.

I stepped up to the microphone and surveyed the franchisees. "People already know who you are. You are an American icon. Dairy Queen means fun. Your advertising should be fun. Not contrived. It should be memorable and bring a smile to your face. Music on the radio is an efficient way to remind folks of your iconic, beloved brand. Rhyme, repetition, and melody are some of the most important tools we have to break through the noise of advertising clutter. Songs about DQ will make people smile. Not jingles. Songs. Sixty-second songs." The franchisees were listening to the bald guy with the guitar.

And now I revealed my secret weapon—Miss Rhoda Jean Kershaw. She was a redheaded country singer I had previously collaborated with on a *Tool TV* song, and she overflowed with genuine good spirit and a downhome voice.

"Hi y'all," she waved to the crowd.

The room murmured "hi" back. I voiced a one-two-three countdown—just like at a corner bar gig—and Rhoda Jean launched into a song that I had just written, *The Cake You Don't Have to Bake,* incorporating the current "Think DQ" tagline.

There's a cake, you don't have to bake.
The smooth creamy Dairy Queen frozen cake.
It's the cake your family will love.
The cool creamy Dairy Queen frozen cake.
If you're having a party soon
Here's what you do
Think DQ!!!!

The room dug it! Whoops and hollers and applause. The franchisees were finding their voice. The suits at the back of the room conferred and huddled and attempted a vibe of indifferent nonchalance. They had no guitars.

Other dramas were also playing out. During the performance, the bearded, truck driving, jeans wearing, outgoing local franchise ad committee chairman—he had just been voted out of office—was in the lobby bar sucking down his third beer, loudly and profanely getting in the face of some IDQ corporate players. This hubbub had wafted into the conference room and added tense vibes. When Rhoda and I began to sing and play, though, the room lost its tension. The franchisees sensed something different brewing after years of corporate despotism. (With a tad of irony, *Something Different* became a new tag line a few years later.) I thanked Rhoda Jean, I thanked the franchisees, I thanked the corporation, I even thanked "the team from Campbell Mithun." With my guitar again slung over my shoulder, like a working man with his pickaxe, I sauntered back down the aisle to the rear of the room as the sound of real applause delighted my ears.

A silver-haired account super for C-M with over thirty years of industry experience complimented me with a bemused look of ... envy? Or so I thought, though he may also have been thinking that it wasn't fair that I got to have more fun at my job than he did.

"Nice tie," I told him.

Especially abhorrent to the corpos was the fact that I was proposing that we use radio. This was sacrilege! IDQ and Campbell Mithun—all big agencies—preferred TV because it was "sexier" than radio, production budgets were more lucrative, it was easier to buy, and creative directors got to travel to LA for the commercial shoot. If you're a hot shot creative director and you don't have cocktails at the Chateau Marmont or the Polo Lounge a few times a year, why are you working?

IDQ and Campbell Mithun were singing from the same hymnal. I was singing a different tune. No matter how much the franchisees dug my presentation, there was still plenty for me to overcome.

Part II: The World's Largest Peanut Buster Parfait

A few weeks after the big meeting John notified me that he had figured out a way to finance a radio buy. He told me that I had $50,000 to spend, not a big budget for the Chicago market—my first TV buy for Mail Boxes Etc. had been twice as much—but at least a start. The money came from the bank account of John's franchise company, a company that I had recently come to realize was not even owned by John. He was just an employee. I was now a bit unsure if he was authorized to use the $50,000. It was shaky ground, but it was shakier for John than it was for me. Let's do it.

The radio ads would be promoting a Peanut Buster Parfait sale. I wrote and produced a sixty second product song—*The Peanut Buster Boogie*—and negotiated the ad buy on eight radio stations.

My name is Buster
Peanut Buster
Peanut Buster Parfait
I'll make your taste buds boogie woogie
For just a dollar ninety-nine today
I am the Dairy Queen
Peanut Buster Parfait

The Peanut Buster Boogie hit the airwaves featuring my lead vocal and female background vocals. I also voiced the announcer donut. The franchisees loved it. The sale was a success. If your client loves your work, you're golden. At least for a while.

As part of the advertising buy, I had also negotiated a promotion with the *Oldies* radio station to give away "The World's Largest Peanut Buster Parfait." This stunt originated from John's fevered imagination. No known size currently held the title as "world's largest." We hadn't a clue in our pre-google world. John had a five-foot tall polystyrene parfait glass manufactured at no small expense. A three-footer would have been enough to set the "record," but John wanted to blow minds. He wanted to create a monster. I admire people who think like that. The thing would tower up to my chin when finished.

For an entire week, in between waiting on customers, DQ employees at a northwest suburban Dairy Queen worked to fill the five-foot cup with smooth and creamy DQ soft serve. Each night the monstrous treat was wheeled back into the walk-in freezer on a mover's dolly, the humongous parfait cup slowly filling. John phoned me with progress reports.

"We put on a layer of fudge and peanuts today. It will be ready by Thursday." The prize delivery was scheduled for Friday.

The contest winner was a sophomore at Weber, an all-boys Catholic High School in Chicago. He wanted the prize delivered to school at lunchtime. John rented a tall truck with a rear lift. When he picked me up on delivery day, he opened the rear door to give me a peek. "Oh my God," I marveled. This looks unmistakably phallic. And to think this is what I now did for a living. I felt like a mad scientist whose creation had come to life. Not the mega parfait. I meant my career.

We raced into the city on a beautiful, warm Friday in May, a perfect day for frozen soft serve to grow softer. A few blocks from Weber High, we encountered a low underpass. We tried a few different routes that ended in dead ends or one-way streets and finally found ourselves once again facing the underpass. If we failed to deliver, Buster would be a bust. What would the radio station say? What would the winner say? What would the ad committee say? What would the corporation say?

After a short deliberation, with four hundred and fifty pounds of melting Peanut Buster Parfait in our hold, John declared. "We can't let those kids down. I'm going for it."

Years ago, when I worked for North American Van Lines, a driver had let air out of the tires to sneak under a low overpass. I suggested we try this, but John reasoned that driving slowly beneath the underpass might minimize the damage although we had little scientific evidence to back this postulation. After a few feet, a nasty scraping sound filled our ears. We slowly scraped our way to a large pothole that lowered our profile for a few feet, then the scraping sound again. John was sweating. His half-baked plan appeared to be melting. There was no time to check the damage when we finally came out into the sunlight. Our thawing prize had to be delivered now.

At Weber's main entrance, we were told to drive around back to access the cafeteria where a priest met us.

"We're delivering the world's largest Peanut Buster Parfait to one of your students and we need help." The be-robed Father crossed himself then quickly rounded up beefy members of the football team. When John opened the door for the assembled crew, they gasped and cackled. This giant, sweating parfait bungee-d to the truck wall looked like a monstrous dildo, a particularly hilarious vision in the presence of a priest. The plastic cup was alive with rivulets of condensation. We wheeled the smooth and creamy dildo to the lift and lowered it down. Now the hard part, getting this slippery monster down the stairs. Two priests and half of the football team helped us get the thing into the cafeteria. We were greeted by catcalls and a general feeling of WTF? A roomful of insolent teenage boys bursting with springtime testosterone is a tough crowd, but they rambunctiously lined up for their treat.

John was all business, climbing a small step stool while gleefully announcing, "And now for the final layer of fudge sauce!" He then began to scoop out lumberjack-size portions of Buster. Like the ad said: smooth and creamy DQ soft serve, rich chocolate fudge and a generous helping of lightly salted, freshly roasted peanuts. By now, it was more like sweet glop on a plate. The kids didn't seem to mind. Everybody digs free ice cream. As the cafeteria cleared out, our work area looked like a sweet, sticky bomb had gone off.

"What is this?" asked an incredulous lunch lady with a Polish accent. There were no Dairy Queen locations within the Chicago city limits at the time. She had never heard of Dairy Queen.

"It's history in the making," I told her.

When the lunch bell rang, half of the concoction remained. John slid it into the walk-in cooler, made some vague pledge to pick it up later, and then we slipped out. Reaching the parking lot, he winced at the rental truck, which had momentarily been forgotten. The damage ran into the thousands.

Soon after the Peanut Buster radio campaign, John was fired. He had been key to my entry into the DQ world and a worthy collaborator. I benefited from his loose business practices but now he was a casualty of his own exuberance. He had a good heart, an active promotional mind and was always doing what he thought best for the franchise. Thank you, John.

A DELIGHTFUL SPREE

Later in the year, I was officially granted the entire Chicago ad budget. With Campbell Mithun sidelined and a gradual corporate acceptance of me—that at times bordered on respect—I set off on a multi-year spree of campaigns using my 60 second product songs. With my producing partner, ace engineer and musician Chuck Kawal, we created a hit factory using a reliable stable of great musicians and a top-notch recording studio. *The Cake You Don't Have to Bake, I See a Chili Dog in Your Future, Do the Moo, I Wanna Dog and a Shake, We Got the Shakes, When Only a Blizzard Will Do,* and at least a dozen more. Each song had its own musical style. Music was making me money. Most of the ad buys were spread across a dozen radio stations with three to eight plays per station per day. During the typical two-week run, we got as much airtime as a hit song. Like all forms of propaganda, frequency is the cornerstone of advertising. Within the Chicago radio industry, I became known as *the DQ guy.*

♪   ♪   ♪

I was now handling Mail Boxes Etc., Berland's House of Tools, Tool TV, Dairy Queen, and often one or two other clients plus the occasional freelance jingle or corporate video production. One month, I counted over two dozen different pieces of my creative work airing on Chicago media. Almost all of it involved original music. In the ad biz, it is exceedingly rare for the person who handles concept, creation, and strategy to also plan and buy the media, proof the invoices, oversee the billing, and coordinate the promotions, but I was a one-man band agency—and I was having a ball!

Working solo allows you to get a lot done without office politics and needless meetings, but it was heartening to create a small team. I hired Jennifer Raaths, a Northwestern grad. She worked with me for a few years then my daughter, Janina, assisted me for a about fifteen months before moving to the west coast and beginning her own non-conforming work life. One remarkable assistant, talented jazz artist, Stephanie Browning, sang on some of the product songs as well as spearheaded, with her husband, an ongoing effort to deliver the Blizzard Flavor of the Month to a dozen radio stations. Free ice cream is a terrific way to negotiate favorable treatment in the scheduling of ad times and spontaneous shout-outs by on-air personalities.

My office, dubbed *The Swingers' Lounge,* had evolved into a hodgepodge of guitars and amps, posters, a large painting of a frog playing the saxophone—acquired from a drunken artist in New Orleans—delightfully mismatched furniture, a bizarrely patterned 1950s modernist couch that looked right out of an episode of *Ren & Stimpy* and Saucer, my African Grey parrot, whose vocabulary included, *I like cheese, gimme a peanut* and *ooh la la*. It was like my brain had exploded all over the room.

Playing in the swinger's lounge

For years, I had been able to befuddle and thwart the IDQ marketing VP, who was more of an accountant type and possessed little promotional flamboyance. Over time, he had begrudgingly allowed me to produce my product songs and use radio rather than TV. Then, my life changed when the corporation replaced this Marketing VP with a "rising star."

The new VP quickly instituted a "Leadership Summit" at Minneapolis headquarters, titled, "Movin' the Needle," where he threw down the gauntlet to the local and regional agencies. I'm calling the shots now, said the new, needle-moving VP. Your client is me, not the local franchisees. Follow my guidelines and you'll survive. The new VP pontificated on the brand as if it were a mysterious presence. He never referenced Dairy Queen. He spoke only of the DQ brand, like a preacher speaks of the deity. I pictured the room genuflecting at a DQ logo alter. The brand was sacred. Another new truth: Dairy Queen was no longer Dairy Queen. It was now DQ, a much hipper offspring of the old Queen. And don't refer to us as a *fast-food chain*. We are a *quick serve restaurant*.

Also attending the summit was a large and very important hierarchy of supervisors, Directors, VPs and assistant VPs from Grey Advertising, the New York Agency behemoth recently hired by the VP—who was himself from the New York area. They presented their re-imagined vision of DQ, showing animatics (a movie of storyboards) of snide, jokey, proposed TV commercials that featured clueless doofuses surrounded by hapless cohorts who were subject to all sorts of surreal mayhem in order to eat DQ treats conjured up in a world of idiocy: a full-scale abandonment of the sweet, small town, summertime vibe projected by the actual Dairy Queen. Full bore, east coast advertising cynicism had come to roost. Nearly all franchisees in attendance were from rural or smaller city outposts. The city slickers were pitching the country folk on how they aimed to change Dairy Queen from an old school, rural icon—whose stores were concentrated in the Bible belt—into a cutting-edge quick serve restaurant. They even shot commercials with young urban professionals eating DQ on their lunch break in the big city, where no DQ stores actually existed.

During a breakout session with the local and regional ad agencies, the new marketing VP professed that he didn't "get" radio. That's like a chef saying that he didn't "get" bread. This sentiment was aimed directly at me, the outsider, the heretic, the rebel. Chicago was the only DQ market in the country that used radio as the primary ad vehicle. He also revealed a new formula whereby local budgets would decrease in order to boost the *national* budget.

"This will exponentially increase our success quotient," said the keeper of the Brand. To each of us local ad agents he was saying, "you will be making less money from now on and you better be happy you have any budget at all." My tenuous grip on the account was slipping further with each new session.

Day two of the Summit featured an utterly unique dining experience: the tasting of eighteen possible new menu items. Attendance was mandatory. I felt like a salmon in a spawning run as we streamed into the smooth and creamy DQ corporate test kitchen. When you take three bites of eighteen different food items or treats that have been fried, grilled, deep fried, glopped, spooned, and sauced, you are taking fifty-four bites. Up that to four bites of each item and you have consumed seventy-two bites: seventy-two bites of creamy caramel sauce and rich butterscotch and fudge sauce and chipotle mayo and golden-brown chicken meat and breaded, deep fried seafood product and burger and cheese sauce and twice deep-fried, crispy golden fries with the new coating and soft serve and brownies. And the new coffee-inspired Moo Latte! Every few minutes a corporate minion would hover over your booth and inquire which delectable treat or food item you most enjoyed. The answers came gushing out, how you loved the flavor profile of this one and the salt meets sweet combo of that one and the obvious wonderfulness of that new Blizzard flavor, the one with graham crackers and double fudge encrusted almond bark with cocoa swirls. Did anyone truly care what a rogue ad guy thought about the taste of a chili lime cheese dog?

The only time I felt relaxed during the three-day Summit was the afternoon I snuck away to watch my friend George Funk play in the Minnesota State Croquet Championship, which he won. This change of scene, from calculated, corporate vibe to a lawn studded with wickets was restorative. George was still making a go of it with an updated iteration of Funk & Rose. Stew had gone east to seek his fortune in the corporate world. We were updated versions from who we had been during our Church Days.

This Summit was the beginning of the end for me. Within six months, I made a deal to transfer my account to a St. Louis agency that managed a handful of DQ markets. Consolidation seemed my only path. This agency had about fifteen employees and was on solid ground because they used TV. So I sold the Chicago account that I had fought so hard to get. Might as well salvage what I could. For a few years, I remained in charge of Chicago and supervised the Milwaukee and Green Bay markets. Then my new agency partner went down in flames. He had collected money from DQ to pay for media buys then failed to pay the radio and TV stations. It was deemed fraud in a court of law. I was not lumped in with his misdeeds but still waited in limbo for months. DQ let me back in with the proviso that I administer my media buys through an agency in Kansas City. And there was no longer a budget for me to create radio songs. Even worse, I was now directed to use uninspired, unmemorable Grey creative produced by their "B" team; the kind of commercials that take up airspace but don't stick in your head.

For several years I did my best to make an impact with the ever-dwindling Chicago budget until finally the budget became so small that there was little to administer. The corporation shifted the remaining, miniscule budget to the KC agency. After a fifteen-year run, my DQ days were done.

♫   ♫   ♫

Losing ad clients is often due to factors beyond your control. Dwight was eager for more personal time, so he hired a management consultant to run Berland's. From my very first meeting with the guy, I knew I would be toast, which I soon became. And after ten-years of Tool TV, the concept finally ran out of gas. It ceased provoking boffo sales results. My ten-year run with Mail Boxes Etc. ended when they were subsumed by UPS and the franchisees who were my early backers had all departed. When Wild Bill left The Kane County Cougars, I was without my main collaborator and the account gradually slipped away. My short run with Gloria Jean's ended when they were bought by a company that didn't believe in radio or TV advertising and who also had their own in-house direct mail department. A couple of restaurant groups I had done multi-year work for decided to *hold back* or *hit pause* or *change direction* or whichever ambiguous phrase you don't want to hear from a client. After a few seasons, one retail client in the outdoor gear and clothing business let me go because my media commission had grown larger than the salaries of the store managers and the client didn't think this was permissible. He wanted me to lower my commission which, on principle, I wouldn't do. On my exit, he expressed how much he loved my creativity and he paid me the incentive that I'd earned for exceeding revenue goals. "We love you, now get outta here."

CODA

AFTER A RIDICULOUS ASSORTMENT OF JOBS, MISFIRES, and dead ends, I managed to eke out my own slice of the universe, creating my own American Dream job that required no brown suit. I worked in, around, through and outside of *the system*. I knew what I didn't want to do, and I didn't do it. At least not for long. All you can ask of a career is the ability to be *the real you*, the ability to keep a parrot in your office if so inclined. It didn't hurt that education, upbringing, and skin color were all in my favor. Along the way, I had worked with many who did not have that privilege. Acquiring *enough* while having fun had been my goal. If your primary goal is to become rich, you might never have *enough*.

What about my youthful notion of going so far out on a limb that I could never get back to bourgeois society? Like the seasons, goals change. Although I became a home-owning suburban dad, my soul remained—and remains—that of a free spirit. The subversive pleasure of making money from the preposterous provided my biggest thrill.

The 60s platitude that burned brightest for me was *Do your own thing*. Not everyone's *thing* is the same. Mine was music and mirth. Corporate

America held little mirth for me. The notion of being a cog in a profit machine, slashing my way up the ladder; the hierarchies, rule books, organizational charts, codes, sucking up, backstabbing and the art of making your boss look good ... were not my style. I was so-so at selling somebody else's time and space but much better at selling my ideas, tapping into my own ingenuity, nurtured by quixotic experience. This had been my game plan from the time I was twenty years old. When you are working, yet it doesn't feel like a job, you are hardly working.

Advertising has changed in the short span since I closed shop. Now it's a stalker's game. It is impossible to escape. It follows you. It is cold and calculating. In my tiny ad universe, I might have nudged you into buying soft serve ice cream or a cordless autofeed screwgun, but fun was my guide. If you have ever seen the "Dancing Tool Babes from Outer Space," episode on Tool TV, it is nothing more than me trying to have fun with an entire crew of pranksters, celebrating absurdity. In the guise of marketing.

With more than a tad of irony, I confess that Linda and I have muted TV commercials since the 70s and now, with digital TV, we fast forward past the commercial pods whenever we watch commercial TV. When someone begins a sentence, "Have you seen that commercial where..." I mostly answer, no. Unless it's the Snoop Dog spots for Corona. A full-blown analysis of the industry would require an entire book and there are already thousands of them so enough said.

♫　♫　♫

The guitar shaped my adult life. Had I never learned to play, I may have never written songs. Had I not become a songwriter, I would have been bereft of my central advertising tool: music composed on the guitar. My passionate avocation became my financial lifeline. There would have been no Roger Bain Communications without my ability to churn out jingles and theme songs.

If I can posit one "self-help" platitude it would be to find something you enjoy—write, sing, draw, paint, sculpt, play an instrument—and do it. You don't even have to show anybody your work. It can be your little secret. You certainly don't have to make money from whatever your thing is. But it will give you a feeling that you are participating in life.

Retiring from a job isn't retiring from life. If you can entertain yourself or others, you'll be fine.

Linda retired from teaching the year my client base went to zero. Suddenly, we were both in the house at the same time, creating a humorous juggling act as we tried to arrange schedules to diminish our house time together, to give each other some space.

"When you get home, I'll go get guitar strings. Then when I come back, you can go to your sister's." Laughter is the glue of marriage.

While working full time you're too busy to deliberate about the big picture. But when you have time for reflection and pondering, when your days aren't automatically filled with the noise of work and you're confronted with yourself and who you are, why you're here, what it all means and what's for dinner, it can be disorienting. In my second retirement, I confronted the same questions I had in my twenties. (Lyrics from the song *Hardly Working*.)

What can I do?
I don't know
I haven't a clue what I can do

Thing is, this go round I *did* have a clue. The joy of creation still burned bright. People like me never retire.

♪　♪　♪

For over a year, Sunflower Dave and I attempted to create an HD cable channel—or website—devoted to showcasing the art of living artists. *The Virtual Gallery*. We made endless videos, wrestled with multiple strategies and with the help of my CEO friend, Jack, got as far as pitching it to the Discovery Channel. They offered to test the concept, but bureaucracy and management changes got in the way. It slipped into the oblivion bin of good ideas never realized. A good old "learning experience." We had fun seeing it go nowhere.

♪　♪　♪

My assistant, Jennifer, had often told me how much her kids dug my tool songs. When my own kids were growing up, I made up countless ditties for the neighborhood gang. I knew I could connect with kids, so I recorded a CD collection of my absurdist songs (with Chuck Kawal) titled, *My Mailman Has a Tail*. Kids music for parents with Monty Python sensibilities. It made little money but at least the world now has songs about a smelly elephant and a dinosaur-eating frog.

And I still have a toe in the advertising waters. Once again, I'm on retainer for long-time client, Berland's. (Often working with son, Anthony.) It's still fun! Amazing what you can accomplish with a phone and a laptop that previously required a film crew and editing suite.

I have recorded over 50 songs with collaborator Geoff DeMuth, including *Hardly Working*, and a half dozen tunes with Chuck Kawal. My gin mill band, *Under the Kitchen*, is currently on hiatus, but we might get back together any day now. Just last week, I jammed with the Springer Brothers in my basement and man, it felt good! I still listen to Blind Blake. I play guitar every day, often a long set of tunes after dinner that vanish into the air, like sand art that disappears from the wind or water. When I put the guitar back on the stand or in its case, I feel nourished, like I've discovered something.

On a nice spring day, I'll still catch myself thinking, "I bet Dairy Queen is doing well today." And I hope they are.

♪　♪　♪

As my kids were growing up, I searched for wisdom to impart. I came up with the three Bs for Anthony: Blues, Books & Basketball. Blues represents the creative nature, books the curious, and basketball the physical and competitive. A balanced life. Creative, curious, and competitive. Maybe it should be the three Cs?

♪　♪　♪

In 1959, the year that Ernie Banks was MVP, my dad took me to Wrigley Field to see Ernie in action. That same year Linda lived just a block away from Wrigley, at the corner of Waveland and Racine. Before and after the games, she set up a Kool Aid stand on Waveland Avenue with her brother. Maybe I passed by her stand? Maybe she caught a glimpse of me, a little league all-star who would one day sleep with her in a field of curious horses in a Rocky Mountain Meadow, who would be there for the birth of their children. She would be with him the night he found out his kids' show wasn't getting greenlighted. And the night he came home without the DQ account. She would be with him when they got their Pfizers. The job of life is best experienced with another.

AFTERWARD

THIS BOOK IS NOT INTENDED TO BE a comprehensive examination of the American workplace or American values. Leave that to academics or pop psychologists. I simply wanted to take stock in what I had done to make money throughout my life. My original motivation was to provide a document for my kids; not a path for them to follow but more an entertainment, much as I made up bedtime stories for them about the magic pig that had people hands and people feet, a top hat, spats and a cane.

My story is not one of breathtaking audacity or world class adventure. Many have done far more interesting or dangerous or worthwhile things to make money. But the story is mine alone. We all have a story.

It is remarkable how memory works. Dwell enough on something and small details return. Not necessarily important details, rather, snapshots from the photo album that is our mind. For the most part, I have written what I remembered. And I have tried to be truthful. But memory and truth are two different things. I confess to augmenting my memory with Google searches from time to time. How else would I have known the number of people employed by the auto industry in the 1960s? But the book isn't meant to dwell on the factual history of the past six decades. Nor is it meant to be a true autobiography. Nor a tome on the human condition, nor a travelogue, nor a rumination on social strata, although I suppose it has elements of all of these. My hope is that readers may conclude that they, too, have a life worth examining through the lens of work.

Each job you have contributes to your understanding of the world regardless of the pay grade or skill required. I have had countless discussions with friends who have offered their own recollections of past jobs, and whenever I read aloud chapters at Writer's Ink, my local writers' group, the ensuing discussion often veered into similar jobs that group members had. They recalled tasks that were bureaucratic or time wasting or bosses or co-workers who were wonderful or not. Of special importance seemed to be jobs that are deemed low skill or incidental or low paying. Summer jobs. Starter jobs. Dirty jobs: the jobs that are the binding agents of society. The jobs deemed essential during a pandemic. As a married couple fondly recalls their younger life, when they didn't have material comforts, when they shared a single bed, had a leaky faucet, and ate a lot of canned tuna, these early jobs become romantic. The romance of youth.

Writing this book became a form of therapy. I tried not to glorify or romanticize myself or stretch the truth to make me look better than the flawed person I am. I grew up to be the person I was meant to be. And still I'm growing, still I'm learning. I might have to find another job soon, who knows?

♫ ♫ ♫

May your soul remain restless, may you continue to seek what's up the road or down the path, may you be passionate about something that may or may not have to do with your job, may you be ever mindful of the needs of others.

ACKNOWLEDGEMENTS

Many people have helped me, either as proofreaders, editors, or beta readers, including; George Funk who gave me encouragement after reading an early draft. Jim Vaughn (the Smock) who read an early draft and his since passed away. Sara Lippmann, a wonderful editor (and writer) who pushed me to dig. John Knight, who provided early edits. Jacob Knabb of the Arlington Heights Public Library writer's group, Writer's Ink. He

Typical afternoon at home with Linda.
Photo by Terry Karow

came up with the title. Jennifer Raaths, who has helped in many ways. Betsy Salmon Miller, who read three different drafts and gave me hope. Beta reader (and author) Shasta Grant for critical commentary and support. Jim Jewell, who took many of the Sunflower Cable-era photos. Suzanne Burdick took the cover photo. And finally, my wife, life partner, and travelling companion, Linda, who read the manuscript many times and encouraged me through umpteen re-writes, And thanks to my parents for their love and understanding.

ABOUT THE AUTHOR

ROGER BAIN IS A BALD CHRONICLER OF the human condition, a songwriter, occasional performer, and an optimistic cynic whose work has appeared on network television, syndicated radio, and print. He was employed in the media and advertising industries for 30 years after a long stretch of career procrastination. He resides in the northwest suburbs of Chicago with his wife, Linda. At one time he owned a parrot.